CONTENTS

2000 Overview 2

Production/Factory Sales

Historical U.S. Production and Factory Sales 3
U.S. and Canadian Passenger Car Production 4,5
U.S. and Canadian Truck and Bus Factory Sales 7
U.S. Factory Sales of Trucks and Buses .
by Gross Vehicle Weight Rating 6
U.S. Factory Sales of Diesel Trucks 7
Motor Vehicle Production by City and State 8,9
Factory Installations of Selected Equipment 10
Recreation Vehicle Production 11
World Production 12,13
Production in Mexico 14
Production Milestones 27

Retail Sales

Historical U.S. Retail Sales 15
U.S. Retail Sales of Passenger Cars 15-21
U.S. Retail Sales of Trucks 15,22-26
Retail Sales Milestones 27
Top Selling Vehicles 28
Sales in Canada 29
Sales in Mexico 30
Leasing 48

Registrations

Registrations in Canada 29
New car and Truck Registrations by State 31-37
Total Registrations by State 38-44,49
Cars and Trucks in Use 45-49
Fleet Registrations 49
World Registrations 50-53
Motor Vehicles Retired from Use 61

Automotive Trade

U.S. Exports by Country of Destination 54-57
U.S. Imports by Country of Origin 58
World Trade in Motor Vehicles 59

Materials

Automotive Consumption of Materials by Type 60,61
Materials Disposition from Recycled Vehicles 61

Ownership

Population Per Vehicle 50-53,72
Licensed Drivers 62
New Car Buyers 63
Motor Vehicle Thefts 69

Transportation Expenditures

Passenger Car Operating Costs 64
Light Truck Operating Costs 65
Automotive Financing 66
Consumer Expenditures 67,68
Fuel and Licensing Taxes 72,82

Travel Trends

Vehicle Miles of Travel 70-72
Public Roads 72,73

Automotive Businesses

Facilities and Employment 74-77,79
Compensation/Payrolls 76-79
Industrial Production 80
Capacity Utilization and Vehicle Output 80
Corporate Profits 81
Research and Development
Expenditures 81

Environment/Regulations

Fuel Consumption 70
Corporate Average Fuel Economy 83,84
Automotive Fuel Prices 85
Gas Guzzler Taxes 85
Safety and Emissions Costs 85
Federal Exhaust Emissions Standards 86
Federal Motor Vehicle Safety Standards 87

Traffic Fatalities

Historical Motor Vehicle Deaths 88
Traffic Death Rates by State 89
Traffic Fatality Characteristics 90
Traffic Deaths in Selected Countries 91
Safety Belt Use Laws 91

Index 92,93

North America Automotive Industry has Best Year in 2000

After a grandiose year in 1999, it was hard to believe 2000 could be better, but it was for the North American automotive industry. Sales and production in North America hit new all-time highs for the second consecutive year in 2000, and all three countries on the continent had individual sales records. The U.S. economy continued its record expansion, and although there were some signs of weakness toward the end of the year, the Federal Reserve began cutting interest rates in the hopes of curbing a recession after its increases the previous year helped to stave off inflation. Low unemployment and high consumer confidence, combined with the ever-increasing competitive nature of the automotive sector — resulted in lower costs to the consumer because of heavy price rebates and low interest rate financing as automakers scrambled to maintain market share — allowed 2000 to be by far the North American automotive industry's best year on record. Adding to the surge were more offerings in the newest hot segment, cross/utility vehicles (CUVs), which are vehicles classified as light trucks by the government but consisting largely of traditional passenger car traits. Also leading the growth were entry-level luxury sedans, sporty performance cars, and the small-car market rebounded thanks in part to an influx of affordable Korean-built makes.

North American Retail Sales

North American sales of all vehicles in 2000 broke the 20.0 million level for the first time by climbing 10.3% to 20.30 million from the prior year's 19.7 million, which also was the previous record. By country, U.S. sales increased 2.3% from 1999 to 17.8 million, Canada sales rose 3.0% to 1.6 million, and vehicle sales in Mexico surged 28.0% to 902,000 units. For the U.S. and Mexico, 2000 sales beat records set in 1999 of 17.4 million and 705,000, respectively. Canada's previous high was 1.6 in 1988, although 1999's volume of 1.5 million was close to that mark. Cars made a resurgence of sorts in North America by climbing 3.3% from the previous year compared to a 3.2% rise in trucks, thanks to a 28.9% increase in Mexico car deliveries and a 5.3% increase in cars for Canada. It was the first time in at least a decade that trucks did not outdo cars on a year-to-year comparison. But as in 1999, trucks spurred growth in the U.S., although cars did climb a modest 1.7% from the previous year. However, it was mostly the CUV segment that spurred the U.S. truck market as sport/utility vehicles, pickups and medium/heavy-duty rigs recorded declines in market penetration, if not overall volume.

North American Production

Production of all vehicles from North American factories hit a new high of 17.7 million in 2000. The 2000 total represented an small increase over 1999's 17.6 million because demand for import vehicles took the lion's share of the double-digit sales gain. The production increase also paled in comparison to the 4.7% increase in global output, which totaled a new world record of 57.5 million compared to 55.0 million the year before. Extracting North American output from the total, production in the rest of the world increased 6.8% and accounted for 69.3% of global output compared to 68.0% in 1999.

Vehicles in Operation

Motor vehicles on U.S. roads increased 1.8% in 2000 from the prior year, the lowest increase since 1.4% in 1997. Total vehicles in operation numbered 213.3 million, with trucks accounting for 40.1% of the population, compared to 39.4% in 1999, and 31.2% just 10 years ago. The percentage of trucks in the vehicle population has increased for 39 consecutive years.

In other highlights from Ward's Motor Vehicles Facts & Figures:

- Sales of imported vehicles in North America increased 17.7% in 2000 to 3.3 million, or 16.4% of the total. That compares to 1999's 2.8 million units and 14.4% share.
- U.S. factory sales in 2000 hit a 22-year high of 12,526,863 units, and was a 3.3% increase vs. 1999's 12,126,859.
- World registrations of all vehicles increased by some 23.6 million in 1999 — the most recent year available — from 1998, or 3.6%. On a regional basis, Western Europe had the biggest volume increase with 9.0 million more registrations than in 1999, led by a 5.7 million rise in the United Kingdom. Asia was the second leading region in volume growth with a 5.62-million increase.
- The dollar value for U.S. motor vehicle imports increased by nearly 10.0% to $125.1 billion in 2000, from $114.0 billion in 1999. The biggest growth in dollars was from Mexico where the monetary value of imports increased by $5.6 billion to $20.9 billion in 2000. The largest percent increase was an 8,000% surge in Brazil imports to $167 million.
- The number of licensed drivers in the U.S. increased to 187.2 million in 2000 from 185.0 million in 1999. The gender mix remained static at 50.3% male and 49.7% female.

U.S. Production and Factory Sales of Passenger Cars, Trucks and Buses

ANNUAL U.S. MOTOR VEHICLE PRODUCTION AND FACTORY SALES

Year	Production Passenger Cars	Production Commercial Vehicles	Production Total	Factory Sales Passenger Cars	Factory Sales Commercial Vehicles	Factory Sales Total
2000	5,542,217	7,228,497	12,770,714	5,504,385	7,022,478	12,526,863
1999	5,637,949	7,387,029	13,024,978	5,427,746	6,699,113	12,126,859
1998	5,554,373	6,448,290	12,002,663	5,676,964	6,435,185	12,112,149
1997	5,927,281	6,191,888	12,119,169	6,069,886	6,152,817	12,222,703
1996	6,083,227	5,749,410	11,832,637	6,140,454	5,775,730	11,916,184
1995	6,350,733	5,634,724	11,985,457	6,309,836	5,713,469	12,023,305
1994	6,613,970	5,648,767	12,262,737	6,548,562	5,640,275	12,188,837
1993	5,981,046	4,916,619	10,897,665	5,961,754	4,895,224	10,856,978
1992	5,664,203	4,037,731	9,701,934	5,685,299	4,062,002	9,747,301
1991	5,438,579	3,371,942	8,810,521	5,407,120	3,387,503	8,794,623
1990	6,077,449	3,705,548	9,782,997	6,049,749	3,725,205	9,774,954
1989	6,823,097	4,050,935	10,874,032	6,807,416	4,061,950	10,869,366
1988	7,113,137	4,100,550	11,213,687	7,104,617	4,120,574	11,225,191
1987	7,098,910	3,825,776	10,924,686	7,085,147	3,821,410	10,906,557
1986	7,828,783	3,505,992	11,334,775	7,516,189	3,500,933	11,017,122
1985	8,184,821	3,467,922	11,652,743	8,002,259	3,464,327	11,466,586
1984	7,773,332	3,151,449	10,924,781	7,621,176	3,175,835	10,797,011
1983	6,781,184	2,443,637	9,224,821	6,739,223	2,433,876	9,173,099
1982	5,073,496	1,912,099	6,985,595	5,049,184	1,906,455	6,955,639
1981	6,253,138	1,689,778	7,942,916	6,255,340	1,700,908	7,956,248
1980	6,375,506	1,634,335	8,009,841	6,400,026	1,667,283	8,067,309
1979	8,433,662	3,046,331	11,479,993	8,419,226	3,036,706	11,455,932
1978	9,176,635	3,722,567	12,899,202	9,165,190	3,706,239	12,871,429
1977	9,213,654	3,489,128	12,702,782	9,200,849	3,441,521	12,642,370
1976	8,497,893	2,999,703	11,497,596	8,500,305	2,979,476	11,479,781
1975	6,716,951	2,269,562	8,986,513	6,712,852	2,272,160	8,985,012
1974	7,324,504	2,746,538	10,071,042	7,331,256	2,727,313	10,058,569
1973	9,667,152	3,014,361	12,681,513	9,657,647	2,979,688	12,637,335
1972	8,828,205	2,482,503	11,310,708	8,823,938	2,446,807	11,270,745
1970	6,550,128	1,733,821	8,283,949	6,546,817	1,692,440	8,239,257
1965	9,335,227	1,785,109	11,120,336	9,305,561	1,751,805	11,057,366
1960	6,703,108	1,202,011	7,905,119	6,674,796	1,194,475	7,869,271
1955	7,950,377	1,253,672	9,204,049	7,920,186	1,249,106	9,169,292
1950	6,628,598	1,377,261	8,005,859	6,665,863	1,337,193	8,003,056
1945	83,786	701,090	784,876	69,532	655,683	725,215
1940	3,728,491	784,404	4,512,895	3,717,385	754,901	4,472,286
1935	3,252,244	694,690	3,946,934	3,273,874	697,367	3,971,241
1930	2,784,745	571,241	3,355,986	2,787,456	575,364	3,362,820
1925	N.A.	N.A.	N.A.	3,735,171	530,659	4,265,830
1920	N.A.	N.A.	N.A.	1,905,560	321,789	2,227,349
1915	N.A.	N.A.	N.A.	895,930	74,000	969,930
1910	N.A.	N.A.	N.A.	181,000	6,000	187,000
1905	N.A.	N.A.	N.A.	24,250	750	25,000
1900	N.A.	N.A.	N.A.	4,192	N.A.	4,192

N.A. - Not available.
SOURCE: *Ward's Automotive Reports.*

U.S. and Canadian Passenger Car Production by Model

U.S. AND CANADIAN PASSENGER CAR PRODUCTION BY MODEL, 1998-2000

	United States			Canada			U.S. and Canada Total		
	1998	1999	2000	1998	1999	2000	1998	1999	2000
Chrysler 300M	0	0	0	51,169	75,191	57,933	51,169	75,191	57,933
Chrysler LHS	0	0	0	23,097	27,720	19,584	23,097	27,720	19,584
Cirrus	47,246	47,124	39,232	0	0	0	47,246	47,124	39,232
Concorde	0	0	0	87,832	61,403	52,768	87,832	61,403	52,768
Sebring Convertible	0	0	7,338	0	0	0	0	0	7,338
Sebring Sedan	0	0	33,778	0	0	0	0	0	33,778
Total Chrysler	**47,246**	**47,124**	**80,348**	**162,098**	**164,314**	**130,285**	**209,344**	**211,438**	**210,633**
Intrepid	0	0	0	138,757	174,607	161,599	138,757	174,607	161,599
Neon	124,729	165,229	179,039	0	0	0	124,729	165,229	179,039
Stratus	115,674	100,196	117,272	0	0	0	115,674	100,196	117,272
Stratus Coupe	0	0	17,596	0	0	0	0	0	17,596
Viper	1,216	1,600	1,731	0	0	0	1,216	1,600	1,731
Total Dodge	**241,619**	**267,025**	**315,638**	**138,757**	**174,607**	**161,599**	**380,376**	**441,632**	**477,237**
Breeze	64,270	47,911	2,030	0	0	0	64,270	47,911	2,030
Neon	78,372	66,905	49,623	0	0	0	78,372	66,905	49,623
Prowler	2,124	2,862	2,890	0	0	0	2,124	2,862	2,890
Total Plymouth	**144,766**	**117,678**	**54,543**	**0**	**0**	**0**	**144,766**	**117,678**	**54,543**
Total Chrysler Corp.	**433,631**	**431,827**	**450,529**	**300,855**	**338,921**	**291,884**	**734,486**	**770,748**	**742,413**
Contour	129,945	114,897	17,410	0	0	0	129,945	114,897	17,410
Crown Victoria	0	0	0	133,351	124,002	104,798	133,351	124,002	104,798
Escort	198,679	114,171	0	0	0	0	198,679	114,171	0
Focus	0	114,682	325,720	0	0	0	0	114,682	325,720
Mustang	149,129	191,432	180,431	0	0	0	149,129	191,432	180,431
Taurus	400,652	382,858	441,480	0	0	0	400,652	382,858	441,480
Total Ford	**878,405**	**918,040**	**965,041**	**133,351**	**124,002**	**104,798**	**1,011,756**	**1,042,042**	**1,069,839**
Continental	36,328	27,121	22,589	0	0	0	36,328	27,121	22,589
Lincoln LS	0	39,266	58,791	0	0	0	0	39,266	58,791
Mark	6,103	0	0	0	0	0	6,103	0	0
Town Car	110,718	81,551	81,391	0	0	0	110,718	81,551	81,391
Total Lincoln	**153,149**	**147,938**	**162,771**	**0**	**0**	**0**	**153,149**	**147,938**	**162,771**
Grand Marquis	0	0	0	135,709	143,627	130,883	135,709	143,627	130,883
Mystique	39,818	38,021	5,388	0	0	0	39,818	38,021	5,388
Sable	111,676	106,427	114,133	0	0	0	111,676	106,427	114,133
Tracer	27,760	14,691	0	0	0	0	27,760	14,691	0
Total Mercury	**179,254**	**159,139**	**119,521**	**135,709**	**143,627**	**130,883**	**314,963**	**302,766**	**250,404**
Total Ford Motor Co.	**1,210,808**	**1,225,117**	**1,247,333**	**269,060**	**267,629**	**235,681**	**1,479,868**	**1,492,746**	**1,483,014**
LeSabre	142,155	157,501	163,919	0	0	0	142,155	157,501	163,919
Park Ave	65,343	61,009	45,418	0	0	0	65,343	61,009	45,418
Regal	0	0	0	211,715	247,461	233,763	211,715	247,461	233,763
Riviera	6,317	0	0	0	0	0	6,317	0	0
Skylark	6	0	0	0	0	0	6	0	0
Total Buick	**213,821**	**218,510**	**209,337**	**211,715**	**247,461**	**233,763**	**425,536**	**465,971**	**443,100**
Eldorado	14,397	17,638	12,043	0	0	0	14,397	17,638	12,043
Fleetwood Deville	105,206	88,922	118,967	0	0	0	105,206	88,922	118,967
Seville	56,429	38,907	28,026	0	0	0	56,429	38,907	28,026
Total Cadillac	**176,032**	**145,467**	**159,036**	**0**	**0**	**0**	**176,032**	**145,467**	**159,036**
Camaro	0	0	0	47,049	44,564	44,136	47,049	44,564	44,136
Cavalier	233,806	269,564	252,028	0	0	0	233,806	269,564	252,028
Corvette	32,046	33,243	34,919	0	0	0	32,046	33,243	34,919
Impala	0	0	0	0	122,673	209,780	0	122,673	209,780
Lumina	0	0	0	248,272	76,118	45,871	248,272	76,118	45,871
Malibu	252,479	251,584	260,546	0	0	0	252,479	251,584	260,546
Monte Carlo	0	0	0	0	69,378	75,994	0	69,378	75,994
Total Chevrolet	**518,331**	**554,391**	**547,493**	**295,321**	**312,733**	**375,781**	**813,652**	**867,124**	**923,274**
Achieva	6	0	0	0	0	0	6	0	0
Alero	56,429	146,329	135,012	0	0	0	56,429	146,329	135,012
Aurora	21,751	12,260	39,921	0	0	0	21,751	12,260	39,921

U.S. and Canadian Passenger Car Production by Model

U.S. AND CANADIAN PASSENGER CAR PRODUCTION BY MODEL, 1998-2000

	United States			Canada			U.S. and Canada Total		
	1998	1999	2000	1998	1999	2000	1998	1999	2000
Cutlass	50,562	20,784	0	0	0	0	50,562	20,784	0
Intrigue	95,255	98,492	59,884	0	0	0	95,255	98,492	59,884
Olds 88	68,140	0	0	0	0	0	68,140	0	0
Total Oldsmobile	**292,143**	**277,865**	**234,817**	**0**	**0**	**0**	**292,143**	**277,865**	**234,817**
Bonneville	57,516	48,120	66,783	0	0	0	57,516	48,120	66,783
Firebird	0	0	0	33,124	36,581	30,831	33,124	36,581	30,831
Grand Am	184,335	259,471	250,452	0	0	0	184,335	259,471	250,452
Grand Prix	136,948	173,876	166,929	0	0	0	136,948	173,876	166,929
Sunfire	96,851	110,089	92,174	0	0	0	96,851	110,089	92,174
Total Pontiac	**475,650**	**591,556**	**576,338**	**33,124**	**36,581**	**30,831**	**508,774**	**628,137**	**607,169**
Saturn	243,976	238,140	174,946	0	0	0	243,976	238,140	174,946
Saturn FV1	125	318	0	0	0	0	125	318	0
Saturn LS	0	60,987	85,953	0	0	0	0	60,987	85,953
Total Saturn	**244,101**	**299,445**	**260,899**	**0**	**0**	**0**	**244,101**	**299,445**	**260,899**
Toyota Cavalier	4,788	6,111	1,111	0	0	0	4,788	6,111	1,111
Total General Motors	**1,924,866**	**2,093,345**	**1,989,031**	**540,160**	**596,775**	**640,375**	**2,465,026**	**2,690,120**	**2,629,406**
Mazda 626	94,175	87,065	67,255	0	0	0	94,175	87,065	67,255
Mercury Cougar	73,093	78,078	40,176	0	0	0	73,093	78,078	40,176
Total AutoAlliance	**167,268**	**165,143**	**107,431**	**0**	**0**	**0**	**167,268**	**165,143**	**107,431**
BMW Z3	54,802	48,394	38,665	0	0	0	54,802	48,394	38,665
Total BMW	**54,802**	**48,394**	**38,665**	**0**	**0**	**0**	**54,802**	**48,394**	**38,665**
Chevrolet Metro	0	0	0	21,136	32,263	27,032	21,136	32,263	27,032
Suzuki Swift	0	0	0	2,481	3,589	4,874	2,481	3,589	4,874
Total CAMI	**0**	**0**	**0**	**23,617**	**35,852**	**31,906**	**23,617**	**35,852**	**31,906**
Acura CL	30,480	15,804	31,440	0	0	0	30,480	15,804	31,440
Acura EL	0	0	0	7,925	7,680	8,097	7,925	7,680	8,097
Acura TL	31,324	78,959	83,893	0	0	0	31,324	78,959	83,893
Total Acura	**61,804**	**94,763**	**115,333**	**7,925**	**7,680**	**8,097**	**69,729**	**102,443**	**123,430**
Accord	424,660	369,324	336,034	0	0	0	424,660	369,324	336,034
Civic	208,239	221,956	225,723	159,412	168,377	158,818	367,651	390,333	384,541
Total Honda	**632,899**	**591,280**	**561,757**	**159,412**	**168,377**	**158,818**	**792,311**	**759,657**	**720,575**
Total Honda	**694,703**	**686,043**	**677,090**	**167,337**	**176,057**	**166,915**	**862,040**	**862,100**	**844,005**
Chrysler Sebring Coupe	36,753	24,853	19,952	0	0	0	36,753	24,853	19,952
Dodge Avenger	23,459	15,801	1,360	0	0	0	23,459	15,801	1,360
Eagle Talon	295	0	0	0	0	0	295	0	0
Mitsubishi Eclipse	50,715	54,019	78,985	0	0	0	50,715	54,019	78,985
Mitsubishi Galant	45,917	65,029	104,143	0	0	0	45,917	65,029	104,143
Total Mitsubishi	**157,139**	**159,702**	**204,440**	**0**	**0**	**0**	**157,139**	**159,702**	**204,440**
Altima	162,273	152,541	150,129	0	0	0	162,273	152,541	150,129
Nissan 200SX	6,102	0	0	0	0	0	6,102	0	0
Sentra	54,358	15,201	0	0	0	0	54,358	15,201	0
Total Nissan	**222,733**	**167,742**	**150,129**	**0**	**0**	**0**	**222,733**	**167,742**	**150,129**
Chevrolet Prizm	45,284	49,967	49,996	0	0	0	45,284	49,967	49,996
Toyota Corolla	158,180	160,759	147,741	0	0	0	158,180	160,759	147,741
Total NUMMI	**203,464**	**210,726**	**197,737**	**0**	**0**	**0**	**203,464**	**210,726**	**197,737**
Legacy	104,229	93,070	107,955	0	0	0	104,229	93,070	107,955
Total Subaru Isuzu	**104,229**	**93,070**	**107,955**	**0**	**0**	**0**	**104,229**	**93,070**	**107,955**
Avalon	83,718	71,227	120,252	0	0	0	83,718	71,227	120,252
Camry	297,012	285,613	251,625	0	0	0	297,012	285,613	251,625
Corolla	0	0	0	150,413	147,718	133,043	150,413	147,718	133,043
Solara	0	0	0	21,326	63,364	50,696	21,326	63,364	50,696
Total Toyota	**380,730**	**356,840**	**371,877**	**171,739**	**211,082**	**183,739**	**552,469**	**567,922**	**555,616**
Volvo S70/V70	0	0	0	8,373	0	0	8,373	0	0
Total Volvo	**0**	**0**	**0**	**8,373**	**0**	**0**	**8,373**	**0**	**0**
Total Passenger Cars	**5,554,373**	**5,637,949**	**5,542,217**	**1,481,141**	**1,626,316**	**1,550,500**	**7,035,514**	**7,264,265**	**7,092,717**

SOURCE: *Ward's AutoInfoBank*

U.S. Factory Sales of Trucks and Buses by Gross Vehicle Weight Rating

U.S. FACTORY SALES OF TRUCKS AND BUSES BY GROSS VEHICLE WEIGHT RATING, 1980-2000

	Gross Vehicle Weight Rating (Pounds)								
	6,000 & Less	6001- 10,000	10,001- 14,000	14,001- 16,000	16,001- 19,500	19,501- 26,000	26,001- 33,000	33,001 & Over	Total
U.S. TOTAL									
2000	4,533,600	1,973,801	100,293	48,572	25,137	36,874	106,750	197,451	7,022,478
1999	4,876,534	1,891,397	116,868	44,250	19,699	25,528	122,411	248,332	7,345,059
1998	4,458,970	1,431,110	147,839	33,513	17,441	19,850	116,412	210,050	6,435,185
1997	4,377,340	1,366,899	47,022	32,286	4,056	16,687	128,245	180,282	6,152,817
1996	4,073,778	1,344,826	38,525	32,912	4,127	12,379	106,657	162,526	5,775,730
1995	3,742,739	1,583,878	901	37,073	1,549	16,369	125,703	205,257	5,713,469
1994	3,811,837	1,478,854	848	29,585	550	13,559	115,334	189,708	5,640,275
1993	3,488,278	1,124,106	—	8,149	—	21,943	93,939	158,809	4,895,224
1992	2,978,214	850,876	—	7,193	2	21,993	81,601	122,123	4,062,002
1991	2,533,904	658,425	—	3,820	56	19,498	77,850	93,950	3,387,503
1990	2,574,071	906,423	—	789	1,726	38,123	87,107	116,966	3,725,205
1989	2,657,084	1,130,606	11	146	4,593	37,788	90,440	141,282	4,061,950
1988	2,704,891	1,105,069	—	182	5,618	55,840	97,771	151,203	4,120,574
1987	2,475,402	1,052,958	—	366	6,085	46,473	103,188	136,938	3,821,410
1986	2,238,922	997,272	—	—	5,931	45,333	96,998	116,477	3,500,933
1985	2,095,856	1,057,556	19,463	—	5,345	53,471	98,406	134,230	3,464,327
1984	1,807,811	1,061,974	1,631	4	5,713	60,457	87,396	150,849	3,175,835
1982	917,908	803,639	280	58	1,556	47,330	58,498	77,186	1,906,455
1980	592,339	794,184	5,661	362	2,946	91,119	58,846	121,826	1,667,283
U.S DOMESTIC									
2000	4,070,026	1,757,683	97967	35407	22,602	35,752	100,175	171,565	6,290,907
1999	4,453,332	1,723,012	112,349	37,328	17,542	24,362	113,147	218,041	6,699,113
1998	4,053,521	1,303,786	141,781	29,629	15,779	18,989	105,874	177,852	5,847,211
1997	3,894,222	1,236,119	44,893	28,428	3,931	15,609	116,922	149,183	5,489,307
1996	3,699,385	1,225,792	37,559	30,309	4,056	11,717	97,720	141,941	5,248,479
1995	3,405,062	1,458,713	780	35,427	1,471	15,046	114,194	180,652	5,211,345
1994	3,475,044	1,353,576	848	28,437	533	12,123	102,745	165,375	5,138,681
1993	3,187,731	1,031,829	—	7,630	—	19,277	84,779	140,247	4,471,493
1992	2,711,172	785,198	—	6,612	2	19,160	71,899	108,003	3,702,046
1991	2,281,761	594,435	—	3,547	28	16,536	69,703	83,875	3,049,885
1990	2,383,892	848,690	—	693	1,644	34,141	78,553	107,025	3,454,638
1989	2,447,962	1,057,077	11	54	4,234	32,721	81,971	127,880	3,751,910
1988	2,496,648	1,020,515	—	86	5,238	49,670	87,994	135,163	3,795,314
1987	2,270,950	976,573	—	322	5,841	40,502	93,044	121,859	3,509,091
1986	2,072,880	927,462	—	—	5,749	40,353	87,831	103,990	3,238,265
1985	1,962,323	989,633	19397	—	5,123	46,340	88,784	121,996	3,233,596
1984	1,711,345	997,626	—	4	5,502	52,053	78,977	139,135	2,984,642
1982	870,054	745,208	—	10	1,333	40,165	53,244	69,182	1,779,196
1980	547,426	679,532	4,803	24	1,761	76,208	51,900	102,154	1,463,808

SOURCE: Ward's Communications.

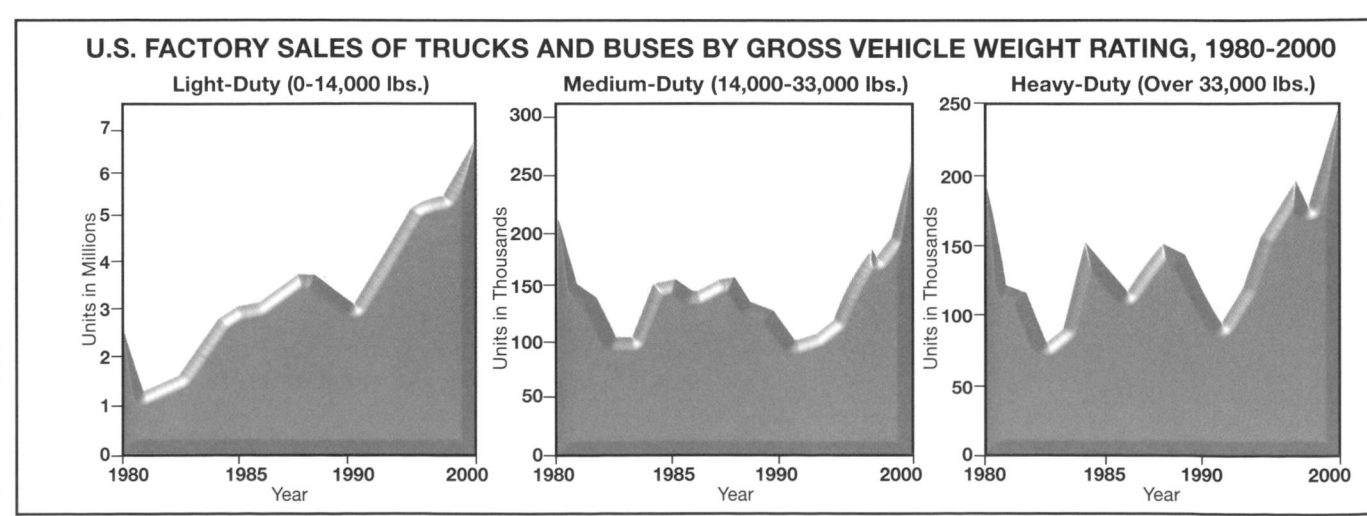

U.S. FACTORY SALES OF TRUCKS AND BUSES BY GROSS VEHICLE WEIGHT RATING, 1980-2000

Light-Duty (0-14,000 lbs.) — Medium-Duty (14,000-33,000 lbs.) — Heavy-Duty (Over 33,000 lbs.)

U.S. Factory Sales of Diesel Trucks and Motor Vehicle Factory Sales from U.S. and Canadian Plants

U.S. FACTORY SALES OF DIESEL TRUCKS BY GROSS VEHICLE WEIGHT RATING, 1965-2000

	Gross Vehicle Weight Rating (Pounds)								
	6,000 & Less	6001- 10,000	10,001- 14,000	14,001- 16,000	16,001- 19,500	19,501- 26,000	26,001- 33,000	33,001 & Over	Total
U.S. TOTAL									
2000	2,580	279,224	50,571	30,223	23,422	19,807	72,509	197,451	675,787
1999	2,843	229,401	68,636	27,424	16,846	23,096	90,493	248,372	707,111
1998	2,486	188,027	104,428	24,020	15,792	17,564	84,083	210,050	646,450
1997	3,294	182,170	11,632	19,590	3,640	13,606	89,713	180,281	503,926
1996	3,139	199,079	9,900	21,770	3,811	8,593	72,753	162,526	481,571
1995	5,995	225,968	150	25,241	1,346	11,403	93,237	205,254	568,594
1994	9,468	140,330	—	8,259	550	8,114	83,317	189,692	439,730
1990	449	102,051	—	81	51	12,567	61,010	116,931	293,140
1985	15,447	132,871	5,870	—	—	16,537	57,238	132,429	360,392
1980	72,501	4,973	—	—	—	15,268	34,544	116,860	244,146
1975	—	1	—	—	159	5,651	11,819	84,878	102,508
1970	8	417	—	168	26	7,875	11,932	85,288	105,714
1965	323	566	146	207	3,739	9,864	16,208	51,098	82,151
U.S DOMESTIC									
2000	271	221,830	48,911	26,997	20,921	18,812	68,678	171,565	577,985
1999	2,199	188,823	66,390	24,753	15,025	22,205	83,867	218,041	621,303
1990	201	155,001	99,898	21,597	14,200	16,791	76,200	177,852	561,800
1997	894	153,845	11,340	18,487	3,515	12,686	80,800	149,182	430,749
1996	1,539	167,634	9,516	20,916	3,740	8,125	66,072	141,941	419,483
1995	4,579	191,758	92	23,913	1,272	10,597	84,213	180,652	497,076
1994	7,366	113,358	—	7,689	533	7,107	73,371	165,371	374,795
1990	337	94,030	—	55	51	11,458	53,957	107,002	266,890
1985	9,663	123,882	5,870	—	—	14,253	50,492	120,311	324,471
1980	68,868	4,397	—	—	—	12,337	30,958	98,002	214,562
1975	—	1	—	—	159	3,517	8,992	59,936	72,605
1970	—	268	—	165	—	3,158	10,245	77,965	91,801
1965	59	509	123	160	2,715	6,206	14,749	47,836	72,357

MOTOR VEHICLE FACTORY SALES FROM U.S. AND CANADIAN PLANTS, 1965-2000

	U.S. Plants				Canadian Plants*			
	U.S Total	Exports to Canada	Other Exports	U.S. Domestic	Canada Total	Exports to U.S.	Other Exports	Canada Domestic
PASSENGER CARS								
2000	5,504,385	285,348	236,589	4,982,448	1,151,889	1,063,547	12,617	75,725
1999	5,427,746	263,160	204,130	4,960,456	1,160,478	1,063,455	15,592	81,431
1998	5,676,964	305,064	176,910	5,194,990	1,109,265	1,017,833	16,216	75,216
1997	6,069,886	342,113	193,853	5,533,920	1,023,828	929,028	18,243	76,557
1996	6,140,454	285,745	238,163	5,616,546	965,849	848,666	23,771	93,412
1995	6,309,839	265,594	256,422	5,787,820	1,028,970	912,939	22,128	93,903
1990	6,049,749	416,459	131,419	5,501,871	901,903	795,621	3,725	102,557
1985	8,002,259	635,546	29,978	7,336,735	1,068,420	878,052	5,878	184,490
1980	6,400,026	488,857	70,864	5,840,305	827,124	539,239	86,297	201,588
1975	6,712,852	549,353	90,199	6,073,300	1,043,245	713,407	58,149	271,689
1970	6,546,817	245,746	113,753	6,187,318	919,232	681,872	30,427	206,933
1965	9,305,561	46,540	158,334	9,100,687	750,777	33,862	39,771	677,144
TRUCKS AND BUSES								
2000	7,022,478	410,698	320,873	6,290,907	1,161,653	954,641	8,899	198,114
1999	7,345,059	416,010	229,936	6,699,113	1,241,442	1,017,982	11,814	211,646
1998	6,435,185	364,865	223,109	5,847,211	1,041,626	814,961	10,223	216,442
1997	6,152,817	402,138	261,372	5,489,307	1,153,540	924,837	11,329	217,374
1996	5,775,730	327,701	199,550	5,248,479	1,058,106	891,117	11,772	155,217
1995	5,713,469	318,470	183,654	5,211,345	1,004,717	871,134	5,180	128,403
1990	3,725,205	207,559	63,008	3,454,638	8,124,697	660,176	26,441	125,850
1985	3,464,327	197,903	32,828	3,233,596	853,974	677,998	7,706	168,270
1980	1,667,283	86,420	117,055	1,463,808	525,968	290,529	47,228	188,211
1975	2,272,160	133,701	135,701	2,002,758	390,065	181,165	47,742	161,158
1970	1,692,440	53,646	73,125	1,565,669	252,079	157,532	32,429	962,118
1965	1,751,805	9,550	126,311	1,615,944	151,214	7,001	15,525	128,688

* Reporting firms do not represent the entire industry.
SOURCE: Ward's Communications.

Passenger Car Production by City and State

PASSENGER CAR PRODUCTION BY CITY AND STATE, 2000

State/City	Model	Units	Percent
CALIFORNIA		**197,737**	**3.6**
Fremont	Corolla	147,741	2.7
	Prizm	49,996	0.9
	Total NUMMI	**197,737**	**3.6**
DELAWARE		**85,953**	**1.6**
Wilmington	Saturn LS	85,953	1.6
	Total General Motors	**85,953**	**1.6**
GEORGIA		**281,801**	**5.1**
Atlanta	Sable	58,556	1.1
	Taurus	223,245	4.0
	Total Ford	**281,801**	**5.1**
ILLINOIS		**724,510**	**13.1**
Belvidere	Dodge Neon	179,039	3.2
	Plymouth Neon	49,623	0.9
	Total Chrysler	**228,662**	**4.1**
Chicago	Sable	55,577	1.0
	Taurus	218,235	3.9
	Total Ford	**273,812**	**4.9**
Normal	Chrysler Sebring	19,952	0.4
	Dodge Avenger	1,360	0.0
	Dodge Stratus Coupe	17,596	0.3
	Mitsubishi Eclipse	78,985	1.4
	Mitsubishi Galant	104,143	1.9
	Total Mitsubishi	**222,036**	**4.0**
INDIANA		**107,955**	**1.9**
Lafayette	Legacy	107,955	1.9
	Total Subaru	**107,955**	**1.9**
KANSAS		**226,813**	**4.1**
Fairfax	Grand Prix	166,929	3.0
	Intrigue	59,884	1.1
	Total General Motors	**226,813**	**4.1**
KENTUCKY		**406,796**	**7.3**
Bowling Green	Corvette	34,919	0.6
	Total General Motors	**34,919**	**0.6**
Georgetown	Avalon	120,252	2.2
	Camry	251,625	4.5
	Total Toyota	**371,877**	**6.7**
MICHIGAN		**1,846,995**	**33.3**
Flat Rock	Cougar	40,176	0.7
	Mazda 626	67,255	1.2
	Total AutoAlliance	**107,431**	**1.9**
Detroit	Prowler	2,890	0.1
	Viper	1,731	0.0
Sterling Heights	Breeze	2,030	0.0
	Cirrus	39,232	0.7
	Sebring Convertible	7,338	0.1
	Sebring Sedan	33,778	0.6
	Stratus	117,272	2.1
	Total Chrysler	**204,271**	**3.7**
Dearborn	Mustang	180,431	3.3
Wayne	Focus	325,720	5.9
Wixom	Continental	22,589	0.4
	Lincoln LS	58,791	1.1
	Town Car	81,391	1.5
	Total Ford	**668,922**	**12.1**
Craft Center	Eldorado	12,043	0.2
Hamtramck	Fleetwood Deville	118,967	2.1
	LeSabre	92,544	1.7
	Seville	28,026	0.5
Lansing	Alero	135,012	2.4
	Cavalier	5	0.0
	Grand Am	250,452	4.5
	Malibu	5,820	0.1
	Sunfire	5	0.0
Orion	Aurora	39,921	0.7
	Bonneville	66,783	1.2
	LeSabre	71,375	1.3
	Park Ave	45,418	0.8
	Total General Motors	**866,371**	**15.6**
MISSOURI		**22,798**	**0.4**
Kansas City	Contour	17,410	0.3
	Mystique	5,388	0.1
	Total Ford	**22,798**	**0.4**
OHIO		**1,022,393**	**18.4**
Lordstown	Cavalier	252,023	4.5
	Sunfire	92,169	1.7
	Toyota Cavalier	1,111	0.0
	Total General Motors	**345,303**	**6.2**
East Liberty	Civic	225,723	4.1
Marysville	Accord	336,034	6.1
	Acura CL	31,440	0.6
	Acura TL	83,893	1.5
	Total Honda	**677,090**	**12.2**
OKLAHOMA		**254,726**	**4.6**
Oklahoma City	Malibu	254,726	4.6
	Total General Motors	**254,726**	**4.6**
SOUTH CAROLINA		**38,665**	**0.7**
Spartanburg	BMW Z3	38,665	0.7
	Total BMW	**38,665**	**0.7**
TENNESSEE		**325,075**	**5.9**
Spring Hill	Saturn	174,946	3.2
	Total General Motors	**174,946**	**3.2**
Smyrna	Altima	150,129	2.7
	Total Nissan	**150,129**	**2.7**
TOTAL		**5,542,217**	**100.0**

Top States in Calendar 2000 U.S. Production

Rank	Cars		Rank	Trucks	
1. Michigan		1,846,995	1. Michigan		1,262,382
2. Ohio		1,022,393	2. Missouri		1,112,230
3. Illinois		724,510	3. Ohio		841,636
4. Kentucky		406,796	4. Kentucky		840,940
5. Tennessee		325,075	5. Indiana		483,372

SOURCE: *Ward's AutoInfoBank.*

Truck Production by City and State

TRUCK PRODUCTION BY CITY AND STATE, 2000

State/City	Model	Units	Percent
ALABAMA		**80,009**	**1.1**
Vance	Mercedes M Class . . .	80,009	1.1
	Total Mercedes	**80,009**	**1.1**
CALIFORNIA		**146,339**	**2.0**
Fremont	Tacoma	146,339	2.0
	Total NUMMI	**146,339**	**2.0**
DELAWARE		**180,346**	**2.5**
Newark	Durango	180,346	2.5
	Total Chrysler	**180,346**	**2.5**
GEORGIA		**263,342**	**3.6**
Doraville	Montana	92,701	1.3
	Silhouette	39,067	0.5
	Venture	131,574	1.8
	Total General Motors	**263,342**	**3.6**
INDIANA		**483,372**	**6.7**
Fort Wayne	Chevy Silverado	190,990	2.6
	GMC Sierra	61,937	0.9
	Total General Motors	**252,927**	**3.5**
Lafayette	Honda Passport	21,197	0.3
	Isuzu Amigo	6,693	0.1
	Isuzu Rodeo	72,831	1.0
	Total Subaru-Isuzu . .	**100,721**	**1.4**
Princeton	Sequoia	15,000	0.2
	Tundra	114,724	1.6
	Total Toyota	**129,724**	**1.8**
KENTUCKY		**840,940**	**11.6**
Kentucky Truck	Excursion	58,992	0.8
	Ford F Series	367,507	5.1
Louisville	Explorer	249,640	3.5
	Mountaineer	41,248	0.6
	Total Ford	**717,387**	**9.9**
Georgetown	Sienna	123,553	1.7
	Total Toyota	**123,553**	**1.7**
LOUISIANA		**205,152**	**2.8**
Shreveport	Chevy S-10	158,739	2.2
	GMC Sonoma	46,413	0.6
	Total General Motors	**205,152**	**2.8**
MARYLAND		**122,334**	**1.7**
Baltimore	Astro	90,050	1.2
	Safari	32,284	0.4
	Total General Motors	**122,334**	**1.7**
MICHIGAN		**1,262,382**	**17.5**
Detroit	Grand Cherokee	293,160	4.1
Warren	Dakota	195,072	2.7
	Dodge Ram	74,941	1.0
	Total Chrysler	**563,173**	**7.8**
Detroit	Ford Chassis	23,730	0.3
Wayne	Expedition	241,460	3.3
	Navigator	45,009	0.6
	Total Ford	**310,199**	**4.3**
Flint	Chevy C/K	45,227	0.6
	Chevy Silverado	17,364	0.2
	GMC Sierra	21,091	0.3
Pontiac East	Chevy Silverado	237,520	3.3
	GMC Sierra	67,808	0.9
	Total General Motors	**389,010**	**5.4**
MINNESOTA		**203,353**	**2.8**
Twin Cities	Ford Ranger	203,353	2.8
	Total Ford	**203,353**	**2.8**
MISSOURI		**1,112,230**	**15.4**
St. Louis North	Dodge Ram	135,588	1.9
St. Louis South	Caravan	123,787	1.7
	Town & Country	51,080	0.7
	Voyager	35,697	0.5
	Total Chrysler	**346,152**	**4.8**
Kansas City 1	Escape	65,986	0.9
	Tribute	36,618	0.5
Kansas City 2	Ford F Series	250,668	3.5
St. Louis	Explorer	239,353	3.3
	Total Ford	**592,625**	**8.2**
Wentzville	Express	129,114	1.8
	Savana	44,339	0.6
	Total General Motors	**173,453**	**2.4**
NEW JERSEY		**364,840**	**5.0**
Edison	Ford Ranger	142,846	2.0
	Mazda Pickup	29,552	0.4
	Total Ford	**172,398**	**2.4**
Linden	Chevy Blazer	73,592	1.0
	Chevy S-10	85,004	1.2
	GMC Jimmy	18,481	0.3
	GMC Sonoma	15,365	0.2
	Total General Motors	**192,442**	**2.7**
OHIO		**841,636**	**11.6**
Toledo	Cherokee	165,590	2.3
	Wranglor	95,440	1.3
	Total Chrysler	**261,030**	**3.6**
Avon Lake	Mercury Villager	27,248	0.4
Lorain Truck	Nissan Quest	41,384	0.6
	Econoline	216,467	3.0
	Total Ford	**285,099**	**3.9**
Moraine	Bravada	30,750	0.4
	Chevy Blazer	179,809	2.5
	GMC Jimmy	84,948	1.2
	Total General Motors	**295,507**	**4.1**
SOUTH CAROLINA		**45,007**	**0.6**
Spartanburg	BMW X5	45,007	0.6
	Total BMW	**45,007**	**0.6**
TENNESSEE		**227,146**	**3.1**
Smyrna	Nissan Frontier	119,162	1.6
	Nissan Xterra	107,984	1.5
	Total Nissan	**227,146**	**3.1**
TEXAS		**102,677**	**1.4**
Arlington	Chevy C/K	20,410	0.3
	Escalade	20,042	0.3
	GMC Sierra	7,079	0.1
	Tahoe	47,410	0.7
	Yukon	7,736	0.1
	Total General Motors	**102,677**	**1.4**
VIRGINIA		**230,628**	**3.2**
Norfolk	Ford F Series	230,628	3.2
	Total Ford	**230,628**	**3.2**
WISCONSIN		**237,454**	**3.3**
Janesville	Chevy CT Series	6,531	0.1
	Chevy Suburban	7,594	0.1
	Chevy Tahoe	130,695	1.8
	Chevy W4 Tiltmaster .	2,574	0.0
	GMC CT Series	18,495	0.3
	GMC W4 Forward . . .	637	0.0
	GMC Yukon	60,209	0.8
	GMC Yukon XL	6,354	0.1
	Isuzu Medium Duty . .	1,574	0.0
	Isuzu NPR	2,791	0.0
	Total General Motors	**237,454**	**3.3**
Other	. . . .	**279,310**	**3.9**
TOTAL	. . . .	**7,228,497**	**100.0**

SOURCE: *Ward's AutoInfoBank.*

Factory Installations of Selected Passenger Car and Light Truck Equipment

FACTORY INSTALLATIONS OF SELECTED EQUIPMENT, 1997-2000 MODEL YEARS*

	1997 Units (000)	1997 % of Total	1998 Units (000)	1998 % of Total	1999 Units (000)	1999 % of Total	2000 Units (000)	2000 % of Total
PASSENGER CARS								
AutomaticTransmission	6,238	88.7	5,933	89.4	6,392	90.2	6,754	91.3
5-Speed Transmission	777	11.0	689	10.3	665	9.4	613	8.3
6-Speed Transmission	15	0.2	18	0.3	31	0.4	32	0.4
Four-Wheel Drive	96	1.4	93	1.4	89	1.3	97	1.3
3-Cylinder Engine	18	0.3	12	0.2	8	0.1	5	0.1
4-Cylinder Engine	3,699	52.6	3,451	52.0	3335	47.7	3,450	46.6
6-Cylinder Engine	2,573	36.6	2,571	38.7	2976	42.6	3,252	44
8-Cylinder Engine	739	10.5	605	9.1	667	9.6	689	9.3
Traction Control	1,271	18.1	1,342	20.2	1848	26.1	2,147	29
Anti-Lock Brakes	3,970	56.5	3,930	59.2	4612	65.1	4,616	62.4
Power Door Locks	5,573	79.3	5,466	82.3	6072	85.7	6,543	88.4
Power Seats, 4 or 6 way	2,683	38.2	2,472	37.2	3047	42	3,576	48.3
Power Windows	5,296	75.3	5,195	78.2	5857	82.6	6,075	82.1
Sun Roof	891	12.7	1,194	18.0	1437	20.3	1,646	22.3
Side Air Bags	100	1.4	428	6.4	639	9	1,371	18.5
Windshield Wiper Delay	6,849	97.4	6,523	98.2	7029	99.2	7,393	99.9
Trip Computer	433	6.2	346	5.2	625	8.8	485	6.6
Keyless Remote	2,875	40.9	3,280	49.4	4080	57.6	5,007	67.7
Air Conditioning,Automatic Temp. Cont	852	12.1	1,069	16.1	1243	17.5	1,240	16.8
Air Conditioning, Manual Temp. Contro	5,877	83.6	5,400	81.3	5692	80.3	6,042	81.7
Limited Slip Differential	120	1.7	114	1.7	165	2.3	218	2.9
Styled Wheels	3,113	44.3	3,078	46.4	3528	49.8	4,148	56.1
Adjustable Steering Column	6,027	85.7	5,928	89.3	6537	92.2	6,862	92.8
Rear Window Defogger	6,655	94.7	8,332	95.4	6749	95.2	7,169	96.9
Cruise Control	5,519	78.5	5,228	78.7	5611	79.2	5,954	80.5
Anti-Theft Device	1,655	23.5	2,012	30.3	2019	28.5	3,012	40.7
LIGHT TRUCKS (0-10,000 lbs. G.V.W.R.)								
AutomaticTransmission	5,340	83.8	5,694	87.2	6,587	89.2	6,935	90.7
Four Wheel Anti-Lock Brakes	3,863	60.6	4,393	67.2	5,270	71.4	5,623	73.5
Rear Anti-Lock Brakes	2,044	32.1	1,610	24.6	1,491	20.6	1,353	17.7
Keyless Entry	2,757	43.3	3,335	51.0	4,458	60.4	4,933	64.5
Anti-Theft Device	832	13.1	1,484	22.7	1,949	26.4	1,949	25.5
Side Air Bag	NA.	NA.	232	3.6	304	4.1	372	4.9
Four-Wheel Drive	2,526	39.6	2,705	41.4	3,195	43.3	3,193	41.7
Diesel Engine	304	4.8	112	1.7	435	5.9	408	5.3
4-Cylinder Gasoline Engine	703	11.0	203	10.8	557	7.5	599	7.8
6-Cylinder Gasoline Engine	2,761	43.3	3,345	51.2	3,478	47.1	3,796	0.6
8-Cylinder Gasoline Engine	2,562	40.2	2,462	37.7	3,220	43.6	3,118	40.8
Air Conditioning	6,007	94.3	6,320	96.7	7,219	96.8	7,525	98.3
Cruise Control	4,870	76.4	5,168	79.1	6,003	81.3	6,289	82.2
Limited Slip Differential	1,817	28.5	1,762	27.0	2,234	30.2	2,257	29.5

* Based on production in the United States, Canada and Mexico for the United States market.
N.A. - Not available.
SOURCE: Ward's Communications.

Recreational Vehicle Shipments

U.S. RECREATIONAL VEHICLE SHIPMENTS BY TYPE, 1977-2000

| | | Travel Trailers | | Folding | | Motor Homes | | | |
Year	Total All Types	Conven- tional	Fifth Wheel[1]	Camping Trailers	Truck Campers	Type A Conven- tional	Type B Van Campers[2]	Type C Chopped Vans[3]	Multi-use Van Con- versions
2000	418,300	114,500	62,300	51,300	11,100	41,000	3,400	16,500	76,400
1999	481,200	117,500	60,500	60,100	11,500	49,400	3,600	18,600	104,100
1998	441,300	98,600	56,500	63,300	10,800	42,900	3,600	17,000	104,600
1997	438,800	78,800	52,800	57,600	10,300	37,600	3,800	13,600	122,300
1996	466,800	75,400	48,500	57,300	11,000	36,500	4,100	14,700	144,000
1995	475,200	75,300	45,900	61,100	11,900	33,000	4,100	15,700	151,100
1994	518,800	79,100	48,900	61,700	11,400	37,300	3,500	17,300	181,800
1993	420,200	69,700	43,900	51,900	10,900	31,900	3,000	16,500	192,400
1992	382,700	63,600	38,900	43,300	10,600	27,300	2,900	16,800	179,300
1991	293,700	49,300	28,300	33,900	9,600	23,500	3,500	15,200	130,400
1990	347,300	52,500	27,900	30,700	9,700	29,000	5,900	17,400	174,200
1989	388,300	53,500	29,100	33,900	0,000	35,400	5,000	20,000	200,400
1988	420,000	58,300	31,300	42,300	11,000	41,500	5,200	26,200	204,200
1987	393,600	59,100	27,100	41,600	10,100	40,800	6,600	26,400	181,900
1986	371,700	55,100	23,100	36,500	7,400	33,300	6,200	28,200	181,900
1985	351,700	54,700	20,700	35,900	6,900	33,600	6,700	28,400	164,800
1984	391,000	65,600	19,600	40,900	7,600	42,100	7,100	32,800	175,300
1983	350,800	64,700	18,100	37,500	6,800	34,400	5,600	30,500	154,200
1982	251,900	47,700	11,700	34,300	5,700	19,300	3,900	18,000	111,300
1981	233,400	48,500	9,600	35,000	5,100	14,300	3,800	17,300	99,800
1980	178,500	42,700	6,300	24,500	5,000	9,800	2,400	16,400	71,400
1979	307,700	74,700	15,500	31,300	13,800	21,500	3,400	39,200	108,500
1978	526,300	132,700	27,100	48,200	24,700	46,600	19,500	91,100	136,400
1977	533,900	145,900	22,000	53,900	31,900	43,000	40,800	76,400	120,000

(1) To be towed by pickup truck with fifth-wheel hitch mounted on the truck bed.
(2) Panel-type trucks with interior converted to living area.
(3) Chopped Vans: (Mini)-unit over 8' high attaches to van chassis of 6,500 lbs. GVWR or more; (Low Profile)-unit less than 8' high attaches to van chassis of 6,500 lbs. GVWR or more: (Compact)-unit attaches to van chassis less than 6,500 lbs. GVWR.

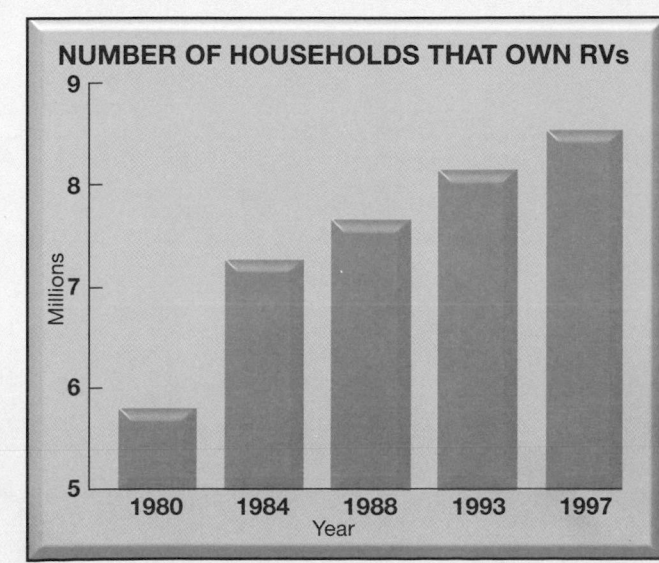

NUMBER OF HOUSEHOLDS THAT OWN RVs

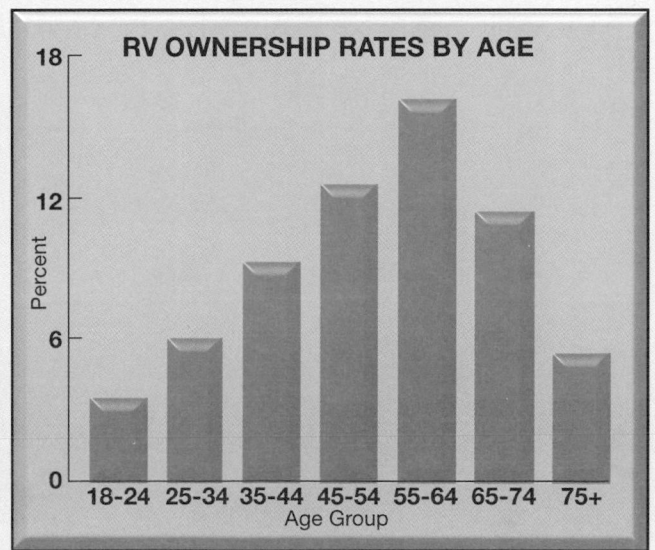

RV OWNERSHIP RATES BY AGE

SOURCE: Recreation Vehicle Industry Association. Permission for further use must be obtained from the Recreation Vehicle Industry Association.

World Motor Vehicle Production by Country

WORLD MOTOR VEHICLE PRODUCTION BY COUNTRY, 2000

Region/Country	Passenger Cars	Commercial Vehicles	Total
North America	**8,223,205**	**9,432,034**	**17,655,239**
Canada	1,550,500	1,411,136	2,961,636
Mexico	1,130,488	792,401	1,922,889
U.S.A.	5,542,217	7,228,497	12,770,714
Western Europe	**14,915,807**	**2,245,619**	**17,161,426**
Austria	115,979	25,047	141,026
Belgium	912,233	121,061	1,033,294
Finland	38,468	458	38,926
France	2,883,419	468,510	3,351,929
Germany	4,802,983	394,702	5,197,685
Italy	1,422,284	316,031	1,738,315
Netherlands	215,085	52,234	267,319
Portugal	191,387	55,812	247,199
Spain	2,445,421	587,453	3,032,874
Sweden	260,000	35,800	295,800
United Kingdom	1,628,548	188,511	1,817,059
Eastern and Central Europe	**2,550,039**	**440,185**	**2,990,224**
Czech Republic	428,223	27,258	455,481
Hungary	134,029	3,369	137,398
Poland	532,845	23,520	556,365
Romania	57,688	13,979	71,667
Russia	965,651	236,938	1,202,589
Serbia	11,178	1,650	12,828
Slovenia	122,949	0	122,949
Turkey	297,476	133,471	430,947
South America	**1,586,844**	**423,881**	**2,010,725**
Argentina	238,921	100,711	339,632
Brazil	1,347,923	323,170	1,671,093
Asia-Oceania	**13,225,148**	**4,140,362**	**17,365,510**
Australia	323,649	24,621	348,270
China	620,000	1,388,500	2,008,500
India	513,948	282,237	796,185
Indonesia	257,058	35,652	292,710
Japan	8,363,485	1,781,362	10,144,847
Malaysia	280,000	15,000	295,000
South Korea	2,602,008	512,990	3,114,998
Taiwan	265,000	100,000	365,000
Africa	**230,577**	**114,383**	**344,960**
South Africa	230,577	114,383	344,960
Total	**40,731,620**	**16,796,464**	**57,528,084**

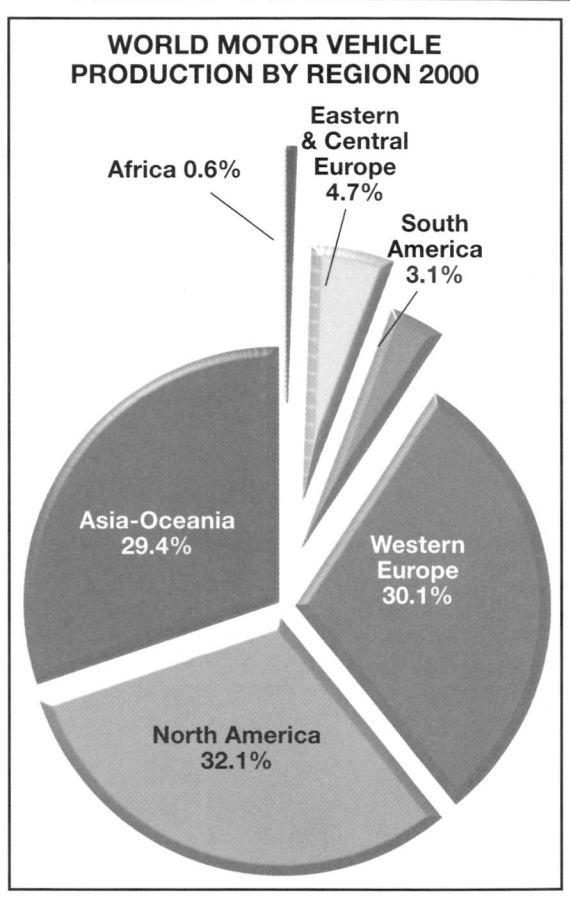

WORLD MOTOR VEHICLE PRODUCTION BY REGION 2000

- Africa 0.6%
- Eastern & Central Europe 4.7%
- South America 3.1%
- Western Europe 30.1%
- North America 32.1%
- Asia-Oceania 29.4%

WORLD MOTOR VEHICLE PRODUCTION, 1950-2000 (In Thousands)

Year	United States	Canada	U.S. & Canada Total	Europe	Japan	Other	World Total	Percent of World Total United States	Percent of World Total U.S. & Canada
2000	12,771	2,962	15,732	17,161	10,145	14,490	57,528	22.2	27.3
1999	13,025	3,057	16,082	19,158	9,905	9,803	54,948	23.7	29.3
1998	12,006	2,173	14,179	18,137	10,050	9,732	52,098	23.1	27.2
1997	12,119	2,571	14,690	17,773	10,975	10,024	53,463	22.7	27.5
1996	11,799	2,397	14,196	17,550	10,346	9,241	51,332	22.0	27.7
1995	11,985	2,408	14,393	17,045	10,196	8,349	49,983	23.0	28.8
1994	12,263	2,321	14,583	16,195	10,554	8,167	49,500	24.8	29.5
1993	10,898	2,246	13,144	15,208	11,228	7,205	46,785	23.3	28.1
1992	9,729	1,961	11,692	17,628	12,499	6,269	48,088	20.2	24.3
1991	8,811	1,888	10,699	17,804	13,245	5,180	46,928	18.8	22.8
1990	9,783	1,928	11,711	18,866	13,487	4,496	48,554	20.1	24.1
1985	11,653	1,933	13,586	16,113	12,271	2,939	44,909	25.9	30.3
1980	8,010	1,324	9,334	15,496	11,043	2,692	38,565	20.8	24.2
1975	8,987	1,385	10,372	13,581	6,942	2,211	33,106	27.1	31.3
1970	8,284	1,160	9,444	13,049	5,289	1,637	29,419	28.2	32.1
1965	11,138	847	11,985	9,576	1,876	834	24,271	45.9	49.4
1960	7,905	398	8,303	6,837	482	866	16,488	47.9	50.4
1955	9,204	452	9,656	3,741	68	163	13,628	67.5	70.9
1950	8,006	388	8,394	1,991	32	160	10,577	75.7	79.4

SOURCE: Compiled by Ward's Communications from various sources.

World Motor Vehicle Production by Manufacturer

WORLD MOTOR VEHICLE PRODUCTION BY MANUFACTURER, 2000

Manufacturer	Passenger Cars	Light Trucks	Heavy Trucks	Buses	Total
General Motors	5,247,245	2,861,116	5,996	0	8,114,357
Ford	4,038,670	3,167,359	0	0	7,206,029
Toyota-Daihatsu-Hino	4,655,935	1,201,765	35,889	3,625	5,897,214
Volkswagen	4,859,478	234,726	8,765	3,780	5,106,749
DaimlerChrysler	2,043,376	2,326,064	254,977	42,223	4,666,640
PSA Peugeot Citroen	2,493,980	385,442	0	0	2,879,422
Nissan	2,041,346	631,119	24,406	1,086	2,697,957
Fiat	2,183,858	339,186	108,054	8,307	2,639,405
Renault	2,101,855	325,323	87,719	0	2,514,897
Hyundai	2,023,042	435,100	19,136	11,043	2,488,321
Honda	2,250,771	218,485	0	0	2,469,256
Mitsubishi	1,094,357	470,483	45,913	2,500	1,613,253
Suzuki-Maruti	1,181,929	252,416	0	0	1,434,345
Mazda	822,187	149,489	0	0	971,676
BMW	834,628	0	0	0	834,628
Daewoo	758,059	66,143	5,336	4,197	833,735
Avtovaz	755,997	0	0	0	755,997
Fuji-Subaru	499,738	81,297	0	0	581,035
Isuzu	35,911	473,775	60,000	2,133	571,819
GAZ	116,319	111,354	0	0	227,673
Proton	212,681	0	0	0	212,681
Changan	100,000	103,127	0	0	203,127
Tata	90,122	57,001	38,857	7,600	193,580
MG Rover	174,885	0	0	0	174,885
Dongfeng	0	157,038	0	0	157,038
Beijing Jeep	0	124,824	0	0	124,824
Harbin	0	122,007	0	0	122,007
PACCAR	0	0	99,895	1,677	101,572
Navistar	0	0	75,383	19,859	95,242
Volvo Truck	0	0	82,006	11,256	93,262
Perodua	70,000	15,000	0	0	85,000
UAZ	40,250	44,622	0	0	84,872
MAN	0	0	65,267	5,295	70,562
Kamaz	33,561	0	23,482	0	57,043
Scania	0	0	51,409	4,172	55,581
Porsche	51,574	0	0	0	51,574

SOURCE: OICA.

Motor Vehicle Production in Mexico

MOTOR VEHICLE PRODUCTION IN MEXICO, 1999-2000

	For Domestic Market		For Export		Total	
	1999	**2000**	**1999**	**2000**	**1999**	**2000**
BMW 3 Series	1,401	1,385	0	0	1,401	1,385
BMW 5 Series	194	209	0	0	194	209
BMW 7 Series	1	0	0	0	1	0
Porsche 911	9	0	0	0	9	0
Total BMW	**1,605**	**1,594**	**0**	**0**	**1,605**	**1,594**
Cirrus	2,416	1,002	0	0	2,416	1,002
Neon (Dodge)	0	0	10,356	0	10,356	0
Neon (Plym)	0	0	5,824	0	5,824	0
Sebring	0	0	56,123	31,089	56,123	31,089
Stratus	17,905	6,020	0	0	17,905	6,020
Total Chrysler	**20,321**	**7,022**	**72,303**	**31,089**	**92,624**	**38,111**
Contour	7,105	5,402	7,644	12,431	14,749	17,833
Escort	4,495	1,952	108,546	103,736	113,041	105,688
Focus	0	1,969	12,924	60,387	12,924	62,356
Ikon	0	705	0	0	0	705
Mystique	3,475	2,683	1,847	2,323	5,322	5,006
Tracer	0	0	975	0	975	0
Total Ford Motor Co. ...	**15,075**	**12,711**	**131,936**	**178,877**	**147,011**	**191,588**
Cavalier	12,513	6,465	53,815	43,694	66,328	50,159
Joy/Swing	55,868	65,967	1,540	500	57,408	66,467
Monza	27,655	23,149	2,407	1,910	30,062	25,059
Sunfire	7,440	6,817	23,444	36,714	30,884	43,531
Total General Motors ..	**103,476**	**102,398**	**81,206**	**82,818**	**184,682**	**185,216**
Accord	8,446	11,524	1,795	7,277	10,241	18,801
Total Honda	**8,446**	**11,524**	**1,795**	**7,277**	**10,241**	**18,801**
Mercedes C Class	107	0	0	0	107	0
Mercedes E Class	83	0	0	0	83	0
Total Mercedes Benz ..	**190**	**0**	**0**	**0**	**190**	**0**
Lucino	1,208	676	0	0	1,208	676
Sentra	28,568	35,604	46,369	142,568	74,937	178,172
Tsubame	2,069	1,653	274	293	2,343	1,946
Tsuru	66,396	84,179	2,559	4,502	68,955	88,681
Total Nissan	**98,241**	**122,112**	**49,202**	**147,363**	**147,443**	**269,475**
Beetle	1,483	1,831	158,664	147,595	160,147	149,426
Golf	209	306	3	0	212	306
Jetta	31,317	42,641	165,670	178,686	196,987	221,327
Sedan	35,993	40,871	453	389	36,446	41,260
VW Cabrio	0	0	16,516	13,384	16,516	13,384
Total Volkswagen	**69,002**	**85,649**	**341,306**	**340,054**	**410,308**	**425,703**
Total Passenger Cars ...	**316,356**	**343,010**	**677,748**	**787,478**	**994,104**	**1,130,488**
Chrysler Corp.	16,714	26,828	223,448	343,433	240,162	370,261
Dina Camiones	1,973	1,799	0	0	1,973	1,799
Ford Motor Co..	30,339	33,729	46,852	53,677	77,191	87,406
General Motors	21,489	14,702	124,850	243,468	146,339	258,170
Kenworth	7,233	7,326	0	0	7,233	7,326
Mercedes Benz	21,751	12,875	0	0	21,751	12,875
Navistar	6,418	9,311	0	0	6,418	9,311
Nissan	32,297	37,406	5,834	6,615	38,131	44,021
Oshmex	542	1,095	0	0	542	1,095
Scania Heavy Truck	**316**	**137**	**0**	**0**	**316**	**137**
Total Trucks	**139,072**	**145,208**	**400,984**	**647,193**	**540,056**	**792,401**
Total Cars and Trucks ..	**455,428**	**488,218**	**1,078,732**	**1,434,671**	**1,534,160**	**1,922,889**

SOURCE: AMIA, ANPACT.

U.S. Retail Sales of Cars and Trucks

ANNUAL U.S. MOTOR VEHICLE RETAIL SALES (In Thousands)

Year	Passenger Cars			Trucks			Motor Vehicles		
	Domestic	Import	Total	Domestic	Import	Total	Domestic	Import	Total
2000	6,830	2,016	8,846	8,092	873	8,965	14,922	2,889	17,811
1999	6,979	1,719	8,698	7,922	795	8,716	14,901	2,513	17,415
1998	6,762	1,380	8,142	7,151	674	7,826	13,913	2,054	15,967
1997	6,917	1,355	8,272	6,632	593	7,226	13,549	1,949	15,498
1996	7,255	1,271	8,526	6,478	452	6,929	13,732	1,723	15,455
1995	7,129	1,506	8,635	6,064	417	6,481	13,193	1,923	15,116
1994	7,255	1,735	8,990	5,995	426	6,421	13,250	2,161	15,411
1993	6,742	1,776	8,518	5,287	394	5,681	12,029	2,170	14,199
1992	6,277	1,937	8,214	4,481	422	4,903	10,758	2,359	13,117
1991	6,137	2,038	8,175	3,813	551	4,364	9,950	2,589	12,539
1990	6,097	2,403	9,300	4,215	631	4,846	11,112	3,034	14,146
1989	7,073	2,699	9,772	4,403	538	4,941	11,476	3,237	14,713
1988	7,526	3,004	10,530	4,508	641	5,149	12,034	3,645	15,679
1987	7,081	3,196	10,277	4,055	858	4,913	11,136	4,054	15,190
1986	8,215	3,245	11,460	3,921	941	4,862	12,136	4,186	16,322
1985	8,205	2,838	11,043	3,902	779	4,681	12,107	3,617	15,724
1984	7,952	2,439	10,391	3,475	618	4,093	11,427	3,057	14,484
1983	6,795	2,387	9,182	2,658	471	3,129	9,453	2,858	12,311
1982	5,759	2,224	7,983	2,146	414	2,560	7,905	2,638	10,543
1981	6,209	2,327	8,536	1,809	451	2,260	8,018	2,778	10,796
1980	6,581	2,398	8,979	2,001	487	2,488	8,582	2,885	11,467
1979	8,341	2,332	10,673	3,010	470	3,480	11,351	2,802	14,153
1978	9,312	2,002	11,314	3,773	336	4,109	13,085	2,338	15,423
1977	9,109	2,074	11,183	3,352	323	3,675	12,461	2,397	14,858
1976	8,611	1,499	10,110	2,944	237	3,181	11,555	1,736	13,291
1975	7,053	1,571	8,624	2,249	229	2,478	9,302	1,800	11,102
1974	7,454	1,399	8,853	2,512	176	2,688	9,966	1,575	11,541
1973	9,676	1,748	11,424	2,916	233	3,149	12,592	1,981	14,573
1972	9,327	1,614	10,941	2,486	143	2,629	11,813	1,757	13,570
1971	8,681	1,561	10,242	2,011	85	2,096	10,692	1,646	12,338
1970	7,119	1,280	8,399	1,746	65	1,811	8,865	1,345	10,210
1969	8,464	1,118	9,582	1,936	34	1,970	10,400	1,152	11,552
1958	8,625	1,031	9,656	1,807	24	1,831	10,432	1,055	11,487
1967	7,568	769	8,337	1,524	21	1,545	9,092	790	9,882
1966	8,377	651	9,028	1,619	17	1,636	9,996	668	10,664
1965	8,763	569	9,332	1,539	14	1,553	10,302	583	10,885
1964	7,617	484	8,101	1,351	42	1,393	8,968	526	9,494
1963	7,334	386	7,720	1,230	40	1,270	8,564	426	8,990
1962	6,753	339	7,092	1,068	32	1,100	7,821	371	8,192
1961	5,556	379	5,935	908	29	937	6,464	408	6,872
1959	5,486	614	6,100	928	37	965	6,414	651	7,065
1957	5,826	207	6,033	878	16	894	6,704	223	6,927
1955	7,408	58	7,466	1,012	3	1,015	8,420	61	8,481
1953	5,775	33	5,808	965	N.A.	965	6,740	33	6,773
1951	5,143	21	5,164	1,111	N.A.	1,111	6,254	21	6,275
1942-1950	N.A.	N.A.	N.A.	N.A.	N.A.	N.A.	N.A.	N.A.	N.A.
1941	3,763	N.A.	3,763	902	N.A.	902	4,665	N.A.	4,665
1939	2,724	N.A.	2,724	521	N.A.	521	3,245	N.A.	3,245
1937	3,508	N.A.	3,508	645	N.A.	645	4,153	N.A.	4,153
1935	2,867	N.A.	2,867	552	N.A.	552	3,419	N.A.	3,419
1933	1,526	N.A.	1,526	261	N.A.	261	1,787	N.A.	1,787
1931	1,903	N.A.	1,903	328	N.A.	328	2,231	N.A.	2,231

.A. - Not available.
SOURCE: Ward's Communications.

U.S. Retail Sales of Passenger Cars

U.S. RETAIL SALES OF PASSENGER CARS, 1996-2000

Model	1996	1997	1998	1999	2000
BMW 3 Series	5,468	824	0	0	0
BMW 3 Series*	44,779	51,648	57,520	77,138	89,681
BMW 5 Series*	22,775	31,347	35,100	38,218	39,703
BMW 7 Series*	17,174	18,273	18,309	18,233	16,619
BMW 8 Series*	525	648	17	7	1
BMW Z3	15,040	19,760	20,613	20,062	16,382
BMW Z8*	0	0	0	0	317
Total BMW	**105,761**	**122,500**	**131,559**	**153,658**	**162,703**
Chrysler 300M	0	0	30,765	55,966	50,682
Chrysler LHS	34,659	30,189	16,753	24,307	20,982
Cirrus	36,007	31,549	38,504	31,859	38,086
Concorde	52,106	38,772	64,912	59,855	50,206
Lebaron	1,062	0	0	0	0
New Yorker	2,554	0	0	0	0
Sebring Convertible	53,852	53,054	51,342	51,750	39,114
Sebring Coupe	31,781	35,365	33,584	25,581	12,870
Sebring Sedan	0	0	0	0	10,632
Total Chrysler	**212,021**	**188,929**	**235,860**	**249,318**	**222,572**
Avenger	35,774	31,943	24,084	17,658	5,512
Intrepid	145,402	118,537	110,499	144,355	143,840
Neon	139,831	121,854	117,964	112,236	113,381
Stealth*	1,276	0	0	0	0
Stratus Coupe	0	0	0	0	5,791
Stratus Sedan	98,065	99,040	106,434	94,413	97,906
Viper	1,597	1,458	1,248	1,315	1,470
Total Dodge	**421,945**	**372,832**	**360,229**	**369,977**	**367,900**
Summit*	1,365	0	0	0	0
Summit Wagon*	2,051	0	0	0	0
Talon	13,842	10,206	2,957	0	0
Vision	11,437	5,146	501	0	0
Total Eagle	**28,695**	**15,352**	**3,458**	**0**	**0**
Breeze	64,500	72,499	59,543	52,054	6,319
Neon	105,472	86,798	78,533	71,561	49,951
Prowler	0	120	1,594	2,365	2,631
Total Plymouth	**169,972**	**159,417**	**139,670**	**125,980**	**58,901**
Total Chrysler Corp.	**832,633**	**736,530**	**739,217**	**745,275**	**649,373**
Lanos*	0	0	388	9,321	22,061
Leganza*	0	0	1,331	12,913	24,826
Nubira*	0	0	523	8,553	21,473
Total Daewoo	**0**	**0**	**2,242**	**30,787**	**68,360**
Aspire*	37,359	33,243	4,917	0	0
Contour	174,187	151,060	139,838	134,487	45,109
Crown Victoria	108,789	107,872	111,531	114,669	92,047
Escort	284,644	283,898	291,936	260,486	110,736
Focus	0	0	0	55,846	286,166
Mustang	122,674	116,610	144,732	166,915	173,676
Probe	32,505	16,361	3,058	0	0
Taurus	401,049	357,162	371,074	368,327	382,035
Thunderbird	79,721	66,334	2,243	0	0
Total Ford	**1,240,928**	**1,132,540**	**1,069,329**	**1,100,730**	**1,089,769**
Jaguar S-Type*	0	0	0	15,541	24,507
Jaguar Vanden Plas*	4,383	3,174	4,789	4,438	3,944

U.S. Retail Sales of Passenger Cars

U.S. RETAIL SALES OF PASSENGER CARS, 1996-2000 — continued

Model	1996	1997	1998	1999	2000
Jaguar XJ12*	374	48	0	0	0
Jaguar XJ6/8*	7,583	8,598	10,191	7,366	7,155
Jaguar XJC Sc*	2,867	49	0	0	0
Jaguar XJR Sedan*	618	768	1,662	1,540	1,393
Jaguar XJS Coupe*	3	0	0	0	0
Jaguar XK8*	2,050	6,864	5,861	6,154	6,729
Total Jaguar	**17,878**	**19,501**	**22,503**	**35,039**	**43,728**
Continental	32,019	31,220	35,210	26,246	22,648
Lincoln Ls	0	0	0	26,368	51,039
Mark	15,859	16,023	10,505	0	0
Town Car	93,598	92,297	97,547	84,629	81,399
Total Lincoln	**141,476**	**139,540**	**143,262**	**137,243**	**155,086**
Cougar	36,015	30,516	38,216	56,831	40,343
Grand Marquis	99,770	109,539	114,162	122,776	122,572
Mystique	57,102	41,038	38,274	30,501	10,208
Sable	114,164	112,400	100,367	101,120	103,030
Tracer	47,797	43,589	33,077	23,146	0
Total Mercury	**354,848**	**337,082**	**324,096**	**343,404**	**282,153**
Volvo 40*	0	0	0	11,988	35,635
Volvo 60*	0	0	0	0	2,994
Volvo 80*	0	0	6,071	33,549	29,000
Volvo 800*	68,403	20,184	410	18	0
Volvo 90*	0	9,017	7,894	32	0
Volvo 900*	20,178	8,698	0	0	0
Volvo S70 V70*	0	52,995	86,797	71,105	48,660
Total Volvo	**88,581**	**90,894**	**101,172**	**116,692**	**116,289**
Total Ford Motor Co.	**1,843,711**	**1,719,557**	**1,660,362**	**1,733,108**	**1,687,025**
Impreza*	24,687	24,242	19,041	19,356	19,220
Legacy	94,950	92,913	88,660	87,267	96,393
SVX*	1,111	640	0	0	0
Total Subaru	**120,748**	**117,795**	**107,701**	**106,623**	**115,613**
Century	72,433	91,232	126,220	157,035	143,085
Lesabre	131,316	150,744	136,551	149,445	148,633
Park Ave	47,732	68,777	58,187	62,868	47,669
Regal	86,847	50,691	65,979	74,016	65,167
Riviera	20,641	14,089	9,390	2,247	58
Roadmaster	17,112	3,200	82	0	0
Skylark	51,269	59,331	1,747	0	0
Total Buick	**427,350**	**438,064**	**398,156**	**445,611**	**404,612**
Catera*	1,676	25,411	24,635	15,068	17,290
Eldorado	20,964	20,609	15,598	15,255	13,289
Fleetwood Brougham	10,200	2,024	22	0	0
Fleetwood Deville	103,730	104,743	100,513	90,755	105,694
Seville	33,809	29,837	38,713	33,532	29,535
Total Cadillac	**170,379**	**182,624**	**179,481**	**154,610**	**165,808**
Camaro	66,866	55,973	47,577	40,726	42,131
Caprice	46,261	11,583	67	0	0
Cavalier	277,222	302,161	256,099	272,122	236,803
Corsica Beretta	149,117	4,844	58	0	0
Corvette	17,805	22,724	29,208	29,963	31,208
Impala	0	0	0	81,247	174,358
Lumina	237,973	228,451	177,631	97,607	46,573
Malibu	2,274	164,654	223,703	218,540	207,376

U.S. Retail Sales of Passenger Cars

U.S. RETAIL SALES OF PASSENGER CARS, 1996-2000 — continued

Model	1996	1997	1998	1999	2000
Metro	88,773	55,629	28,515	31,989	33,878
Monte Carlo	79,593	71,543	64,022	68,309	66,364
Prizm	79,288	62,992	49,552	44,246	52,116
Total Chevrolet	**1,045,172**	**980,554**	**876,432**	**884,749**	**890,807**
Achieva	40,344	63,196	888	34	0
Alero	0	0	28,134	118,907	122,722
Aurora	23,717	25,404	21,374	16,321	28,250
Ciera	89,577	4,322	63	0	0
Cutlass	434	26,708	53,438	32,677	1,243
Intrigue	0	23,460	90,563	90,057	64,109
Olds 88	58,525	67,223	65,877	23,915	477
Olds 98	12,626	633	48	0	0
Supreme	81,263	40,717	1,601	78	0
Total Oldsmobile	**306,486**	**251,663**	**261,986**	**281,989**	**216,801**
Bonneville	73,849	75,882	59,638	45,111	65,606
Firebird	32,622	32,524	31,692	33,850	31,013
Grand Am	222,477	204,078	180,428	234,936	214,923
Grand Prix	104,979	142,018	122,915	148,197	148,521
Sunfire	95,783	102,160	82,748	90,256	82,364
Total Pontiac	**529,710**	**556,662**	**477,421**	**552,350**	**542,427**
Saab 9-3*	0	0	12,826	22,473	19,406
Saab 9-5*	0	0	7,928	16,778	19,993
Saab 900*	22,436	23,049	9,009	238	62
Saab 9000*	6,003	5,404	993	52	18
Total Saab	**28,439**	**28,453**	**30,756**	**39,541**	**39,479**
Saturn EV1	0	289	264	137	411
Saturn LS	0	0	0	24,456	94,034
Saturn S	278,574	250,810	231,522	207,977	177,355
Total Saturn	**278,574**	**251,099**	**231,786**	**232,570**	**271,800**
Total General Motors	**2,786,110**	**2,689,119**	**2,456,018**	**2,591,420**	**2,531,734**
Acura CL	16,740	28,939	26,644	20,968	24,677
Acura NSX*	460	415	303	238	221
Acura RL*	15,948	16,004	15,024	13,366	14,827
Acura TL	0	0	16,718	56,556	67,033
Acura TL*	24,700	23,151	15,165	0	0
Integra*	46,966	38,331	34,904	26,184	25,975
Legend*	629	4	0	0	0
Total Acura	**105,443**	**106,844**	**108,758**	**117,312**	**132,733**
Accord	381,912	363,016	370,984	316,339	317,483
Accord*	386	21,593	30,087	87,853	87,032
Civic	266,859	273,356	317,134	308,807	306,748
Civic*	11,673	42,190	17,428	9,501	17,780
Del Sol*	7,818	5,598	548	1	0
Honda EV Plus*	0	105	133	62	2
Honda S2000*	0	0	0	3,400	6,797
Insight*	0	0	0	17	3,788
Prelude*	12,063	16,678	15,399	11,378	9,692
Total Honda	**680,711**	**722,536**	**751,713**	**737,358**	**749,322**
Total Honda	**786,154**	**829,380**	**860,471**	**854,670**	**882,055**
Accent*	53,230	40,355	30,231	41,235	66,736
Elantra*	39,801	41,303	37,501	83,292	104,099
Excel*	22	0	0	0	0
Scoupe*	458	9	0	0	0
Sonata*	14,616	22,128	14,144	30,022	45,983

U.S. Retail Sales of Passenger Cars

U.S. RETAIL SALES OF PASSENGER CARS, 1996-2000 — continued

Model	1996	1997	1998	1999	2000
Tiburon*	341	9,391	8,341	9,641	15,237
XG300*	0	0	0	0	2,004
Total Hyundai	**108,468**	**113,186**	**90,217**	**164,190**	**234,059**
Isuzu Stylus*	1	0	0	0	0
Total Isuzu	**1**	**0**	**0**	**0**	**0**
Optima*	0	0	0	0	97
Rio*	0	0	0	0	16,624
Sephia*	26,366	35,494	54,311	82,211	67,893
Spectra*	0	0	0	0	13,642
Total Kia Motors	**26,366**	**35,494**	**54,311**	**82,211**	**98,256**
Mazda 626	79,354	75,800	91,147	86,735	71,046
Mazda 929*	1,232	7	0	0	0
Mazda MX3*	2,399	7	0	0	0
Mazda MX6	6,550	3,546	443	14	0
Mazda RX7*	369	12	0	0	0
Miata*	18,408	17,218	19,845	17,738	18,299
Millenia*	13,019	18,020	16,717	19,198	16,558
Protégé*	59,644	53,930	58,349	65,242	62,851
Total Mazda	**180,975**	**168,540**	**186,501**	**188,927**	**168,754**
Mercedes C Class*	28,715	32,543	34,487	29,770	34,600
Mercedes CL*	0	0	0	367	2,204
Mercedes CLK*	0	1,236	11,622	16,714	17,796
Mercedes E Class*	37,956	42,883	47,563	50,214	49,592
Mercedes S Class*	17,317	16,119	15,010	28,713	30,319
Mercedes SL Class*	6,856	8,025	7,809	7,853	5,409
Mercedes SLK*	0	6,890	10,620	10,600	12,930
Total Mercedes Benz	**90,844**	**107,696**	**127,111**	**144,231**	**152,850**
Diamante*	2,718	11,402	8,563	9,921	9,219
Eclipse	63,116	58,569	57,955	61,874	71,307
Expo*	2	1	0	0	0
Galant	62,518	42,588	44,201	74,782	96,452
Galant*	3,174	19	1	0	0
Mirage*	30,338	31,717	33,072	47,136	49,369
Mitsubishi 3000 GT*	8,317	6,086	4,164	3,419	117
Total Mitsubishi	**170,183**	**150,382**	**147,956**	**197,132**	**226,464**
Infiniti G20*	13,467	419	7,217	16,108	13,095
Infiniti I30*	27,057	31,303	26,350	31,042	39,532
Infiniti J30*	7,564	4,594	1,783	17	1
Infiniti Q45*	5,896	10,443	8,244	6,271	4,178
Total Infiniti	**53,984**	**46,759**	**43,594**	**53,438**	**56,806**
Altima	147,910	144,483	144,451	153,525	136,971
Altra EV*	0	0	0	30	50
Maxima*	128,395	123,215	113,843	131,182	129,235
Nissan 200SX	31,388	26,032	18,734	1,193	8
Nissan 240SX*	7,029	3,533	2,266	954	18
Nissan 300ZX*	2,074	1,010	124	15	3
Nissan NX*	1	0	0	0	0
Sentra	129,593	122,468	88,363	63,134	98,803
Sentra*	3	0	0	0	0
Total Nissan	**446,393**	**420,741**	**367,781**	**350,033**	**365,088**

U.S. Retail Sales of Passenger Cars

U.S. RETAIL SALES OF PASSENGER CARS, 1996-2000 — continued

Model	1996	1997	1998	1999	2000
Total Nissan	**500,377**	**467,500**	**411,375**	**403,471**	**421,894**
Boxster*	0	6,989	9,696	12,681	13,312
Porsche 911*	7,141	5,977	7,547	8,194	9,098
Porsche 928*	5	0	0	0	0
Porsche 968*	6	10	0	0	0
Total Porsche	**7,152**	**12,976**	**17,243**	**20,875**	**22,410**
Esteem*	6,996	6,968	13,915	12,320	16,877
Swift	3,379	1,615	2,254	2,290	3,379
Swift*	13	1	0	0	0
Total Suzuki	**10,388**	**8,584**	**16,169**	**14,610**	**20,256**
Lexus ES300*	44,773	58,428	48,644	45,860	41,320
Lexus GS300*	2,044	3,823	20,696	24,990	21,921
Lexus GS400*	0	3,890	9,926	6,894	6,158
Lexus LS300*	0	0	0	0	15,540
Lexus LS400*	22,237	19,618	20,790	16,357	15,871
Lexus SC300*	2,390	2,999	1,766	1,731	450
Lexus SC400*	2,557	2,042	1,243	826	181
Total Lexus	**74,001**	**90,800**	**103,065**	**96,658**	**101,441**
Avalon	73,308	71,309	77,752	68,038	104,078
Camry	280,021	305,416	295,108	320,156	298,123
Camry*	79,412	91,740	134,467	128,006	124,838
Celica*	14,343	9,021	4,290	16,418	52,406
Corolla	202,417	217,207	250,500	249,127	230,156
Corolla*	6,631	1,254	1	1	0
Echo*	0	0	0	10,490	48,876
MR2 Spyder*	0	0	0	0	7,233
Paseo*	6,069	2,786	200	5	0
Prius*	0	0	0	0	5,562
Supra*	861	1,389	688	24	2
Tercel*	56,492	31,651	1,743	46	0
Toyota MR2*	37	9	0	0	0
Total Toyota	**719,591**	**731,782**	**764,749**	**792,311**	**871,274**
Total Toyota	**793,592**	**822,582**	**867,814**	**888,969**	**972,715**
Audi A4*	15,319	20,871	26,635	32,137	34,460
Audi A6*	9,908	9,949	18,050	26,131	30,487
Audi A8*	559	2,085	2,172	2,481	2,362
Audi Cabrio*	1,183	1,255	660	71	3
Audi S4*	410	0	0	0	0
Audi TT*	0	0	0	5,139	12,027
Total Audi	**27,379**	**34,160**	**47,517**	**65,959**	**79,339**
Beetle	0	0	55,842	83,434	81,134
Corrado*	2	1	0	0	0
Golf	24,208	20,702	18,282	0	0
Golf*	0	0	0	18,990	28,124
Jetta	85,022	90,984	89,311	130,054	144,853
Passat*	19,850	14,868	39,272	68,151	84,521
VW Cabrio	975	9,538	15,230	11,539	14,133
VW Cabrio*	4,853	0	0	0	0
VW Fox*	2	0	0	0	0
Total Volkswagen	**134,912**	**136,093**	**217,937**	**312,168**	**352,765**
Total Volkswagen	**162,291**	**170,253**	**265,454**	**378,127**	**432,104**
Total Passenger Cars	**8,525,754**	**8,272,074**	**8,141,721**	**8,698,284**	**8,846,625**

*Units imported from outside North America.
SOURCE: Ward's AutoInfoBank.

U.S. Retail Sales of Passenger Cars by Country of Origin, Market Class and Purchasing Sector

U.S. RETAIL SALES OF PASSENGER CARS, 1971-2000

Year	Domestic	Imports From Japan	Imports From Germany	Imports From Other Countries	Total Imports	U.S. Total	Import Percent Total	Import Percent Japan	Import Percent Germany
2000	6,830,505	862,780	516,614	636,726	2,016,120	8,846,625	22.8	9.8	5.8
1999	6,979,357	757,568	466,870	494,489	1,718,927	8,698,284	19.8	8.7	5.4
1998	6,761,940	691,162	366,724	321,895	1,379,781	8,141,721	16.9	8.5	4.5
1997	6,916,769	726,104	297,028	332,173	1,355,305	8,272,074	16.4	8.8	3.6
1996	7,253,582	726,940	237,984	308,247	1,273,171	8,526,753	14.9	8.5	2.8
1995	7,128,707	981,506	207,482	317,269	1,506,257	8,634,964	17.4	11.4	2.4
1994	7,255,303	1,239,450	192,275	303,489	1,735,214	8,990,517	19.3	13.8	2.1
1993	6,741,667	1,328,445	186,177	261,570	1,776,192	8,517,859	20.9	15.6	2.2
1992	6,276,557	1,451,766	200,851	283,938	1,936,555	8,213,112	23.6	17.7	2.4
1991	6,136,757	1,500,309	192,776	344,814	2,037,899	8,174,656	24.9	18.4	2.4
1990	6,896,888	1,719,384	265,116	418,823	2,403,323	9,300,211	25.8	18.5	2.9
1989	7,072,902	1,897,143	248,561	553,660	2,699,364	9,772,266	27.6	19.4	2.5
1988	7,526,038	2,022,602	280,099	700,991	3,003,692	10,529,730	28.5	19.2	2.7
1987	7,080,858	2,190,405	347,881	657,465	3,195,751	10,276,609	31.1	21.3	3.4
1986	8,214,897	2,382,614	443,721	418,286	3,244,621	11,459,518	28.3	20.8	3.9
1985	8,204,542	2,217,837	423,983	195,925	2,837,745	11,042,287	25.7	20.1	3.8
1984	7,951,523	1,906,206	344,416	188,220	2,438,842	10,390,365	23.5	18.3	3.3
1983	6,795,295	1,915,621	279,748	191,403	2,386,772	9,182,067	26.0	20.9	3.1
1981	6,208,760	1,858,896	282,881	185,502	2,327,279	8,536,039	27.3	21.8	3.3
1979	8,341,139	1,755,818	366,084	209,727	2,331,629	10,672,768	21.8	16.5	3.4
1977	9,109,022	1,387,856	459,707	226,827	2,074,390	11,183,412	18.5	12.4	4.1
1975	7,053,016	807,931	492,507	271,034	1,571,472	8,624,488	18.2	9.4	5.7
1973	9,675,790	742,621	787,562	217,878	1,748,061	11,423,851	15.3	6.5	6.9
1971	8,681,409	578,977	769,457	212,362	1,560,796	10,242,205	15.2	5.7	7.5

SOURCE: Ward's Communications.

U.S. CAR SALES BY MARKET CLASS, 1983-2000

Year	Small	Middle	Large	Luxury	Total
2000	28.1	47.8	7.0	17.1	100.0
1999	24.2	51.7	7.6	16.5	100.0
1998	24.7	51.1	8.2	16.0	100.0
1997	26.3	49.5	9.5	14.8	100.0
1995	27.1	48.5	10.8	13.6	100.0
1993	32.8	43.3	11.1	12.8	100.0
1991	33.0	44.9	8.3	13.9	100.0
1989	36.6	41.9	11.9	11.6	100.0
1987	38.4	42.3	9.1	10.2	100.0
1985	37.9	42.1	9.8	10.2	100.0
1983	38.8	40.6	10.7	9.9	100.0

SOURCE: Ward's Communications.

U.S. CAR SALES BY SECTOR, 1960-2000

Year	Units by Consuming Sector (000) Consumer	Business	Government	Total	% of Total Sales Consumer	Business
2000	4,665	3,999	189	8,852	54.5	45.2
1999	4,366	4,155	175	8,697	50.2	47.8
1998	3,988	3,992	161	8,142	48.0	49.0
1997	3,910	4,216	147	8,273	47.3	50.0
1996	4,079	4,273	176	8,527	47.8	50.1
1995	4,351	4,186	151	8,687	50.1	48.2
1994	4,600	4,268	124	8,991	51.2	47.5
1993	4,657	3,748	113	8,518	54.7	44.0
1992	4,566	3,529	119	8,214	55.6	42.0
1991	4,424	3,648	103	8,175	54.1	44.6
1990	5,677	3,477	147	9,301	61.0	37.4
1989	6,288	3,362	127	9,777	64.3	34.4
1988	6,746	3,669	131	10,546	63.0	34.8
1987	6,625	3,416	130	10,171	65.1	33.6
1985	7,092	3,754	132	10,978	64.6	34.2
1980	6,100	2,758	124	8,982	67.9	30.7
1975	5,907	2,508	123	8,538	69.2	29.4
1970	6,252	2,056	94	8,403	74.4	24.5
1965	7,106	2,149	89	9,344	76.1	22.0
1960	4,950	1,616	66	6,632	74.6	24.4

SOURCE: U.S. Department of Commerce, Bureau of Economic Analysis.

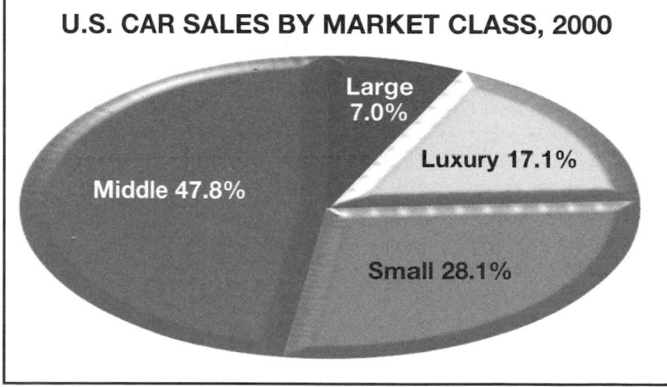

U.S. CAR SALES BY MARKET CLASS, 2000

Large 7.0%
Luxury 17.1%
Middle 47.8%
Small 28.1%

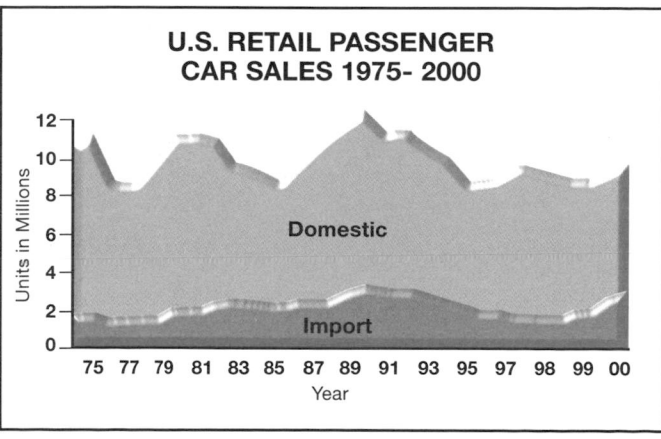

U.S. RETAIL PASSENGER CAR SALES 1975- 2000

Domestic
Import

U.S. Light Truck Sales by Segment

U.S. LIGHT TRUCK SALES BY SEGMENT, 1996-2000

Models	1996	1997	1998	1999	2000
CROSS UTILITY VEHICLES					
BMW X5	0	0	0	1,312	26,720
Total BMW	**0**	**0**	**0**	**1,312**	**26,720**
Chrysler PT Cruiser	0	0	0	0	91,996
Total Chrysler Corp.	**0**	**0**	**0**	**0**	**91,996**
Ford Escape	0	0	0	0	42,635
Volvo XC*	0	0	0	0	6,890
Total Ford Motor Co.	**0**	**0**	**0**	**0**	**49,525**
Subaru Forester*	0	15,988	40,132	50,183	56,605
Total Subaru	**0**	**15,988**	**40,132**	**50,183**	**56,605**
Pontiac Aztek	0	0	0	0	11,201
Total General Motors	**0**	**0**	**0**	**0**	**11,201**
Acura MDX	0	0	0	0	9,750
Honda CRV*	0	66,752	100,582	120,754	118,260
Total Honda	**0**	**66,752**	**100,582**	**120,754**	**128,010**
Hyundai Santa Fe*	0	0	0	0	10,332
Total Hyundai	**0**	**0**	**0**	**0**	**10,332**
Isuzu Vehicross*	0	0	0	1,271	1,223
Total Isuzu	**0**	**0**	**0**	**1,271**	**1,223**
Mazda Tribute	0	0	0	0	21,048
Total Mazda	**0**	**0**	**0**	**0**	**21,048**
Lexus RX300*	0	0	42,191	73,498	89,864
Toyota Rav4*	56,709	67,487	64,990	57,138	53,777
Total Toyota	**56,709**	**67,487**	**107,181**	**130,636**	**143,641**
Audi Allroad*	0	0	0	0	1,033
Total Volkswagen	**0**	**0**	**0**	**0**	**1,033**
Total Cross Utility	**56,709**	**150,227**	**247,895**	**304,156**	**541,334**
SPORT UTILITY VEHICLES					
Dodge Durango	0	20,263	156,923	189,840	173,567
Jeep Cherokee XJ	148,544	130,041	146,298	165,261	141,457
Jeep Grand Cherokee	279,195	260,875	229,135	300,031	271,723
Jeep Wrangler	81,444	81,956	83,861	89,174	82,254
Total Chrysler Corp.	**509,183**	**493,135**	**616,217**	**744,306**	**669,001**
Ford Bronco	36,833	0	0	0	0
Ford Excursion	0	0	0	18,315	50,786
Ford Expedition	45,974	214,524	225,703	233,125	213,483
Ford Explorer	402,663	383,852	431,488	428,772	445,157
Land Rover Defender*	606	2,501	122	0	0
Land Rover Discovery*	15,491	14,703	14,230	21,931	20,860
Range Rover*	7,085	6,621	7,070	7,449	6,287
Lincoln Navigator	0	26,831	43,859	39,250	37,923
Mercury Mountaineer	26,700	45,363	47,595	49,281	46,547
Total Ford Motor Co.	**535,352**	**694,395**	**770,067**	**798,123**	**821,043**
Cadillac Escalade	0	0	3,089	23,897	23,346
Chevrolet Blazer	23	0	0	0	0
Chevrolet Suburban	94,010	99,068	108,933	138,977	133,123
Chevrolet S Blazer	246,307	221,400	219,710	232,140	225,948
Chevrolet Tahoe	124,038	124,125	133,235	122,213	149,834
Chevrolet Tracker	47,188	33,354	20,296	40,024	48,020
GMC Suburban	43,161	43,137	42,423	44,886	4,776
GMC S Jimmy	77,838	75,817	72,301	79,375	79,489
GMC Yukon	36,566	41,072	49,355	53,280	56,297
GMC Yukon XL	0	0	0	1,857	47,016
Hummer H1	0	0	0	0	875
Oldsmobile Bravada	15,471	28,481	30,202	29,258	31,194
Total General Motors	**684,602**	**666,454**	**679,544**	**765,907**	**799,918**
Acura SLX*	2,565	1,299	1,634	694	198

U.S. Light Truck Sales by Segment

U.S. LIGHT TRUCK SALES BY SEGMENT, 1996-2000 — continued

Models	1996	1997	1998	1999	2000
Honda Passport	28,184	22,622	26,094	22,974	21,892
Total Honda	**30,749**	**23,921**	**27,728**	**23,668**	**22,090**
Isuzu Amigo	0	0	7,088	8,298	9,244
Isuzu Amigo*	35	0	0	0	0
Isuzu Rodeo	61,073	63,597	59,889	64,771	59,570
Isuzu Trooper*	18,495	10,956	18,191	20,755	23,100
Total Isuzu	**79,603**	**74,553**	**85,168**	**93,824**	**91,914**
Kia Sportage*	9,908	19,831	28,582	52,383	62,350
Total Kia Motors	**9,908**	**19,831**	**28,582**	**52,383**	**62,350**
Mazda Navajo	68	4	0	0	0
Total Mazda	**68**	**4**	**0**	**0**	**0**
Mercedes M Class	0	14,569	43,134	45,206	52,764
Total Mercedes Benz	**0**	**14,569**	**43,134**	**45,206**	**52,764**
Mitsubishi Montero*	12,083	6,915	4,120	5,115	21,578
Mitsubishi Montero Sport*	232	31,659	38,439	59,007	66,375
Total Mitsubishi	**12,315**	**38,574**	**42,559**	**64,122**	**87,953**
Infiniti QX4*	1,983	18,793	20,055	19,199	21,545
Nissan Pathfinder*	73,686	73,365	68,003	65,968	68,533
Nissan Xterra	0	0	0	47,806	88,578
Total Nissan	**75,669**	**92,158**	**88,058**	**132,973**	**178,656**
Suzuki Samurai*	22	0	0	0	0
Suzuki Sidekick	11,476	6,307	5,316	224	0
Suzuki Sidekick*	11,222	11,757	9,619	621	89
Suzuki Suzuki X90*	3,602	2,625	591	35	3
Suzuki Vitara	0	0	3	6,948	9,015
Suzuki Vitara*	0	0	5,910	27,450	31,482
Total Suzuki	**26,322**	**20,689**	**21,439**	**35,278**	**40,589**
Lexus LX450*	7,528	6,785	312	0	0
Lexus LX470*	0	0	10,692	15,734	14,732
Toyota 4Runner*	99,597	128,496	118,484	124,221	111,797
Toyota Land Cruiser*	12,850	11,510	14,327	18,602	15,509
Toyota Sequoia	0	0	0	0	9,925
Total Toyota	**119,975**	**146,791**	**143,815**	**158,557**	**151,963**
Total Sport Utility	**2,083,746**	**2,285,074**	**2,546,311**	**2,914,347**	**2,978,241**
VANS					
Chrysler Town & Country	84,828	76,653	71,981	71,957	99,252
Chrysler Voyager	0	0	0	129	70,477
Dodge Caravan	300,117	285,736	293,819	293,100	285,739
Dodge Ram Van	61,400	56,088	52,110	52,248	49,602
Dodge Ram Wagon	20,089	17,372	16,937	19,824	20,641
Plymouth Voyager	153,862	156,056	156,971	138,644	28,345
Total Chrysler Corp.	**620,296**	**591,905**	**591,818**	**575,902**	**554,056**
Ford Aerostar	73,685	44,829	1,060	0	0
Ford Econoline	176,480	186,690	206,026	202,024	187,027
Ford Windstar	209,033	205,356	190,173	213,844	222,298
Mercury Villager	65,587	55,168	38,495	45,315	30,443
Total Ford Motor Co.	**524,785**	**492,043**	**435,754**	**461,183**	**439,768**
Chevrolet Astro	125,962	111,390	95,977	102,427	92,585
Chevrolet Van	77,510	77,667	73,812	92,627	98,730
Chevrolet Express	2,693	5,975	8,658	13,214	14,502
Chevrolet Lumina	27,442	1,243	12	0	0
Chevrolet Venture	3,788	76,171	97,362	96,643	97,450
GMC Safari	39,999	35,787	30,921	31,840	32,444
GMC Savana	16,171	33,951	35,656	39,058	42,391
GMC Vandura Rally	13,486	488	0	0	0
Oldsmobile Silhouette	9,330	24,615	37,554	40,950	41,177
Pontiac Montana	0	0	10,819	62,547	59,849

U.S. Light Truck Sales by Segment

U.S. LIGHT TRUCK SALES BY SEGMENT, 1996-2000 — continued

Models	1996	1997	1998	1999	2000
Pontiac Trans Sport	21,397	51,961	48,229	1,516	71
Total General Motors	**337,778**	**419,248**	**439,000**	**480,822**	**479,199**
Honda Odyssey	0	0	7,154	77,626	126,686
Honda Odyssey*	27,025	20,333	13,665	175	19
Total Honda	**27,025**	**20,333**	**20,819**	**77,801**	**126,705**
Isuzu Oasis*	2,128	2,943	1,671	1,076	147
Total Isuzu	**2,128**	**2,943**	**1,671**	**1,076**	**147**
Mazda MPV*	14,427	15,599	12,425	16,055	35,600
Total Mazda	**14,427**	**15,599**	**12,425**	**16,055**	**35,600**
Nissan Quest	46,636	46,858	30,466	44,467	42,800
Total Nissan	**46,636**	**46,858**	**30,466**	**44,467**	**42,800**
Toyota Previa*	8,520	3,780	95	0	1
Toyota Sienna	0	15,180	81,391	98,809	103,137
Total Toyota	**8,520**	**18,960**	**81,486**	**98,809**	**103,138**
Volkswagen Eurovan*	995	1,792	1,742	3,395	2,714
Total Volkswagen	**995**	**1,792**	**1,742**	**3,395**	**2,714**
Total Van	**1,582,590**	**1,609,681**	**1,615,181**	**1,759,510**	**1,784,127**
PICKUPS					
Dodge Dakota	104,754	131,961	152,629	144,148	177,395
Dodge Ram Pickup	383,960	350,257	410,130	428,930	380,874
Total Chrysler Corp.	**488,714**	**482,218**	**562,759**	**573,078**	**558,269**
Ford F Series	744,189	710,156	787,552	806,579	820,248
Ford Ranger	288,393	298,796	328,136	348,358	330,125
Total Ford Motor Co.	**1,032,582**	**1,008,952**	**1,115,688**	**1,154,937**	**1,150,373**
Chevrolet CK Pickup	519,106	527,842	454,311	98,285	84,928
Chevrolet S10 Pickup	190,178	192,314	228,093	233,669	211,587
Chevrolet Silverado	0	0	78,866	530,106	549,190
GMC Sierra	169,054	168,478	156,244	204,128	185,187
GMC Sonoma	44,629	41,714	54,819	57,992	51,093
Total General Motors	**922,967**	**930,348**	**972,333**	**1,124,180**	**1,081,985**
Isuzu Hombre	10,165	13,975	14,991	7,766	4,782
Isuzu Pickup*	1,993	12	0	0	0
Total Isuzu	**12,158**	**13,987**	**14,991**	**7,766**	**4,782**
Mazda Pickup	42,815	37,697	41,620	38,726	30,124
Total Mazda	**42,815**	**37,697**	**41,620**	**38,726**	**30,124**
Mitsubishi Pickup*	3,629	207	0	0	0
Total Mitsubishi	**3,629**	**207**	**0**	**0**	**0**
Nissan Frontier	0	25,249	91,629	96,301	108,738
Nissan Pickup	127,081	96,612	0	0	0
Total Nissan	**127,081**	**121,861**	**91,629**	**96,301**	**108,738**
Toyota Tacoma	142,356	145,870	152,770	155,476	147,295
Toyota Pickup*	640	41	0	0	0
Toyota T100*	37,926	28,381	7,959	225	9
Toyota Tundra	0	0	0	42,769	100,445
Total Toyota	**180,922**	**174,292**	**160,729**	**198,470**	**247,749**
Total Pickup	**2,810,868**	**2,769,562**	**2,959,749**	**3,193,458**	**3,182,020**
COMMERCIAL CHASSIS					
General Motors	29,333	26,833	22,489	12,247	7,636
Isuzu Truck*	5,252	6,312	6,648	7,593	6,419
Freightliner Truck	164	143	670	945	576
Mitsu-Fuso Truck*	1,768	1,815	2,270	2,210	2,079
Nissan Diesel Truck*	0	0	73	788	698
Total Comm. Chasis	**36,517**	**35,103**	**32,150**	**23,783**	**17,408**
TOTAL LIGHT TRUCKS	**6,570,430**	**6,849,647**	**7,401,286**	**8,195,254**	**8,503,130**

*Units imported from outside North America.
SOURCE: Ward's AutoInfoBank.

U.S. Retail Sales of Trucks by Manufacturer and Gross Vehicle Weight Rating

U.S. RETAIL SALES OF TRUCKS BY MANUFACTURER AND GROSS VEHICLE WEIGHT RATING, 2000

	Gross Vehicle Weight Rating (Pounds)								
	6,000 & Less	6,001- 10,000	10,000- 14,000	14,001- 16,000	16,001- 19,500	19,501- 26,000	26,001- 33,000	33,001 & Over	Total
DOMESTIC*									
BMW	26,720	0	0	0	0	0	0	0	26,720
Chrysler	1,248,638	588,483	36,201	0	0	0	0	0	1,873,322
Ford	1,258,940	1,104,418	63,314	22,347	20,665	21,533	3,523	0	2,494,740
Freightliner	0	0	576	2,555	1,286	12,344	29,992	76,451	123,204
General Motors	1,644,082	728,550	3,038	11,721	0	9,912	19,561	0	2,416,864
Honda	158,328	0	0	0	0	0	0	0	158,328
Isuzu Truck	0	0	2,052	1,545	0	1,336	217	0	5,150
Kenworth	0	0	0	0	0	0	1,852	20,904	22,830
Mack	0	0	0	0	0	0	0	28,210	28,210
Mazda	51,172	0	0	0	0	0	0	0	51,172
Mercedes-Benz	52,764	0	0	0	0	0	0	0	52,764
Navistar	0	0	0	0	496	2,497	64,218	34,417	101,628
Nissan	240,116	0	0	0	0	0	0	0	240,116
Peterbilt	0	0	0	0	0	0	2,148	24,763	26,911
Subaru-Isuzu	73,596	0	0	0	0	0	0	0	73,596
Suzuki	9,015	0	0	0	0	0	0	0	9,015
Toyota	360,802	0	0	0	0	0	0	0	360,802
Volvo	0	0	0	0	0	0	0	22,565	22,565
Western Star	0	0	0	0	0	0	88	2,961	3,049
Other Domestic	0	0	0	0	0	0	0	1,151	1,151
Total Domestic	**5,124,173**	**2,421,451**	**105,181**	**38,168**	**22,447**	**47,622**	**121,599**	**211,502**	**8,092,143**
IMPORT									
Bering	0	0	0	971	40	415	0	51	1,477
General Motors	0	0	4,269	0	296	0	0	0	4,565
Hino	0	0	0	375	448	879	282	0	1,984
Honda	118,477	0	0	0	0	0	0	0	118,477
Hyundai	10,332	0	0	0	0	0	0	0	10,332
Isuzu	24,470	0	0	0	0	0	0	0	24,470
Isuzu Truck	0	0	4,367	6,239	3,836	0	0	0	14,442
Kia	62,350	0	0	0	0	0	0	0	62,350
Land Rover	34,037	0	0	0	0	0	0	0	34,037
Mack	0	0	0	0	0	616	510	0	1,126
Mazda	35,600	0	0	0	0	0	0	0	35,600
Mitsubishi	87,953	0	0	0	0	0	0	0	87,953
Mitsubishi Fuso	0	0	2,079	1,184	1,100	927	132	0	5,422
Nissan	90,078	0	0	0	0	0	0	0	90,078
Nissan Diesel	0	0	698	480	998	710	91	0	2,977
Subaru-Isuzu	56,605	0	0	0	0	0	0	0	56,605
Suzuki	31,574	0	0	0	0	0	0	0	31,574
Toyota	285,689	0	0	0	0	0	0	0	285,689
Volkswagen	3,747	0	0	0	0	0	0	0	3,747
Total Import	**840,912**	**0**	**11,413**	**9,249**	**6,718**	**3,547**	**1,015**	**51**	**872,905**
Total Trucks	**5,965,085**	**2,421,451**	**116,594**	**47,417**	**29,165**	**51,169**	**122,614**	**211,553**	**8,965,048**

*Units produced in the United States, Canada and Mexico.
NOTE: Includes school bus chassis.
SOURCE: Ward's AutoInfoBank

U.S. Retail Sales of Trucks by Gross Vehicle Weight Rating and Body Type

U.S. RETAIL SALES OF DOMESTIC LIGHT TRUCKS BY GROSS VEHICLE WEIGHT RATING AND BODY TYPE, 1995-2000

GVWR/Body type	1995	1996	1997	1998	1999	2000
0-6,000 Lbs.						
Utility	1,257,823	1,391,565	1,368,240	1,428,600	1,610,855	1,826,127
Compact Pickup	961,518	984,957	984,203	1,058,425	1,082,436	1,061,139
Mini Van	73,302	63,878	64,008	43,876	46,364	45,164
Van	12,293	18,369	47,410	39,035	42,662	41,104
Conventional Pickup	613,649	840,361	924,412	896,143	885,198	859,886
Mini Passenger Carrier	1,112,768	1,097,788	1,123,014	1,146,438	1,273,450	1,287,589
Passenger Carrier	17	971	2,407	2,659	3,283	3,164
Total 0-6,000 lbs.	**4,031,370**	**4,397,889**	**4,513,694**	**4,615,176**	**4,944,248**	**5,124,173**
6,001-10,000 Lbs.						
Utility	144,290	243,434	426,815	614,267	679,920	705,236
Van	274,190	253,777	230,194	252,639	282,808	274,228
Van Cutaway	46,167	36,676	38,264	36,883	25,412	29,614
Conventional Pickup	966,874	935,994	792,634	903,121	1,120,524	1,161,471
Station Wagon	108,979	137,171	142,205	151,356	185,720	184,915
Passenger Carrier	63,143	57,703	59,945	61,983	64,830	64,783
Multi-Stop	27,660	24,984	21,986	17,491	6,450	1,204
Total 6,001-10,000 lbs.	**1,631,303**	**1,689,739**	**1,712,043**	**2,037,740**	**2,365,664**	**2,421,451**
10,001 - 14,000 lbs.						
Conventional Pickup	27,101	39,954	39,687	89,989	105,075	99,515
Other Body Types	1,129	4,064	5,281	2,699	5,044	5,384
Total 10,001 - 14,000 lbs.	**28,230**	**44,018**	**44,968**	**92,688**	**110,119**	**104,899**
Total Domestic Light Trucks	**5,690,903**	**6,131,646**	**6,270,705**	**6,745,604**	**7,420,031**	**7,650,523**

* Units produced in U.S., Canada and Mexico.

U.S. RETAIL SALES OF DOMESTIC AND IMPORTED TRUCKS, 1986-2000

	Domestic				Imports		
	Gross Vehicle Weight Rating						
Year	0-14,000 lbs.	14,001-33,000 lbs.	33,001 lbs. & Over	Total Domestic	From Japan	Total Imports	Total U.S. Sales
2000	7,650,523	229,836	211,456	8,091,815	759,836	872,905	8,964,720
1999	7,420,031	239,562	262,316	7,921,909	707,866	794,535	8,716,444
1998	6,745,284	196,321	209,483	7,151,088	621,187	674,478	7,825,566
1997	6,270,705	183,800	178,551	6,633,056	546,015	592,755	7,225,811
1996	6,131,646	176,147	170,009	6,477,802	416,211	451,789	6,929,591
1995	5,690,903	171,948	201,303	6,064,154	393,573	417,203	6,481,357
1994	5,657,634	151,897	185,696	5,995,227	406,682	425,630	6,420,857
1993	5,000,430	129,063	157,886	5,287,379	381,433	393,615	5,680,994
1992	4,247,097	115,198	119,030	4,481,325	412,961	422,037	4,903,362
1991	3,605,779	108,751	98,643	3,813,173	539,556	551,499	4,364,672
1990	3,956,835	137,031	121,137	4,215,003	610,688	631,159	4,846,162
1989	4,113,467	145,104	144,728	4,403,299	514,532	537,921	4,941,220
1988	4,199,643	160,544	147,872	4,508,059	623,540	640,905	5,148,964
1987	3,790,606	133,872	130,260	4,054,738	840,297	857,636	4,912,374
1986	3,676,129	133,465	111,814	3,921,408	926,729	941,309	4,862,717

SOURCE: Ward's AutoInfoBank.

Annual and Monthly Records for U.S. Production and Sales

RECORD U.S. PRODUCTION YEARS

Passenger Cars		Trucks	
Year	**Units**	**Year**	**Units**
1973	9,667,152	1999	7,387,029
1965	9,335,227	2000	7,228,497
1977	9,213,654	1998	6,448,290
1978	9,176,635	1997	6,196,654
1968	8,848,620	1996	5,747,322
1972	8,828,205	1995	5,655,281
1966	8,604,712	1994	5,638,068

RECORD U.S. RETAIL SALES YEARS

Passenger Cars		Trucks	
Year	**Units**	**Year**	**Units**
1986	11,459,518	2000	8,965,048
1973	11,423,851	1999	8,716,444
1978	11,314,079	1998	7,825,566
1977	11,183,412	1997	7,225,786
1985	11,042,287	1996	6,929,359
1972	10,940,482	1995	6,481,361
1979	10,672,768	1994	6,420,857

RECORD U.S. PRODUCTION BY MONTH

Month	Year	Units
	Passenger Cars	
January	1973	917,273
February	1973	856,117
March	1965	963,101
April	1978	870,689
May	1973	941,019
June	1977	949,440
July	1965	740,576
August	1950	684,970
September	1972	758,578
October	1973	951,434
November	1965	913,146
December	1964	866,632
	Trucks	
January	2000	599,213
February	2000	666,296
March	2000	758,273
April	1999	639,703
May	2000	707,996
June	2000	696,694
July	1999	365,279
August	1999	687,772
September	1999	647,573
October	1999	685,153
November	1999	613,129
December	1999	551,236

RECORD U.S. PRODUCTION BY MONTH

Month	Year	Units
	Passenger Cars	
January	1973	874,084
February	1973	918,681
March	1973	1,140,386
April	1978	1,043,341
May	1978	1,159,996
June	1978	1,138,504
July	1973	958,270
August	1986	1,000,658
September	1987	1,217,171
October	1972	1,068,400
November	1972	1,029,689
December	1987	995,415
	Trucks	
January	2000	617,438
February	2000	770,225
March	2000	877,168
April	2000	764,429
May	2000	831,041
June	2000	821,848
July	1999	758,093
August	2000	776,206
September	2000	758,364
October	1999	708,264
November	1999	677,843
December	1999	760,561

U.S. FACTORY SALES MILESTONES

Passenger Cars		Trucks		Total Motor Vehicles	
Year	**Units**	**Year**	**Units**	**Year**	**Units**
1912	1 millionth	1915	100,000th	1906	100,000th
1920	10 millionth	1920	1 millionth	1912	1 millionth
1925	25 millionth	1929	5 millionth	1920	10 millionth
1935	50 millionth	1938	10 millionth	1931	50 millionth
1952	100 millionth	1949	20 millionth	1948	100 millionth
1960	150 millionth	1957	30 millionth	1955	150 millionth
1967	200 millionth	1965	40 millionth	1962	200 millionth
1973	250 millionth	1971	50 millionth	1968	250 millionth
1979	300 millionth	1979	75 millionth	1972	300 millionth
1986	350 millionth	1988	100 millionth	1982	400 millionth
1994	400 millionth	1998	150 millionth	1992	500 millionth

SOURCE: Ward's Communications.

Top Selling Vehicles and Automotive Color Popularity

TOP 20 SELLING PASSENGER CARS IN THE U.S., 1998-2000

1998		1999		2000	
Toyota Camry	429,575	Toyota Camry	448,162	Toyota Camry	422,961
Honda Accord	401,071	Honda Accord	404,192	Honda Accord	404,515
Ford Taurus	371,074	Ford Taurus	368,327	Ford Taurus	382,035
Honda Civic	334,562	Honda Civic	318,308	Honda Civic	324,528
Ford Escort	291,936	Chevrolet Cavalier	272,122	Ford Focus	286,166
Chevrolet Cavalier	256,099	Ford Escort	260,486	Chevrolet Cavalier	236,803
Toyota Corolla	250,501	Toyota Corolla	249,128	Toyota Corolla	230,156
Saturn S	231,522	Pontiac Grand Am	234,936	Pontiac Grand Am	214,923
Chevrolet Malibu	223,703	Chevrolet Malibu	218,540	Chevrolet Malibu	207,376
Pontiac Grand Am	180,428	Saturn S	207,977	Saturn S	177,355
Chevrolet Lumina	177,631	Ford Mustang	166,915	Chevrolet Impala	174,358
Ford Mustang	144,732	Buick Century	157,035	Ford Mustang	173,676
Nissan Altima	144,451	Nissan Altima	153,525	Buick Lesabre	148,633
Ford Contour	139,838	Buick Lesabre	149,445	Pontiac Grand Prix	148,521
Buick Lesabre	136,551	Pontiac Grand Prix	148,197	Volkswagen Jetta	144,853
Buick Century	126,220	Dodge Intrepid	144,355	Dodge Intrepid	143,840
Pontiac Grand Prix	122,915	Ford Contour	134,487	Buick Century	143,085
Dodge Neon	117,964	Nissan Maxima	131,182	Nissan Altima	136,971
Mercury Grand Marquis	114,162	Volkswagen Jetta	130,054	Nissan Maxima	129,235
Nissan Maxima	113,843	Mercury Grand Marquis	122,776	Oldsmobile Alero	122,722

TOP 10 SELLING LIGHT TRUCKS IN THE U.S., 1998-2000

1998		1999		2000	
Ford F Series	787,552	Ford F Series	806,579	Ford F Series	820,248
Chevy C/K Pickup/Silverado	533,177	Chevy C/K Pickup/Silverado	533,177	Chevy C/K Pickup/Silverado	634,118
Ford Explorer	431,488	Dodge Ram Pickup	428,930	Ford Explorer	445,157
Dodge Ram Pickup	410,130	Ford Explorer	428,772	Dodge Ram Pickup	380,874
Ford Ranger	328,136	Ford Ranger	348,358	Ford Ranger	330,125
Dodge Caravan	293,819	Jeep Grand Cherokee	300,031	Dodge Caravan	285,739
Jeep Grand Cherokee	229,135	Dodge Caravan	293,100	Jeep Grand Cherokee	271,723
Chevrolet S10 Pickup	228,093	Chevrolet S10 Pickup	233,669	Chevrolet S Blazer	225,948
Ford Expedition	225,703	Ford Expedition	233,125	Ford Windstar	222,298
Chevrolet S Blazer	219,710	Chevrolet S Blazer	232,140	Ford Expedition	213,483

Source: Ward's AutoInfoBank.

AUTOMOTIVE PAINT COLOR POPULARITY BY VEHICLE TYPE, 2000 MODEL YEAR

Luxury Cars		Full Size/Intermediate Cars		Compact/Sports Cars		Light Trucks	
Color	Percent	Color	Percent	Color	Percent	Color	Percent
White Metallic	19.8	Silver	21.5	Silver	22.3	White	23.1
Silver	17.2	White	13.0	Black	14.4	Silver	14.1
Black	10.8	Black	11.5	White	11.4	Medium/Dark Blue	11.1
Light Brown	8.6	Medium/Dark Green	10.7	Light Brown	9.9	Black	10.6
White	7.1	Light Brown	8.5	Medium/Dark Green	9.7	Medium/Dark Green	8.3
Medium/Dark Blue	7.1	Medium/Dark Blue	7.0	Medium Red	8.3	Medium Red	6.2
Medium/Dark Gray	6.6	Medium Red	6.9	Bright Red	7.5	Bright Red	5.4
Medium Red	6.1	Medium/Dark Gray	4.3	Medium/Dark Blue	5.0	Gold	4.1
Gold	5.3	Bright Red	3.8	Teal	2.6	Medium/DarkGrey	3.9
Medium/Dark Green	4.3	Gold	3.5	Bright Blue	2.1	Dark Red	3.2
Other	7.1	Other	9.3	Other	6.8	Other	10.0

Source: Du Pont Automotive Products.

Motor Vehicle Sales and Registrations in Canada

NEW MOTOR VEHICLE SALES IN CANADA, 1972-2000

Year	Passenger Cars			Commercial Vehicles			Total Vehicles
	Domestic[1]	Imports	Total	Domestic[1]	Imports	Total	
2000	640,916	208,216	849,132	673,631	63,320	736,951	1,586,083
1999	620,880	185,560	806,440	676,243	57,696	733,939	1,540,379
1998	591,272	150,775	742,047	684,592	55,954	704,546	1,446,593
1997	629,488	109,062	738,550	628,214	57,616	685,830	1,424,380
1996	572,581	88,188	660,769	517,738	26,050	543,788	1,204,557
1995	553,265	116,925	670,190	469,590	26,755	496,345	1,166,535
1994	573,361	175,305	748,666	475,444	35,946	511,390	1,260,056
1993	493,759	245,290	739,049	402,112	51,773	453,885	1,192,934
1992	503,460	294,563	798,023	370,422	58,974	429,396	1,227,419
1991	573,297	299,887	873,184	347,671	66,036	414,000	1,287,790
1990	580,397	304,167	884,564	361,403	71,902	433,305	1,317,869
1989	675,340	312,794	988,134	422,398	73,343	495,741	1,483,875
1988	724,733	331,577	1,056,310	459,777	49,414	509,191	1,565,501
1987	700,930	364,163	1,065,093	417,189	51,355	468,544	1,533,637
1986	761,169	334,144	1,095,313	368,423	52,184	420,607	1,515,920
1985	794,965	342,251	1,137,216	344,871	48,323	393,194	1,530,410
1984	724,932	246,278	971,210	273,604	38,688	312,292	1,283,502
1983	625,088	218,230	843,318	192,609	45,161	237,770	1,081,088
1982	489,435	224,046	713,481	166,986	40,435	207,421	920,902
1981	646,942	257,253	904,195	250,775	35,912	288,687	1,190,882
1980	740,767	191,293	932,060	310,273	21,474	331,747	1,263,807
1979	863,554	139,454	1,003,008	381,562	11,832	393,394	1,396,402
1978	815,994	172,896	988,890	364,241	13,413	377,654	1,366,544
1977	797,752	193,646	991,398	337,914	15,647	353,561	1,344,959
1975	835,679	153,601	989,280	310,590	16,759	327,349	1,316,629
1972	653,933	205,026	858,959	189,577	17,085	206,662	1,065,621

(1) Units produced in the United States, Canada and Mexico.

TOTAL REGISTRATIONS BY PROVINCE, 1999

Province	Total Vehicle Registrations by Weight			
	less than 10,000 lbs.	10,001-33,000 lbs.*	Buses	Total
Newfoundland	240,212	97,474	1,379	339,065
Prince Edward Island	70,600	6,449	51	77,100
Nova Scotia	499,193	41,595	1,814	542,602
New Brunswick	421,796	54,495	2499	478,790
Quebec	3,843,729	1,170,856	16,618	5,031,203
Ontario	6,174,461	717,173	23,791	6,915,425
Manitoba	566,581	100,027	3343	669,951
Saskatchewan	615,965	76,235	3,853	696,053
Alberta	1,878,151	235,307	11,509	2,124,967
British Columbia	2,185,877	100,034	8007	2,293,918
Yukon	22,488	3,047	234	25,769
Northwest Territories	16,896	2,189	65	19,150
Nunavut	2,105	1,741	11	3,857
Total	16,538,054	2,606,622	73,174	19,217,850

TOTAL REGISTRATIONS IN CANADA, 1976-1999

Year	Passenger Cars (000)	Commercial Vehicles (000)	Total (000)
1999	16,538	2,679	19,217
1998	13,887	3,694	17,581
1997	13,487	3,591	17,078
1996	13,217	3,644	16,861
1995	13,183	3,485	16,668
1994	13,122	3,466	16,588
1992	12,781	3,413	16,194
1990	12,622	3,931	16,553
1988	12,086	3,766	15,852
1986	11,586	3,213	14,799
1984	10,781	3,099	13,880
1982	10,530	3,293	13,823
1980	10,256	2,955	13,211
1978	9,745	2,771	12,516
1976	9,016	2,319	11,335

* Figures include Farm and Off-Road Vehicles
NOTE: Data for 1999 and later were reclassified from vehicle type to weight class.

Motor Vehicle Sales in Canada and Mexico

MOTOR VEHICLE SALES IN CANADA, 2000

	Passenger Cars			Commercial Vehicles			Total		
	Domestic	Import*	Total	Domestic	Import*	Total	Domestic	Import*	Total
Auto Vaz	0	25	25	0	76	76	0	101	101
BMW	547	8,635	9,182	1,840	0	1,840	2,387	8,635	11,022
Chrysler Corp.	80,853	0	80,853	187,935	0	187,935	268,788	0	268,788
Daewoo	0	4,011	4,011	0	0	0	0	4,011	4,011
Ford Motor Co.	99,738	10,613	110,351	183,304	1,383	184,687	283,042	11,996	295,038
Fuji	7,477	2,521	9,998	0	4,611	4,611	7,477	7,132	14,609
General Motors	254,568	2,224	256,792	216,602	274	216,876	471,170	2,498	473,668
Honda	99,970	6,844	106,814	14,492	13,613	28,105	114,462	20,457	134,919
Hyundai	0	38,233	38,233	0	833	833	0	39,066	39,066
Isuzu	0	0	0	1,110	143	1,253	1,110	143	1,253
Kia Motors	0	8,370	8,370	0	4,973	4,973	0	13,343	13,343
Mazda	2,953	32,923	35,876	7,079	9,115	16,194	10,032	42,038	52,070
Mercedes Benz	0	8,310	8,310	14,730	0	14,730	14,730	8,310	23,040
Mitsubishi	0	0	0	0	48	48	0	48	48
Navistar	0	0	0	9,313	0	9,313	9,313	0	9,313
Nissan	19,579	10,591	30,170	5,457	11,777	17,234	25,036	22,368	47,404
PACCAR	0	0	0	6,025	0	6,025	6,025	0	6,025
Porsche	0	1,292	1,292	0	0	0	0	1,292	1,292
Renault	0	0	0	2,848	105	2,953	2,848	105	2,953
Suzuki	1,302	3,483	4,785	2,130	3,660	5,790	3,432	7,143	10,575
Toyota	44,509	50,514	95,023	15,947	12,626	28,573	60,456	63,140	123,596
Volkswagen	29,420	19,627	49,047	0	83	83	29,420	19,710	49,130
Volvo Truck	0	0	0	2,835	0	2,835	2,835	0	2,835
Western Star	0	0	0	1,984	0	1,984	1,984	0	1,984
Total Canada	**640,916**	**208,216**	**849,132**	**673,631**	**63,320**	**736,951**	**1,314,547**	**271,536**	**1,586,083**

MOTOR VEHICLE SALES IN MEXICO, 2000

	Passenger Cars			Commercial Vehicles			Total		
	Domestic	Import*	Total	Domestic	Import*	Total	Domestic	Import*	Total
BMW	2,220	1,546	3,766	265	0	265	2,485	1,546	4,031
Chrysler Corp.	55,082	11,170	66,252	55,077	0	55,077	110,159	11,170	121,329
Dina Camiones	0	0	0	1,533	0	1,533	1,533	0	1,533
Ford Motor Co.	49,465	17,768	67,233	78,118	3,782	81,900	127,583	21,550	149,133
General Motors	120,185	16,316	136,501	66,279	11,518	77,797	186,464	27,834	214,298
Honda	23,234	0	23,234	2,302	0	2,302	25,536	0	25,536
Mercedes Benz	0	2,222	2,222	12,124	3	12,127	12,124	2,225	14,349
Navistar	0	0	0	7,902	0	7,902	7,902	0	7,902
Nissan	125,167	3,368	128,535	42,179	5,086	47,265	167,346	8,454	175,800
Oshkosh Truck	0	0	0	931	0	931	931	0	931
PACCAR	0	0	0	7,062	0	7,062	7,062	0	7,062
Peugeot S.A.	0	3,454	3,454	0	0	0	0	3,454	3,454
Porsche	0	9	9	0	0	0	0	9	9
Rover Cars	0	596	596	0	0	0	0	596	596
Scania AB	0	0	0	154	0	154	154	0	154
Volkswagen	84,445	83,038	167,483	0	6,993	6,993	84,445	90,031	174,476
Volvo Truck	0	0	0	1,779	0	1,779	1,779	0	1,779
Total Mexico	**459,798**	**139,487**	**599,285**	**275,705**	**27,382**	**303,087**	**735,503**	**166,869**	**902,372**

*Units imported from outside North America.
SOURCE: Ward's AutoInfoBank, AMIA, ANPACT.

New Passenger Car and Truck Registrations by State

NEW PASSENGER CAR AND TRUCK REGISTRATIONS BY STATE, 1999-2000

State	Passenger Cars		Trucks		Total	
	1999	2000	1999	2000	1999	2000
Alabama	104,320	105,533	129,370	139,679	233,690	245,212
Alaska	11,024	11,470	20,990	23,700	32,014	35,170
Arizona	136,856	151,284	164,976	181,173	301,832	332,457
Arkansas	54,451	52,328	92,711	91,432	147,162	143,760
California	994,487	1,126,167	867,184	1,006,077	1,861,671	2,132,244
Colorado	125,700	132,037	173,248	174,315	298,948	306,352
Connecticut	117,752	121,588	86,810	88,546	204,562	210,134
Delaware	30,292	30,258	31,428	33,686	61,720	63,944
Florida	760,686	754,560	524,497	588,378	1,285,183	1,342,938
Georgia	245,935	253,981	297,492	305,267	543,427	559,248
Hawaii	41,140	48,942	30,263	37,878	71,403	86,820
Idaho	17,518	20,303	36,932	39,867	54,450	60,170
Illinois	410,130	416,271	348,020	343,367	758,150	759,638
Indiana	154,578	160,360	184,866	210,582	339,444	370,942
Iowa	59,603	57,854	83,384	85,941	142,987	143,795
Kansas	58,322	57,161	78,153	78,989	136,475	136,150
Kentucky	83,567	82,459	92,459	92,884	176,026	175,343
Louisianna	112,496	110,113	141,903	146,090	254,399	256,203
Maine	25,049	26,587	34,764	37,747	59,813	64,334
Maryland	223,951	237,398	168,020	189,073	391,971	426,471
Massachusetts	217,151	236,381	167,052	173,057	384,203	409,438
Michigan	378,368	350,018	499,635	481,897	878,003	831,915
Minnesota	141,677	158,837	171,905	199,255	313,582	358,092
Mississippi	52,011	54,819	72,590	77,166	124,601	131,985
Missouri	152,791	164,482	161,691	179,407	314,482	343,889
Montana	12,935	13,976	27,646	28,765	40,581	42,741
Nebraska	37,543	36,183	53,275	55,966	90,818	92,149
Nevada	62,858	75,972	62,992	71,204	125,850	147,176
New Hampshire	44,849	48,383	50,101	51,088	94,950	99,471
New Jersey	361,413	396,306	239,375	281,991	600,788	678,297
New Mexico	41,023	44,815	50,570	55,603	91,593	100,418
New York	508,876	525,793	396,155	411,775	905,031	937,568
North Carolina	219,470	228,320	255,499	270,985	474,969	499,305
North Dakota	9,570	9,444	19,300	19,957	28,870	29,401
Ohio	426,350	408,144	400,328	368,089	826,678	776,233
Oklahoma	64,760	63,950	112,929	119,808	177,689	183,758
Oregon	78,992	85,137	104,919	102,932	183,911	188,069
Pennsylvania	401,637	428,727	341,037	365,927	742,674	794,654
Rhode Island	30,655	39,148	19,206	23,777	49,861	62,925
South Carolina	98,345	107,862	117,634	133,264	215,979	241,126
South Dakota	11,825	11,856	22,977	24,512	34,802	36,368
Tennessee	145,521	142,030	165,333	167,810	310,854	309,840
Texas	570,811	604,420	754,221	846,087	1,325,032	1,450,507
Utah	44,787	50,323	60,529	68,356	105,316	118,679
Vermont	17,473	18,830	22,569	23,777	40,042	42,607
Virginia	236,087	249,574	185,879	205,377	421,966	454,951
Washington	121,371	137,998	143,941	159,272	265,312	297,270
West Virginia	39,679	41,765	48,879	50,317	88,558	92,082
Wisconsin	140,874	142,599	175,976	178,616	316,850	321,215
Wyoming	6,733	7,093	14,753	15,929	21,486	23,022
District of Colombia	11,537	11,812	4,599	5,391	16,136	17,203
Federal Government*	16,249	5,516	18,597	23,540	34,846	29,056
Total	8,472,078	8,857,167	8,529,562	9,135,568	17,001,640	17,992,735

*Federal government registrations not included in any state.
Source: The Polk Company. Permission for further use must be obtained from The Polk Company.

New Passenger Car Registrations by Manufacturer and State

NEW PASSENGER CAR REGISTRATIONS BY MANUFACTURER AND STATE, 2000

STATE	Chrysler	Dodge	Plymouth	Total DCC*	Ford	Lincoln	Mercury	Total Ford
Alabama	1,868	3,926	508	6,302	14,155	2,152	3,634	19,941
Alaska	197	818	177	1,192	2,128	64	276	2,468
Arizona	2,855	7,071	1,167	11,093	17,401	1,998	3,876	23,275
Arkansas	1,299	2,391	289	3,979	7,642	1,269	2,212	11,123
California**	20,839	32,027	5,628	58,494	135,657	14,454	25,387	175,498
Colorado	2,405	6,874	1,360	10,639	16,441	1,443	2,977	20,861
Connecticut	2,978	4,313	874	8,165	8,752	1,260	2,773	12,785
Delaware	1,616	1,746	418	3,780	3,085	405	1,026	4,516
Florida	17,989	21,645	3,979	43,613	72,836	17,306	24,289	114,431
Georgia	5,166	10,498	1,848	17,512	36,203	5,394	7,608	49,205
Hawaii	1,238	5,225	1,391	7,854	7,670	742	1,330	9,742
Idaho	441	985	236	1,662	2,555	253	461	3,269
Illinois	11,304	20,733	2,983	35,020	53,777	7,419	16,236	77,432
Indiana	5,731	7,464	1,354	14,549	20,786	2,734	6,054	29,574
Iowa	1,839	2,789	328	4,956	8,035	809	2,478	11,322
Kansas	1,657	2,574	304	4,535	8,857	1,172	2,057	12,086
Kentucky	1,647	3,430	447	5,524	11,469	1,302	2,990	15,761
Louisianna	1,998	4,087	559	6,644	15,017	2,733	4,577	22,327
Maine	615	1,678	158	2,451	3,666	202	960	4,828
Maryland	5,765	14,112	1,873	21,750	31,440	2,706	7,091	41,237
Massachusetts	5,168	9,552	1,577	16,297	24,502	2,897	8,286	35,685
Michigan	16,573	14,710	2,421	33,704	56,662	15,878	17,311	89,851
Minnesota	4,094	6,984	615	11,693	19,208	1,446	4,572	25,226
Mississippi	1,065	1,876	224	3,165	8,509	1,351	2,646	12,506
Missouri	4,617	9,055	1,813	15,485	27,416	3,029	7,455	37,900
Montana	309	796	109	1,214	1,718	121	335	2,174
Nebraska	1,311	1,782	389	3,482	4,895	444	1,199	6,538
Nevada	1,959	5,082	1,334	8,375	7,472	1,408	2,457	11,337
New Hampshire	1,093	2,337	331	3,761	5,979	455	1,402	7,836
New Jersey	10,216	12,009	2,886	25,111	43,546	7,688	16,575	67,809
New Mexico	1,000	2,364	388	3,752	6,328	504	1,195	8,027
New York	14,475	22,362	3,618	40,455	45,157	10,386	14,830	70,373
North Carolina	5,144	8,164	1,093	14,401	34,323	3,342	5,853	43,518
North Dakota	246	476	52	774	1,240	137	482	1,859
Ohio	11,958	16,755	3,230	31,943	55,679	6,828	14,980	77,487
Oklahoma	1,780	3,853	580	6,213	10,009	1,660	3,025	14,694
Oregon	1,696	2,827	589	5,112	11,826	739	2,228	14,793
Pennsylvania	16,740	22,346	5,317	44,403	49,958	5,629	13,664	69,251
Rhode Island	1,058	1,767	344	3,169	4,005	422	1,413	5,840
South Carolina	2,235	3,862	665	6,762	16,512	2,316	3,464	22,292
South Dakota	434	461	125	1,020	1,475	159	319	1,953
Tennessee	2,967	5,875	696	9,538	18,838	2,528	5,252	26,618
Texas	10,871	23,161	4,038	38,070	91,909	11,967	21,335	125,211
Utah	903	2,737	348	3,988	6,829	490	1,315	8,634
Vermont	398	991	210	1,599	2,106	143	521	2,770
Virginia	7,007	10,807	2,040	19,854	31,550	2,939	7,174	41,663
Washington	2,686	3,672	767	7,125	17,808	1,151	2,816	21,775
West Virginia	1,577	2,875	546	4,998	5,313	357	1,137	6,807
Wisconsin	4,147	6,782	1,068	11,997	16,726	1,838	4,979	23,543
Wyoming	216	259	69	544	802	79	252	1,133
District of Colombia	338	190	72	600	953	226	348	1,527
Federal Government	42	268	23	333	3,809	77	172	4,058
TOTAL	223,770	361,423	63,458	648,651	1,110,634	154,451	287,284	1,552,369

* DaimlerChrysler is former Chrysler Corp. operations only. ** Estimated. Source: The Polk Company. Permission for further use must be obtained from The Polk Company.

New Passenger Car Registrations by Manufacturer and State

NEW PASSENGER CAR REGISTRATIONS BY MANUFACTURER AND STATE, 2000 — continued

STATE	Buick	Cadillac	Chevrolet	Oldsmobile	Pontiac	Saturn	Total GM	Acura	Honda	Total Honda
Alabama	5,741	2,540	12,470	2,419	6,412	2,470	32,052	1,410	9,735	11,145
Alaska	356	56	1,136	203	783	424	2,958	87	659	746
Arizona	5,912	3,395	17,109	2,771	8,571	3,994	41,752	2,188	14,093	16,281
Arkansas	2,827	1,356	6,372	1,207	4,211	1,169	17,142	442	4,822	5,264
California**	24,686	14,651	67,764	13,988	34,399	30,529	186,017	23,772	152,938	176,710
Colorado	4,002	1,719	12,761	3,031	6,998	6,027	34,538	2,034	9,925	11,959
Connecticut	4,463	1,345	8,293	2,027	3,529	2,646	22,303	2,901	11,932	14,833
Delaware	1,354	403	2,679	910	1,732	730	7,808	518	2,670	3,188
Florida	49,722	21,127	84,446	22,274	43,918	19,197	240,684	12,107	50,950	63,057
Georgia	11,436	4,317	23,582	5,515	16,336	5,765	66,951	4,284	24,847	29,131
Hawaii	1,291	409	3,353	1,183	1,845	1,087	9,168	573	4,298	4,871
Idaho	837	247	2,073	399	1,289	737	5,582	176	1,689	1,865
Illinois	26,806	8,585	53,283	12,208	38,699	13,194	152,775	4,568	23,439	28,007
Indiana	11,950	3,603	22,369	6,705	18,571	6,319	69,517	861	9,330	10,191
Iowa	5,668	1,178	8,133	2,203	5,717	2,092	24,991	333	3,197	3,530
Kansas	3,292	984	6,520	1,604	4,626	2,219	19,245	1,028	4,841	5,869
Kentucky	4,452	1,583	10,178	1,831	5,550	1,917	25,511	618	5,942	6,560
Louisianna	4,518	1,860	12,296	2,753	7,279	3,971	32,677	1,112	10,598	11,710
Maine	1,341	185	2,600	419	1,297	808	6,650	48	1,657	1,705
Maryland	8,296	3,032	25,850	3,730	13,780	6,799	61,487	3,978	21,556	25,534
Massachusetts	8,075	2,815	15,169	4,103	8,520	7,988	46,670	3,593	21,135	24,728
Michigan	24,889	15,425	45,286	18,894	42,272	14,353	161,119	1,552	10,930	12,482
Minnesota	11,492	2,215	17,835	6,249	14,929	7,057	59,777	1,470	7,430	8,900
Mississippi	2,963	1,260	5,922	1,525	3,706	1,125	16,501	487	3,101	3,588
Missouri	9,743	3,050	22,294	5,036	14,213	4,860	59,196	1,788	9,096	10,884
Montana	873	182	1,722	591	982	98	4,448	31	913	944
Nebraska	2,761	636	4,391	1,585	3,137	1,495	14,005	302	2,605	2,907
Nevada	3,397	1,632	7,609	2,540	4,277	3,134	22,589	733	4,948	5,681
New Hampshire	1,540	409	3,553	618	1,910	1,268	9,298	564	4,107	4,671
New Jersey	12,690	6,537	30,527	8,120	16,170	12,916	86,960	9,249	33,695	42,944
New Mexico	1,733	621	5,386	1,425	4,417	1,287	14,869	358	3,348	3,706
New York	20,899	8,460	45,724	12,509	23,580	17,205	128,377	10,618	44,968	55,586
North Carolina	11,637	4,648	20,370	4,540	11,350	6,491	59,036	3,553	22,353	25,906
North Dakota	1,017	183	1,444	445	1,088	295	4,472	12	613	625
Ohio	24,530	8,765	56,342	13,701	38,198	13,539	155,075	3,978	30,846	34,824
Oklahoma	3,273	1,315	7,255	1,410	5,678	1,384	20,315	589	5,277	5,866
Oregon	2,359	925	5,555	1,454	2,997	2,139	15,429	1,788	9,193	10,981
Pennsylvania	20,791	6,523	51,537	11,710	30,033	13,482	134,076	6,472	28,508	34,980
Rhode Island	1,541	324	2,419	728	2,016	1,495	8,523	589	3,873	4,462
South Carolina	6,166	2,326	9,975	2,190	5,964	3,495	30,116	1,091	10,472	11,563
South Dakota	1,265	240	1,538	712	1,270	349	5,374	24	920	944
Tennessee	7,258	3,388	17,390	3,064	9,809	4,994	45,903	1,570	11,334	12,904
Texas	22,179	12,043	62,525	10,844	36,148	16,416	160,155	8,802	54,253	63,055
Utah	1,680	576	4,534	1,364	2,566	1,775	12,495	518	4,604	5,122
Vermont	672	90	1,609	372	920	460	4,123	128	1,585	1,713
Virginia	9,468	3,670	25,179	6,842	14,068	5,793	65,020	4,565	23,955	28,520
Washington	4,019	1,605	10,337	2,257	4,881	5,228	28,327	2,009	15,306	18,255
West Virginia	2,398	444	6,606	1,015	4,120	802	15,385	143	2,216	2,359
Wisconsin	10,779	2,496	18,842	4,611	14,964	7,516	59,208	1,321	8,561	9,882
Wyoming	533	139	876	285	653	529	3,015	24	452	476
District of Colombia	234	249	711	93	127	232	1,646	212	1,188	1,400
Federal Government	44	23	257	34	69	2	429	8	124	132
TOTAL	411,848	165,789	893,986	218,246	550,574	271,296	2,511,739	132,059	751,087	883,146

SOURCE: The Polk Company. Permission for further use must be obtained from The Polk Company.

New Passenger Car Registrations by Manufacturer and State

NEW PASSENGER CAR REGISTRATIONS BY MANUFACTURER AND STATE, 2000 — continued

STATE	Infiniti	Nissan	Total Nissan	Lexus	Toyota	Total Toyota	Mazda	Mitsubishi	Others	TOTAL
Alabama	804	4,867	5,671	1,027	11,240	12,267	2,820	3,189	12,146	105,533
Alaska	2	98	100	54	707	761	155	77	3,013	11,470
Arizona	1,833	10,598	12,431	1,777	14,843	16,620	2,361	3,469	24,002	151,284
Arkansas	203	2,088	2,291	410	4,938	5,348	981	980	5,220	52,328
California**	10,176	46,235	56,411	21,004	163,679	184,683	18,947	26,326	243,081	1,126,167
Colorado	522	4,926	5,448	1,072	10,434	11,506	2,323	3,169	31,594	132,037
Connecticut	811	8,414	9,225	1,354	11,778	13,132	1,980	4,206	34,959	121,588
Delaware	126	1,274	1,400	244	2,306	2,550	739	638	5,639	30,258
Florida	5,391	34,950	40,341	10,920	83,492	94,412	18,669	21,331	118,022	754,560
Georgia	2,146	12,417	14,563	2,592	24,354	26,946	6,393	8,050	35,230	253,981
Hawaii	209	2,806	3,015	754	5,757	6,511	966	215	6,600	48,942
Idaho	9	595	604	124	1,837	1,961	395	434	4,531	20,303
Illinois	2,769	14,575	17,344	3,901	31,460	35,361	5,048	8,980	56,304	416,271
Indiana	510	3,956	4,466	800	8,916	9,716	1,972	3,129	17,246	160,360
Iowa	104	1,682	1,786	275	3,690	3,965	782	851	5,671	57,854
Kansas	260	1,491	1,751	413	5,503	5,916	1,035	781	5,943	57,161
Kentucky	488	3,035	3,523	612	10,732	11,344	1,759	2,046	10,431	82,459
Louisianna	705	4,372	5,077	1,164	13,602	14,766	3,646	3,734	9,532	110,113
Maine	78	797	875	90	2,237	2,327	595	250	6,906	26,587
Maryland	1,047	9,466	10,513	1,977	26,230	28,207	4,661	6,586	37,423	237,398
Massachusetts	1,443	11,591	13,034	2,315	27,822	30,137	4,033	5,039	60,758	236,381
Michigan	483	3,494	3,977	1,558	10,485	12,043	3,835	1,942	31,065	350,018
Minnesota	482	3,570	4,052	901	10,301	11,202	2,554	12,022	23,411	158,837
Mississippi	312	2,850	3,162	374	5,685	6,059	1,823	1,151	6,864	54,819
Missouri	1,026	4,749	5,775	846	11,022	11,868	2,982	3,554	16,838	164,482
Montana	6	300	306	30	1,131	1,161	212	145	3,372	13,976
Nebraska	91	1,085	1,176	303	2,373	2,676	1,000	685	3,714	36,183
Nevada	516	3,625	4,141	639	7,029	7,668	1,208	3,070	11,903	75,972
New Hampshire	72	2,696	2,768	260	5,739	5,999	655	757	12,638	48,383
New Jersey	4,715	22,162	26,877	5,683	37,464	43,147	6,853	9,252	87,353	396,306
New Mexico	266	1,596	1,862	331	3,359	3,690	896	1,131	6,882	44,815
New York	5,174	32,845	38,019	6,865	48,176	55,041	6,504	12,898	118,540	525,793
North Carolina	954	11,580	12,534	2,155	24,148	26,303	7,812	5,690	33,120	228,320
North Dakota	4	186	190	27	568	595	108	70	751	9,444
Ohio	1,719	9,889	11,608	2,895	36,090	38,985	4,516	7,340	46,366	408,144
Oklahoma	301	2,417	2,718	734	4,910	5,644	1,268	1,249	5,983	63,950
Oregon	247	2,068	2,315	651	9,687	10,338	1,938	1,778	22,453	85,137
Pennsylvania	1,821	16,576	18,397	2,730	32,957	35,687	5,994	7,919	78,020	428,727
Rhode Island	222	2,425	2,647	288	4,042	4,330	922	857	8,398	39,148
South Carolina	743	4,681	5,424	993	11,490	12,483	3,322	2,917	12,983	107,862
South Dakota	4	187	191	23	788	811	160	173	1,230	11,856
Tennessee	1,065	8,778	9,843	1,364	13,411	14,775	3,593	3,289	15,567	142,030
Texas	5,039	23,823	28,862	9,259	60,149	69,408	16,659	19,078	83,922	604,420
Utah	242	1,646	1,888	317	4,621	4,938	1,165	2,435	9,658	50,323
Vermont	52	877	929	24	1,641	1,665	336	132	5,563	18,830
Virginia	1,030	11,086	12,116	2,029	23,804	25,833	6,224	6,471	43,873	249,574
Washington	568	4,375	4,943	1,657	13,372	15,029	3,004	3,318	36,222	137,998
West Virginia	17	1,217	1,234	124	3,644	3,768	431	650	6,133	41,765
Wisconsin	317	2,764	3,081	729	12,048	12,777	1,836	2,465	17,810	142,599
Wyoming	4	146	150	16	519	535	48	97	1,095	7,093
District of Colombia	64	485	549	151	1,269	1,420	539	244	3,887	11,812
Federal Government	2	33	35	9	174	183	17	5	324	5,516
TOTAL	57,194	364,444	421,638	96,844	867,653	964,497	168,674	216,264	1,490,189	8,857,167

SOURCE: The Polk Company. Permission for further use must be obtained from The Polk Company.

New Truck Registrations by Manufacturer and State

NEW TRUCK REGISTRATIONS BY MANUFACTURER AND STATE, 2000

State	Chrysler	Dodge	Jeep	Plymouth	Total DCC*	Ford	Lincoln	Mercury
Alabama	2,378	13,028	6,306	290	22,002	39,108	560	1,033
Alaska	413	3,300	811	71	4,595	7,042	41	112
Arizona	2,985	23,442	7,943	541	34,911	44,049	640	656
Arkansas	1,367	15,478	4,671	286	21,802	22,285	319	454
California	17,756	99,540	42,089	2,886	162,271	265,690	6,221	6,612
Colorado	2,600	22,818	14,285	433	40,136	49,847	483	1,066
Connecticut	3,699	10,646	8,602	537	23,484	16,404	313	675
Delaware	1,252	4,323	2,563	219	8,357	6,304	48	278
Florida	17,087	62,295	30,876	2,448	112,706	149,916	3,830	4,619
Georgia	6,544	28,620	15,204	856	51,224	92,472	1,928	2,306
Hawaii	839	3,653	2,323	166	6,981	8,238	70	264
Idaho	684	7,042	1,418	131	9,275	11,223	126	170
Illinois	12,120	50,344	20,724	2,196	85,384	79,633	1,491	3,572
Indiana	7,300	31,220	11,827	3,223	53,570	51,563	658	2,080
Iowa	3,908	13,588	3,367	307	21,170	22,411	143	882
Kansas	2,586	11,401	3,164	334	17,485	23,130	228	612
Kentucky	2,172	14,031	4,685	262	21,150	23,954	273	672
Louisiana	2,173	18,239	5,473	465	26,350	40,961	841	953
Maine	783	4,594	2,413	131	7,921	8,815	43	244
Maryland	5,387	25,696	11,713	1,052	43,848	46,168	609	1,254
Massachusetts	5,789	21,977	12,795	959	41,520	39,756	584	1,671
Michigan	16,728	59,383	36,705	2,155	114,971	149,225	2,575	10,332
Minnesota	7,359	26,094	8,687	1,172	43,312	55,889	476	1,977
Mississippi	1,075	8,690	3,148	227	13,140	22,161	372	596
Missouri	5,244	25,265	7,530	940	38,979	53,405	574	1,538
Montana	452	5,459	878	79	6,868	7,404	59	132
Nebraska	2,431	7,585	2,645	303	12,964	15,747	105	370
Nevada	1,383	9,419	3,507	186	14,495	19,060	355	594
New Hampshire	1,286	7,096	3,556	283	12,221	12,875	102	351
New Jersey	10,294	31,632	24,148	1,367	67,441	70,548	1,352	4,384
New Mexico	944	7,254	2,666	163	11,027	16,076	140	247
New York	13,967	50,543	37,185	2,465	104,160	89,431	1,812	4,546
North Carolina	7,379	31,286	15,266	904	54,835	74,702	829	1,265
North Dakota	600	3,086	566	46	4,298	5,729	29	226
Ohio	13,920	44,833	23,048	2,293	84,094	97,757	1,155	4,341
Oklahoma	2,613	15,848	3,290	395	22,146	27,671	444	672
Oregon	2,874	14,281	4,904	521	22,580	30,772	262	473
Pennsylvania	15,197	47,318	27,563	2,331	92,409	87,787	964	3,711
Rhode Island	897	3,303	1,609	166	5,975	5,568	58	234
South Carolina	2,799	15,572	6,636	706	25,713	36,530	529	855
South Dakota	880	3,446	816	70	5,212	8,154	39	116
Tennessee	3,170	18,668	8,038	575	30,451	42,952	656	1,409
Texas	14,515	100,699	31,759	2,316	149,289	276,357	4,834	5,322
Utah	938	10,350	4,697	195	16,180	17,878	162	397
Vermont	522	3,162	1,534	124	5,342	5,419	21	187
Virginia	7,376	23,468	13,286	1,257	45,387	48,765	645	1,522
Washington	3,630	21,754	8,132	685	34,201	43,365	492	800
West Virginia	1,472	6,827	3,257	262	11,818	12,007	81	253
Wisconsin	9,137	26,675	8,669	1,254	45,735	40,989	439	1,804
Wyoming	179	2,941	508	27	3,655	4,499	37	66
District of Columbia	191	501	508	46	1,246	1,160	50	80
Federal Government	59	1,630	115	9	1,813	17,057	4	23
TOTAL	249,333	1,119,343	508,108	41,315	1,918,099	2,445,908	39,101	79,008

Note: Toyota includes Lexus, Nissan includes Infiniti. * DaimlerChrysler is former Chrysler Corp. operations only. ** PACCAR is Kenworth and Peterbilt.
Source: The Polk Company. Permission for further use must be obtained from The Polk Company.

New Truck Registrations
by Manufacturer and State

NEW TRUCK REGISTRATIONS BY MANUFACTURER AND STATE, 2000 — continued

State	Total Ford	Cadillac	Chevrolet	GMC	Olds	Pontiac	Total GM	Toyota
Alabama	40,701	420	30,785	9,590	745	744	42,284	8,703
Alaska	7,195	37	5,136	1,885	136	89	7,283	1,335
Arizona	45,345	603	34,930	13,346	885	933	50,697	14,393
Arkansas	23,058	278	21,407	8,072	361	402	30,520	4,047
California	278,523	3,716	159,164	50,984	3,317	4,751	221,932	124,647
Colorado	51,396	666	28,898	9,738	1,010	763	41,075	12,798
Connecticut	17,392	106	14,292	3,165	494	351	18,408	5,998
Delaware	6,630	31	5,819	1,529	240	226	7,845	1,195
Florida	158,365	1,662	100,811	35,682	8,776	6,037	152,968	35,917
Georgia	96,706	914	57,970	19,882	1,572	2,072	82,410	16,866
Hawaii	8,572	20	4,279	1,013	353	586	6,251	5,016
Idaho	11,519	78	7,106	3,937	203	178	11,502	2,149
Illinois	84,696	833	67,605	17,323	4,105	3,677	93,543	12,645
Indiana	54,301	454	46,685	16,487	3,517	3,134	70,277	4,923
Iowa	23,436	140	20,520	4,678	1,140	906	27,384	1,953
Kansas	23,970	101	16,901	5,052	680	615	23,349	3,463
Kentucky	24,899	182	20,283	4,253	744	712	26,174	6,725
Louisiana	42,755	321	32,789	12,650	515	599	46,874	8,791
Maine	9,102	19	7,503	5,583	151	150	13,406	1,912
Maryland	48,031	399	34,120	8,031	1,135	1,176	44,861	12,536
Massachusetts	42,011	277	22,975	9,018	1,039	933	34,242	14,636
Michigan	162,132	1,927	104,992	44,937	8,093	10,551	170,500	5,126
Minnesota	58,342	283	50,861	10,469	2,197	1,702	65,512	5,129
Mississippi	23,129	275	16,908	6,161	319	295	23,958	4,166
Missouri	55,517	384	39,938	10,823	1,704	1,547	54,396	5,636
Montana	7,595	53	6,182	2,370	139	165	8,909	1,212
Nebraska	16,222	135	11,347	2,879	593	459	15,413	1,177
Nevada	20,009	443	13,121	4,626	546	397	19,133	5,330
New Hampshire	13,328	55	8,988	2,597	231	206	12,077	4,322
New Jersey	76,284	596	38,629	13,841	1,854	1,964	56,884	14,701
New Mexico	16,463	152	10,916	4,453	325	326	16,172	4,032
New York	95,789	920	69,750	21,593	3,549	3,450	99,262	19,809
North Carolina	76,796	785	52,763	12,453	1,648	1,338	68,987	17,399
North Dakota	5,984	26	5,963	1,374	256	186	7,805	374
Ohio	103,253	818	79,720	19,757	5,074	4,444	109,813	15,245
Oklahoma	28,787	197	26,346	7,595	381	545	35,064	3,339
Oregon	31,507	179	15,561	4,229	449	311	20,729	8,898
Pennsylvania	92,462	631	67,821	23,816	3,516	3,023	98,807	17,509
Rhode Island	5,860	54	2,574	1,405	99	169	4,301	1,657
South Carolina	37,914	409	29,382	7,900	822	896	39,409	8,066
South Dakota	8,309	41	5,975	1,611	289	228	8,144	615
Tennessee	45,017	606	31,287	10,421	1,101	971	44,386	9,655
Texas	286,513	2,827	188,843	45,518	2,464	2,839	242,491	39,650
Utah	18,437	135	10,955	4,291	268	193	15,842	4,102
Vermont	5,627	15	4,976	1,404	142	143	6,680	2,057
Virginia	50,932	422	31,676	9,484	1,657	2,066	45,305	16,037
Washington	44,657	296	27,658	6,735	832	537	36,058	12,564
West Virginia	12,341	55	12,078	2,670	368	356	15,527	4,020
Wisconsin	43,232	256	41,197	11,984	2,193	2,387	58,017	7,236
Wyoming	4,602	38	3,331	1,863	99	79	5,410	777
District of Columbia	1,290	26	565	114	23	12	740	439
Federal Government	17,084	4	3,101	301	5	8	3,419	67
TOTAL	2,564,017	24,300	1,753,382	541,572	72,354	70,827	2,462,435	540,994

Note: Toyota includes Lexus, Nissan includes Infiniti. *PACCAR is Kenworth and Peterbilt.
Source: The Polk Co. Further use prohibited without written permission from The Polk Company.

New Truck Registrations by Manufacturer and State

NEW TRUCK REGISTRATIONS BY MANUFACTURER AND STATE, 2000 — continued

State	Nissan	Freight-liner	Inter-national	Mack	PACCAR*	Volvo	Other	Total
Alabama	5,871	1,736	2,363	1,110	959	727	13,223	139,679
Alaska	281	119	152	10	137	0	2,585	23,700
Arizona	12,223	2,377	898	188	787	386	18,968	181,173
Arkansas	2,701	2,035	1,097	261	499	566	4,846	91,432
California	50,332	6,667	6,551	475	4,267	1,134	149,278	1,006,077
Colorado	5,482	1,166	1,471	274	1,056	161	19,300	174,315
Connecticut	5,015	261	1,437	302	155	57	16,037	88,546
Delaware	939	2,280	2,525	119	93	477	3,226	33,686
Florida	26,340	3,858	4,025	1,836	1,461	1,096	89,806	588,378
Georgia	14,262	3,263	3,682	1,844	1,248	1,020	32,742	305,267
Hawaii	3,659	55	148	7	63	33	7,093	37,878
Idaho	640	281	271	211	702	173	3,144	39,867
Illinois	7,544	7,054	6,998	2,948	2,812	1,699	38,044	343,367
Indiana	2,400	3,979	3,133	926	1,496	845	14,732	210,582
Iowa	997	2,157	1,883	696	1,042	382	4,841	85,941
Kansas	1,376	765	822	111	929	65	6,654	78,989
Kentucky	2,901	782	984	247	365	230	8,427	92,884
Louisiana	5,723	904	1,440	395	570	106	12,182	146,090
Maine	783	320	446	116	174	130	3,437	37,747
Maryland	7,193	1,885	2,737	644	640	195	26,503	189,073
Massachusetts	6,518	942	1,745	771	352	170	30,150	173,057
Michigan	2,293	2,415	2,711	472	1,277	706	19,294	481,897
Minnesota	1,821	2,170	2,927	585	1,697	415	17,345	199,255
Mississippi	3,770	1,609	1,130	318	560	340	5,046	77,166
Missouri	2,996	2,627	2,125	312	2,100	515	14,204	179,407
Montana	418	453	179	14	394	190	2,533	28,765
Nebraska	953	3,395	636	205	1,225	61	3,715	55,966
Nevada	2,881	184	305	7	43	5	8,812	71,204
New Hampshire	1,774	278	615	234	149	24	6,066	51,088
New Jersey	13,449	3,346	2,501	1,317	867	645	44,556	281,991
New Mexico	1,785	539	550	85	218	155	4,577	55,603
New York	19,282	2,725	5,172	2,058	1,420	508	61,590	411,775
North Carolina	12,703	4,265	2,669	974	1,444	1,083	29,830	270,985
North Dakota	87	206	142	28	231	82	720	19,957
Ohio	4,922	3,771	5,871	1,549	1,766	1,420	36,385	368,089
Oklahoma	3,605	8,262	2,979	975	4,198	1,149	9,304	119,808
Oregon	2,747	1,615	698	63	772	154	13,169	102,932
Pennsylvania	10,111	5,810	5,213	1,576	2,152	488	39,390	365,927
Rhode Island	866	462	447	262	71	114	3,762	23,777
South Carolina	5,401	1,025	1,313	606	653	258	12,906	133,264
South Dakota	192	270	296	24	243	41	1,166	24,512
Tennessee	10,347	4,228	2,089	1,696	1,768	2,542	15,631	167,810
Texas	28,555	5,134	6,169	2,612	4,138	746	80,790	846,087
Utah	1,634	2,403	675	156	1,193	427	7,307	68,356
Vermont	676	191	438	61	75	30	2,600	23,777
Virginia	9,896	1,417	2,573	677	685	340	32,128	205,377
Washington	5,185	2,079	1,103	123	1,766	271	21,265	159,272
West Virginia	1,432	257	470	145	260	70	3,977	50,317
Wisconsin	1,524	3,563	2,926	898	2,028	546	12,911	178,616
Wyoming	228	160	90	13	229	21	744	15,929
District of Columbia	259	8	26	5	1	0	1,377	5,391
Federal Government	47	371	148	16	3	19	553	23,540
TOTAL	315,019	108,124	99,994	31,557	53,433	23,025	1,018,871	9,135,568

Note: Toyota includes Lexus, Nissan includes Infiniti. *PACCAR is Kenworth and Peterbilt.
Source: The Polk Co. Further use prohibited without written permission from The Polk Company.

REGISTRATIONS

Car, Truck and Bus Registrations by State

TOTAL MOTOR VEHICLE REGISTRATIONS BY STATE, 1998-1999

State	Passenger Cars		Trucks and Buses		Total	
	1998	1999	1998	1999	1998	1999
Alabama	2,062,734	1,918,032	1,796,194	2,039,217	3,858,928	3,957,249
Alaska	232,170	238,202	313,695	333,267	545,865	571,469
Arizona	1,728,185	2,037,370	1,215,831	1,568,857	2,944,016	3,606,227
Arkansas	928,958	945,871	825,257	871,954	1,754,215	1,817,825
California	16,174,220	16,657,441	9,426,030	9,705,027	25,600,250	26,362,468
Colorado	1,843,385	2,053,579	1,622,709	1,804,569	3,466,094	3,858,148
Connecticut	1,998,457	1,994,380	702,176	771,791	2,700,633	2,766,171
Delaware	416,709	401,917	199,783	213,694	616,492	615,611
District of Columbia	192,097	197,070	36,619	38,428	228,716	235,498
Florida	7,437,597	7,304,601	3,838,792	4,085,112	11,276,389	11,389,713
Georgia	4,032,998	4,011,725	2,860,321	2,960,985	6,893,319	6,972,710
Hawaii	449,731	454,341	254,105	263,766	703,836	718,107
Idaho	501,509	494,220	617,384	635,423	1,118,893	1,129,643
Illinois	6,425,276	6,307,479	2,881,434	3,047,781	9,306,710	9,355,260
Indiana	3,273,026	3,224,493	2,098,627	2,270,594	5,371,653	5,495,087
Iowa	1,737,582	1,723,848	1,315,553	1,326,119	3,053,135	3,049,967
Kansas	1,127,367	1,187,320	994,043	1,037,028	2,121,410	2,224,348
Kentucky	1,715,524	1,592,519	1,129,088	1,069,470	2,844,612	2,661,989
Louisiana	1,966,954	1,964,922	1,463,763	1,539,740	3,430,717	3,504,662
Maine	565,338	550,537	364,267	364,918	929,605	915,455
Maryland	2,621,923	2,665,572	1,128,352	1,230,725	3,750,275	3,896,297
Massachusetts	3,782,940	3,822,524	1,376,228	1,510,664	5,159,168	5,333,188
Michigan	5,104,781	5,069,808	3,023,369	3,219,836	8,128,150	8,289,644
Minnesota	2,412,412	2,265,392	1,765,429	1,744,325	4,177,841	4,009,717
Mississippi	1,250,200	1,299,441	1,005,544	1,017,331	2,255,744	2,316,772
Missouri	2,600,722	2,601,830	1,776,798	1,802,414	4,377,520	4,404,244
Montana	458,116	455,430	530,161	542,475	988,277	997,905
Nebraska	834,188	833,415	691,810	736,138	1,525,998	1,569,553
Nevada	665,940	620,131	554,337	542,245	1,220,277	1,162,376
New Hampshire	687,770	678,497	350,695	372,401	1,038,465	1,050,898
New Jersey	4,215,195	4,341,182	1,565,141	1,761,576	5,780,336	6,102,758
New Mexico	821,031	761,012	773,761	815,470	1,594,792	1,576,482
New York	7,664,320	7,892,118	2,757,713	2,863,908	10,422,033	10,756,026
North Carolina	3,530,711	3,423,588	2,331,119	2,266,852	5,861,830	5,690,440
North Dakota	330,275	342,786	341,883	361,626	672,158	704,412
Ohio	6,664,356	6,651,554	3,375,132	3,584,049	10,039,488	10,235,603
Oklahoma	1,548,949	1,524,424	1,370,237	1,407,062	2,919,186	2,931,486
Oregon	1,588,313	1,559,972	1,391,751	1,452,987	2,980,064	3,012,959
Pennsylvania	6,131,725	6,071,724	2,847,089	2,936,876	8,978,814	9,008,600
Rhode Island	522,292	535,034	192,725	211,976	715,017	747,010
South Carolina	1,822,640	1,872,502	1,070,421	1,153,745	2,893,061	3,026,247
South Dakota	381,752	379,168	386,755	402,793	768,507	781,961
Tennessee	2,695,539	2,621,508	1,773,526	1,805,011	4,469,065	4,426,519
Texas	7,455,714	7,738,292	5,868,453	6,330,428	13,324,167	14,068,720
Utah	850,487	856,699	681,766	720,481	1,532,253	1,577,180
Vermont	295,664	301,914	200,489	215,701	496,153	517,615
Virginia	3,774,372	3,769,276	2,043,922	2,101,881	5,818,294	5,871,157
Washington	2,776,482	2,741,257	2,047,505	2,120,893	4,823,987	4,862,150
West Virginia	776,583	759,648	601,252	619,483	1,377,835	1,379,131
Wisconsin	2,544,109	2,520,717	1,659,210	1,745,055	4,203,319	4,265,772
Wyoming	219,220	195,762	339,771	332,432	558,991	528,194
Total	131,838,538	132,432,044	79,778,015	83,876,579	211,616,553	216,308,623

NOTE: Registrations include both privately and publicly owned motor vehicles, except those owned by the military.
SOURCE: U.S. Department of Transportation, Federal Highway Administration.

Total Motor Truck Registrations by State

TOTAL MOTOR TRUCK REGISTRATIONS BY STATE, 1996-1999

State	Privately Owned(1)				Privately and Publicly Owned(2)			
	1996	1997	1998	1999	1996	1997	1998	1999
Alabama	1,528,218	1,729,251	1,761,393	2,003,958	1,553,872	1,755,052	1,787,553	2,030,509
Alaska	292,426	307,569	303,406	321,679	300,506	315,550	311,499	330,895
Arizona	1,194,588	1,268,172	1,193,078	1,545,445	1,212,276	1,285,967	1,211,377	1,564,306
Arkansas	754,320	759,701	808,095	854,135	765,273	770,702	819,262	865,486
California	9,526,351	8,946,151	9,125,074	9,394,333	9,771,261	9,194,701	9,380,604	9,658,010
Colorado	1,501,899	1,572,048	1,591,459	1,772,618	1,526,688	1,597,019	1,616,989	1,798,766
Connecticut	633,231	661,320	666,394	735,188	658,434	686,847	692,437	761,780
Delaware	190,231	205,146	195,013	208,972	192,760	207,859	197,772	211,708
Dist. of Columbia	28,793	28,712	27,587	29,154	35,021	34,971	34,037	35,819
Florida	3,425,551	3,318,329	3,653,773	3,895,826	3,561,872	3,457,115	3,795,715	4,041,067
Georgia	2,369,057	2,479,223	2,782,908	2,881,162	2,426,027	2,537,703	2,843,253	2,943,465
Hawaii	269,965	239,863	243,178	252,726	276,329	245,956	249,998	259,582
Idaho	553,008	565,420	595,881	613,991	572,857	582,923	613,780	631,843
Illinois	2,490,532	2,556,208	2,847,783	3,013,920	2,507,383	2,572,445	2,863,926	3,030,090
Indiana	1,986,007	2,034,018	2,033,144	2,203,115	2,023,886	2,072,643	2,072,722	2,243,692
Iowa	1,179,936	1,181,547	1,281,006	1,291,165	1,206,182	1,207,001	1,307,450	1,318,004
Kansas	930,161	993,048	972,283	1,014,353	947,909	1,011,023	990,239	1,033,178
Kentucky	1,070,144	1,127,853	1,109,302	1,048,799	1,077,620	1,135,323	1,117,054	1,056,945
Louisiana	1,373,494	1,438,931	1,420,838	1,495,739	1,394,443	1,460,296	1,442,837	1,518,412
Maine	367,020	407,405	350,265	350,723	377,873	418,357	361,368	361,988
Maryland	1,031,321	1,124,273	1,094,112	1,196,240	1,053,197	1,146,316	1,116,616	1,219,249
Massachusetts	1,113,269	1,191,773	1,328,611	1,461,670	1,147,344	1,226,683	1,364,674	1,498,954
Michigan	2,821,785	2,814,169	2,923,241	3,118,205	2,895,058	2,888,109	2,998,227	3,194,300
Minnesota	1,549,661	1,575,102	1,727,750	1,706,749	1,572,845	1,596,411	1,750,710	1,729,661
Mississippi	886,616	942,680	973,509	989,502	904,335	960,747	995,359	1,006,787
Missouri	1,745,728	1,771,282	1,746,695	1,769,769	1,762,022	1,788,008	1,763,632	1,788,863
Montana	517,814	505,023	510,327	522,253	533,205	521,740	527,363	539,664
Nebraska	648,881	672,574	668,681	711,799	665,057	689,821	686,251	730,341
Nevada	460,782	470,873	538,350	525,827	474,686	484,829	552,631	540,474
New Hampshire	363,123	375,641	338,082	358,865	373,530	386,466	348,960	370,688
New Jersey	1,307,948	1,429,763	1,443,844	1,644,811	1,403,947	1,528,365	1,545,560	1,741,011
New Mexico	748,474	710,562	748,747	789,934	768,981	731,361	770,129	811,946
New York	2,506,142	2,662,545	2,609,294	2,713,666	2,606,026	2,763,560	2,709,077	2,813,177
North Carolina	2,160,114	2,229,780	2,252,915	2,190,920	2,215,933	2,275,679	2,300,380	2,236,865
North Dakota	329,680	347,640	330,960	350,632	338,648	356,213	339,584	359,337
Ohio	3,060,630	3,304,262	3,269,087	3,475,109	3,127,633	3,372,811	3,339,602	3,547,685
Oklahoma	1,338,044	1,295,728	1,309,696	1,345,136	1,380,673	1,339,234	1,354,302	1,390,893
Oregon	1,281,116	1,271,533	1,348,984	1,409,617	1,310,438	1,300,275	1,378,996	1,440,067
Pennsylvania	2,610,941	2,680,277	2,750,082	2,839,317	2,669,913	2,740,670	2,811,780	2,901,946
Rhode Island	177,610	186,913	185,961	205,010	183,211	192,489	190,894	210,076
South Carolina	988,205	1,045,542	1,030,258	1,112,521	1,011,972	1,069,700	1,055,022	1,137,929
South Dakota	365,910	324,952	370,925	386,805	378,151	337,967	384,059	400,072
Tennessee	1,761,726	1,706,190	1,699,764	1,731,891	1,816,551	1,761,492	1,755,950	1,787,631
Texas	5,595,062	5,516,791	5,535,162	5,985,835	5,831,593	5,759,985	5,788,362	6,247,839
Utah	618,369	663,148	665,811	704,089	632,491	677,474	680,534	719,239
Vermont	193,713	196,667	191,907	206,781	200,281	203,207	198,558	213,763
Virginia	1,886,139	2,026,468	1,990,599	2,048,144	1,920,994	2,061,273	2,026,139	2,084,027
Washington	1,920,843	1,964,049	1,999,193	2,071,877	1,958,448	2,003,060	2,038,417	2,111,756
West Virginia	567,909	564,789	566,256	585,068	600,736	597,001	597,953	616,272
Wisconsin	1,444,412	1,626,452	1,602,748	1,688,032	1,485,803	1,668,552	1,645,772	1,732,023
Wyoming	316,872	317,065	325,356	317,584	328,032	328,457	337,110	329,722
Total	73,983,771	75,335,221	77,038,767	81,090,659	75,940,206	77,307,408	79,062,475	83,147,802

(1) Excludes farm trucks registered in certain states and restricted for use in vicinity of owner's farm.
(2) Includes federal, state, county and municipal vehicles; excludes vehicles owned by military.
SOURCE: U.S. Department of Transportation, Federal Highway Administration.

Truck Registrations by State and Type

TOTAL MOTOR TRUCK REGISTRATIONS BY STATE AND TYPE, 1999

State	Truck Tractors	Farm Trucks	Pickups	Vans	Sport Utilities	Other Light	Total
Alabama	73,847	20,416	1,023,566	277,609	192,627	394,697	1,982,762
Alaska	2,891	510	171,848	46,012	92,941	3,439	317,641
Arizona	18,091	0	844,291	260,151	388,554	11,438	1,522,525
Arkansas	18,181	21,320	565,173	114,901	157,620	4,651	881,846
California	113,500	0	3,915,770	2,031,283	2,303,046	53,233	8,416,832
Colorado	6,569	91,292	793,035	270,676	592,963	11,203	1,765,738
Connecticut[1]	2,586	0	280,530	182,885	260,342	6,397	732,740
Delaware	3,946	3,047	86,209	52,223	61,351	1,363	208,139
District of Columbia	180	0	5,788	10,501	11,871	699	29,039
Florida	67,358	0	1,488,070	926,272	950,360	22,765	3,454,825
Georgia[2]	70,320	0	1,447,568	511,477	671,680	16,586	2,717,631
Hawaii	790	0	120,593	63,721	63,281	2,142	250,527
Idaho	6,233	0	359,315	71,724	130,407	3,590	571,269
Illinois	60,878	37,932	1,170,610	862,445	727,210	21,652	2,880,727
Indiana	55,947	47,103	1,065,235	492,457	394,471	11,968	2,067,181
Iowa	60,841	24,150	657,643	250,829	208,848	7,030	1,209,341
Kansas	21,397	87,884	528,839	179,847	172,267	5,751	995,985
Kentucky	26,809	83,942	612,035	171,519	189,884	6,037	1,090,226
Louisiana	31,427	96,540	931,334	225,658	266,635	8,759	1,560,353
Maine	3,222	5,355	198,041	59,170	75,789	2,086	343,663
Maryland	15,928	10,805	464,814	335,836	354,502	8,555	1,190,440
Massachusetts	12,441	9,068	524,079	386,253	514,681	11,416	1,457,938
Michigan	69,870	49,905	1,296,847	822,733	743,824	13,458	2,996,637
Minnesota	30,300	50,690	734,830	362,019	366,221	9,629	1,553,689
Mississippi[2]	12,166	0	653,668	128,314	168,053	7,096	969,297
Missouri	46,831	123,629	949,722	349,486	339,919	12,122	1,821,709
Montana	15,794	110,120	306,407	54,963	97,215	2,926	587,425
Nebraska	29,285	148,433	359,009	120,768	132,851	3,946	794,292
Nevada	6,455	0	240,353	72,015	143,948	2,986	465,757
New Hampshire[1]	5,606	1,976	163,287	77,953	99,957	2,368	351,147
New Jersey[1]	10,461	13,311	448,175	513,225	655,493	14,580	1,655,245
New Mexico	13,043	18,993	433,114	99,021	162,864	4,392	731,427
New York[1]	14,675	49,038	592,785	599,516	633,076	19,884	1,908,974
North Carolina	60,235	86,768	1,112,903	403,980	472,493	15,702	2,152,081
North Dakota	9,357	39,067	185,125	47,070	57,363	1,634	339,616
Ohio	43,370	33,816	1,548,231	962,470	743,572	19,420	3,350,879
Oklahoma	11,198	174,055	783,160	180,746	205,543	8,061	1,362,763
Oregon	19,828	18,357	724,792	250,042	316,176	10,078	1,339,273
Pennsylvania[1]	66,937	0	1,029,128	664,500	822,198	17,903	2,600,666
Rhode Island[1]	2,689	0	86,903	51,016	54,409	1,300	196,317
South Carolina	18,168	25,623	601,397	208,037	252,928	7,472	1,113,625
South Dakota	16,422	0	183,089	51,186	65,166	1,653	317,516
Tennessee	55,192	44,280	980,538	293,798	371,646	9,861	1,755,315
Texas	152,281	201,440	3,325,808	927,834	1,452,373	33,808	6,093,544
Utah	35,519	13,000	336,503	103,728	208,783	3,963	701,496
Vermont	3,106	2,915	105,656	37,685	53,484	1,266	204,112
Virginia	33,307	25,345	933,247	443,643	545,346	13,066	1,993,954
Washington	24,713	20,559	1,023,537	405,068	501,118	14,210	1,989,205
West Virginia	9,770	2,614	336,813	83,498	127,435	2,995	563,125
Wisconsin	40,395	95,740	747,761	414,898	361,918	8,609	1,669,321
Wyoming	3,356	4,920	190,685	31,038	73,613	1,832	305,444
Total	**1,533,711**	**1,893,958**	**37,667,859**	**16,543,699**	**19,010,315**	**881,677**	**77,531,219**

NOTE: The registrations given in this table are as reported by the States in most instances, but have been supplemented in some cases by estimates based on data from other sources. In this partial classification a vehicle may be included more than once; for instance, a truck-tractor in farm use could appear in both columns.

(1) Except for Georgia and Mississippi (Footnote 2), farm registrations are shown for all States that have a special "Farm" classification. The numbers of vehicles shown do not necessarily represent the total number or registered vehicles used on the farm. The following farm trucks, registered at a nominal fee and restricted to use in the vicinity of the owner's farm, are not included in this table: Connecticut, 5,552; New Hampshire, 5,576; New Jersey, 6,777; New York, 19,536; Pennsylvania, 23,163; and Rhode Island, 1,132.

(2) Although Georgia and Mississippi have a special "Farm" classification, their registration reports do not show a complete segregation of farm trucks from private carriers.

SOURCE: U.S. Department of Transportation, Federal Highway Administration.

Private, Commercial and Publicly Owner Trailer Registrations by State

TRAILER REGISTRATIONS BY STATE, 1999

| State | Private and Commercial Trailers[1] | | | | Publicly Owned Trailers | | | Grand Total |
	Commercial Trailers[2]	Car and Light Farm Trailers[3]	House Trailers[4]	Total	Federal Government	State, County and Municipal	Total	
Alabama	62,902	64,746	19,674	147,322	14	1,076	1,090	148,412
Alaska	18,945	88,897	0	107,842	128	1,546	1,674	109,516
Arizona	63,611	221,367	100,544	385,522	94	3,831	3,925	389,447
Arkansas	40,432	362,292	19,694	422,418	5	272	277	422,695
California	665,602	1,446,776	527,539	2,639,917	361	49,385	49,746	2,689,663
Colorado	95,975	184,174	77,549	357,698	79	2,107	2,186	359,884
Connecticut	47,948	130,332	0	178,280	12	2,724	2,736	181,016
Delaware	19,749	31,797	0	51,546	7	892	899	52,445
District of Columbia ..	79	850	0	929	147	339	486	1,415
Florida	100,113	1,133,096	0	1,233,209	178	28,419	28,597	1,261,806
Georgia	133,324	444,365	31,362	609,051	126	3,939	4,065	613,116
Hawaii	3,242	14,708	0	17,950	4	807	811	18,761
Idaho	13,152	48,366	56,620	118,138	58	2,642	2,700	120,838
Illinois	115,176	518,659	122,176	756,011	226	414	640	756,651
Indiana	114,003	338,973	90,868	543,844	38	2,142	2,100	546,024
Iowa	120,832	287,149	68,436	476,417	20	5,108	5,128	481,545
Kansas	82,473	23,822	18,740	125,035	23	897	920	125,955
Kentucky	24,722	28,889	33,385	86,996	59	121	180	87,176
Louisiana	194,980	274,659	10,819	480,458	25	2,731	2,756	483,214
Maine	630,450	103,246	0	733,696	8	2,248	2,256	735,952
Maryland	19,353	224,026	0	243,379	100	401	501	243,880
Massachusetts	24,881	258,692	0	283,573	71	185	256	283,829
Michigan	116,621	845,254	139,336	1,101,211	83	4,476	4,559	1,105,770
Minnesota	165,373	675,801	86,945	928,119	80	2,825	2,905	931,024
Mississippi	32,480	74,345	10,959	117,784	31	1,725	1,756	119,540
Missouri	96,067	221,006	0	317,073	121	464	585	317,658
Montana	22,917	121,611	54,178	198,706	51	2,579	2,630	201,336
Nebraska	88,813	177,420	0	266,233	12	1,035	1,047	267,280
Nevada	9,379	70,619	31,403	111,401	46	1,154	1,200	112,601
New Hampshire	10,911	114,200	0	125,111	3	1,193	1,196	126,307
New Jersey	20,048	320,166	0	340,214	156	100	256	340,470
New Mexico	44,334	36,368	46,857	127,559	135	3,154	3,289	130,848
New York	19,224	386,661	0	405,885	345	6,556	6,901	412,786
North Carolina	92,160	538,975	1,404	632,539	44	7,445	7,489	640,028
North Dakota	23,577	28,466	17,535	69,578	9	952	961	70,539
Ohio	118,952	482,343	108,440	709,735	121	8,892	9,013	718,748
Oklahoma	100,015	63,745	12,621	176,381	34	1,967	2,001	178,382
Oregon	49,858	152,519	125,105	327,482	96	10,280	10,376	337,858
Pennsylvania	137,186	496,187	215,210	848,583	199	4,067	4,266	852,849
Rhode Island	6,824	41,832	0	48,656	8	916	924	49,580
South Carolina	27,266	30,561	129	57,956	32	1,148	1,180	59,136
South Dakota	45,851	79,068	34,064	158,983	29	1,279	1,308	160,291
Tennessee	68,990	38,303	209	107,502	69	341	410	107,912
Texas	237,560	1,312,967	0	1,550,527	176	57,808	57,984	1,608,511
Utah	40,022	54,913	55,065	150,000	73	449	522	150,522
Vermont	4,933	68,038	0	72,971	2	1,027	1,029	74,000
Virginia	86,582	177,372	75,839	339,793	59	2,700	2,759	342,552
Washington	56,804	445,810	84,113	586,727	154	1,969	2,123	588,850
West Virginia	45,251	60,601	30,338	136,190	9	3,762	3,771	139,961
Wisconsin	185,673	17,290	39,883	242,846	27	1,615	1,642	244,488
Wyoming	15,049	202,210	25,152	242,411	86	1,044	1,130	243,541
Total	4,560,664	13,564,532	2,372,191	20,497,387	4,073	245,148	249,221	20,746,608

(1) The completeness of data on trailer registrations varies greatly. Data are reported to the extent available and in some cases are supplemented by estimates of the Federal Highway Administration.
(2) This column includes all commercial type vehicles and semitrailers that are in private or for-hire use.
(3) Several States do not require the registration of light farm or automobile trailers.
(4) Mobile homes and house trailers are shown in this column for States which require them to be registered and are able to segregate them from other trailers. In States where this classification is not available, house trailers are included with light car trailers.
SOURCE: U.S. Department of Transportation, Federal Highway Administration.

Bus Registrations by State

TOTAL MOTOR BUS REGISTRATIONS BY STATE, 1999

| State | Private and Commercial | | Publicly Owned | | Total Privately and Publicly Owned | | |
	Commercial Buses[1]	School and Other[2]	Federal	School[3]	Commercial and Federal	School	Total Buses
Alabama	2,151	214	40	6,303	2,191	6,517	8,708
Alaska	1,591	503	77	201	1,668	704	2,372
Arizona	1,085	216	386	2,864	1,471	3,080	4,551
Arkansas	46	1,324	30	5,068	76	6,392	6,468
California	22,040	8,593	476	15,908	22,516	24,501	47,017
Colorado	704	1,034	43	4,022	747	5,056	5,803
Connecticut	3,073	6,106	13	819	3,086	6,925	10,011
Delaware	429	972	7	578	436	1,550	1,986
District of Columbia	2,074	147	280	108	2,354	255	2,609
Florida	4,570	1,251	212	38,012	4,782	39,263	44,045
Georgia	1,313	2,687	108	13,412	1,421	16,099	17,520
Hawaii	2,544	672	29	939	2,573	1,611	4,184
Idaho	758	516	152	2,154	910	2,670	3,580
Illinois	6,620	10,190	87	794	6,707	10,984	17,691
Indiana	4,112	4,893	56	17,841	4,168	22,734	26,902
Iowa	1,157	281	14	6,663	1,171	6,944	8,115
Kansas	371	1,075	13	2,391	384	3,466	3,850
Kentucky	955	757	161	10,652	1,116	11,409	12,525
Louisiana	1,073	14,601	25	5,629	1,098	20,230	21,328
Maine	176	457	13	2,284	189	2,741	2,930
Maryland	2,848	3,777	154	4,697	3,002	8,474	11,476
Massachusetts	4,069	7,110	85	446	4,154	7,556	11,710
Michigan	3,268	7,086	79	15,103	3,347	22,189	25,536
Minnesota	2,437	4,710	8	7,509	2,445	12,219	14,664
Mississippi	970	2,719	80	6,775	1,050	9,494	10,544
Missouri	1,080	3,735	37	8,699	1,117	12,434	13,551
Montana	433	665	19	1,694	452	2,359	2,811
Nebraska	569	629	10	4,589	579	5,218	5,797
Nevada	1,329	175	144	123	1,473	298	1,771
New Hampshire	365	996	2	350	367	1,346	1,713
New Jersey	4,573	12,918	58	3,016	4,631	15,934	20,565
New Mexico	525	1,986	315	698	840	2,684	3,524
New York	13,636	8,385	225	28,485	13,861	36,870	50,731
North Carolina	2,129	7,350	56	20,452	2,185	27,802	29,987
North Dakota	145	498	67	1,579	212	2,077	2,289
Ohio	11,465	2,741	85	22,073	11,550	24,814	36,364
Oklahoma	405	1,816	140	13,808	545	15,624	16,169
Oregon	1,536	2,399	71	8,914	1,607	11,313	12,920
Pennsylvania	9,560	17,790	126	7,454	9,686	25,244	34,930
Rhode Island	375	1,514	6	5	381	1,519	1,900
South Carolina	897	3,630	33	11,256	930	14,886	15,816
South Dakota	338	409	121	1,853	459	2,262	2,721
Tennessee	2,106	1,445	81	13,748	2,187	15,193	17,380
Texas	3,040	13,799	255	65,495	3,295	79,294	82,589
Utah	345	97	39	761	384	858	1,242
Vermont	92	545	5	1,296	97	1,841	1,938
Virginia	2,434	243	249	14,928	2,683	15,171	17,854
Washington	837	2,474	201	5,625	1,038	8,099	9,137
West Virginia	800	63	46	2,302	846	2,365	3,211
Wisconsin	1,391	7,084	24	4,533	1,415	11,617	13,032
Wyoming	855	119	11	1,725	866	1,844	2,710
Total	**131,694**	**175,396**	**5,054**	**416,633**	**136,748**	**592,029**	**728,777**

(1) Includes municipally owned transit buses.
(2) In some instances church, industrial and other private buses are included here; and in other instances privately-owned school buses could not be segregated from commercial buses, and are included with the latter.
(3) This column consists primarily of publicly owned school buses but includes a few privately owned school, institutional, and industrial buses registered free or at a reduced rate.
SOURCE: U.S. Department of Transportation, Federal Highway Administration.

School Bus Ownership and Usage by State

SCHOOL BUS OWNERSHIP AND USAGE BY STATE, 1998-1999 SCHOOL YEAR

	Pupils Transported at Public Expense	Bus Ownership			Total Miles of Service	Total Expenditures for Pupil Transportation
		Publicly Owned	Contractor	Total		
Alabama	395,400	7,666	277	7,943	64,032,594	180,280,565
Alaska	43,311	139	792	931	11,227,267	N.A.
Arizona	N.A.	N.A.	N.A.	6,500	63,802,000	N.A.
Arkansas	310,190	6,066	200	6,266	32,001,120	90,000,000
California	981,901	16,067	8,152	24,219	259,312,384	901,895,386
Colorado	278,090	5,730	220	5,950	48,828,051	142,351,679
Connecticut	369,205	520	4,712	5,232	N.A.	212,582,024
Delaware	96,239	477	1,065	1,542	20,673,173	51,000,000
Florida	976,068	16,790	1,516	18,306	271,420,105	609,719,599
Georgia	1,034,632	88	14,788	14,876	140,814,540	304,484,769
Hawaii	31,000	7	783	790	6,048,000	20,900,000
Idaho	108,305	1,928	644	2,572	22,677,770	55,936,461
Illinois	1,200,000	8,500	8,500	17,000	181,721,305	500,375,000
Indiana	712,082	9,139	2,692	11,831	79,137,036	327,446,538
Iowa	254,630	N.A.	N.A.	5,819	46,319,445	79,482,034
Kansas	211,851	5,058	1,411	6,469	48,164,239	116,268,812
Kentucky	428,325	9,300	201	9,501	101,845,000	191,773,765
Louisiana	478,906	4,745	3,254	7,999	33,101,640	236,017,131
Maine	182,288	2,017	592	2,609	N.A.	59,919,872
Maryland	598,262	3,433	2,961	6,394	113,156,876	298,883,209
Massachusetts	631,779	1,681	6,519	8,200	75,600,000	N.A.
Michigan	N.A.	14,369	1,416	15,785	183,885,757	531,219,202
Minnesota	761,810	4,168	6,282	10,450	133,711,321	348,019,171
Mississippi	405,484	5,196	74	5,270	47,943,135	113,255,060
Missouri	570,334	7,106	4,740	11,846	104,055,873	267,339,557
Montana	54,589	1,195	937	2,132	18,756,756	41,653,269
Nebraska	39,012	4,010	347	4,357	27,702,389	60,895,974
Nevada	92,646	1,496	0	1,496	26,222,140	N.A.
New Hampshire	135,418	414	1,710	2,124	N.A.	51,100,000
New Jersey	622,870	4,191	15,092	19,283	N.A.	654,069,967
New Mexico	167,192	822	2,178	3,000	31,702,465	83,966,906
New York	1,733,005	22,497	23,000	45,497	204,829,897	1,523,426,952
North Carolina	686,176	13,014	0	13,014	146,283,032	207,900,000
North Dakota	49,117	1,107	362	1,469	23,864,619	28,222,184
Ohio	1,132,679	15,840	2,200	18,040	181,558,260	521240302
Oklahoma	330,763	7,462	100	7,562	54,343,446	120,840,479
Oregon	252,921	4,137	2,237	6,374	50,564,993	168,917,274
Pennsylvania	1,313,969	5,130	14,146	19,276	335,024,855	701,000,000
Rhode Island	106,408	310	1,326	1,636	N.A.	51,633,233
South Carolina	492,179	5,591	0	5,591	13,284,720	117,156,120
South Dakota	47,120	1,100	500	1,600	N.A.	27,521,402
Tennessee	575,671	6,840	842	7,682	42,571,620	180,061,337
Texas	1,350,000	N.A.	N.A.	32,500	276,500,000	714,500,000
Utah	165,830	2,019	40	2,059	23,100,000	65,707,354
Vermont	79,016	483	863	1,346	N.A.	24,767,233
Virginia	885,328	13,784	0	13,784	113,378,676	355,052,572
Washington	490,043	7,326	1,207	8,533	74,513,183	251,605,000
West Virginia	228,569	3,691	0	3,691	41,914,356	129,464,816
Wisconsin	550,000	2,000	8,200	10,200	N.A.	N.A.
Wyoming	34,503	1,769	0	1,769	12,833,903	26,713,931
Total	**22,675,116**	**256,418**	**147,078**	**448,315**	**3,788,427,941**	**11,746,567,005**

N.A. Not available.
SOURCE: Bobit Publishing Company, School Bus Fleet Fact Book.

Government Ownership of Motor Vehicles by State

GOVERNMENT OWNERSHIP OF MOTOR VEHICLES BY STATE, 1999

State	Federal[1] Passenger Cars	Trucks	Buses	Total	State, County and Municipal[2] Passenger Cars	Trucks	Buses	Total	Total Publicly Owned Vehicles
Alabama	1,840	5,347	40	7,227	13,686	21,204	6,303	41,193	48,420
Alaska	556	3,442	77	4,075	1,890	5,774	201	7,865	11,940
Arizona	2,461	10,026	386	12,873	14,249	8,835	2,864	25,948	38,821
Arkansas	1,026	2,992	30	4,048	8,549	8,359	5,068	21,976	26,024
California	13,992	48,557	476	63,025	169,905	215,120	15,908	400,933	463,958
Colorado	1,924	9,539	43	11,506	8,144	16,609	4,022	28,775	40,281
Connecticut	975	4,758	13	5,746	10,423	21,834	819	33,076	38,822
Delaware	300	840	7	1,147	7,573	1,896	578	10,047	11,194
District of Columbia	2,804	4,067	280	7,151	1,607	2,598	108	4,313	11,464
Florida	5,217	16,256	212	21,685	93,639	128,985	38,012	260,636	282,321
Georgia	2,744	7,911	108	10,763	21,905	54,392	13,412	89,709	100,472
Hawaii	566	1,874	29	2,469	5,521	4,982	939	11,442	13,911
Idaho	731	5,338	152	6,221	5,115	12,514	2,154	19,783	26,004
Illinois	3,868	11,538	87	15,493	60,243	4,632	794	65,669	81,162
Indiana	1,521	4,818	56	6,395	21,040	35,759	17,841	74,640	81,035
Iowa	761	3,573	14	4,348	12,167	23,266	6,663	42,096	46,444
Kansas	878	3,440	13	4,331	6,857	15,385	2,391	24,633	28,964
Kentucky	1,743	4,739	161	6,643	20,767	3,407	10,652	34,826	41,469
Louisiana	1,788	5,248	25	7,061	35,829	17,425	5,629	58,883	65,944
Maine	472	1,313	13	1,798	4,419	9,952	2,284	16,655	18,453
Maryland	2,831	7,440	154	10,425	10,600	15,569	4,697	30,866	41,291
Massachusetts	2,925	7,428	85	10,438	14,260	29,856	446	44,562	55,000
Michigan	2,874	9,479	79	12,432	43,961	66,616	15,103	125,680	138,112
Minnesota	1,650	5,927	8	7,585	8,189	16,985	7,509	32,683	40,268
Mississippi	1,465	3,773	80	5,318	9,024	13,512	6,775	29,311	34,629
Missouri	3,346	5,108	37	8,491	4,249	13,986	8,699	26,934	35,425
Montana	966	5,352	19	6,337	4,427	12,059	1,694	18,180	24,517
Nebraska	1,178	2,966	10	4,154	10,845	15,576	4,589	31,010	35,164
Nevada	1,255	6,889	144	8,288	8,590	7,758	123	16,471	24,759
New Hampshire	649	1,180	2	1,831	3,552	10,643	350	14,545	16,376
New Jersey	2,410	10,984	58	13,452	42,962	85,216	3,016	131,194	144,646
New Mexico	1,485	7,244	315	9,044	12,302	14,768	698	27,768	36,812
New York	9,157	19,429	225	28,811	60,999	80,082	28,485	169,566	198,377
North Carolina	1,980	5,752	56	7,788	26,108	40,193	20,452	86,753	94,541
North Dakota	651	2,050	67	2,768	3,323	6,655	1,579	11,557	14,325
Ohio	3,380	9,626	85	13,091	42,147	62,950	22,073	127,170	140,261
Oklahoma	1,645	5,194	140	6,979	9,846	40,563	13,808	64,217	71,196
Oregon	1,496	9,629	71	11,196	24,204	20,821	8,914	53,939	65,135
Pennsylvania	5,513	13,547	126	19,186	38,894	49,082	7,454	95,430	114,616
Rhode Island	260	1,184	6	1,450	3,300	3,882	5	7,187	8,637
South Carolina	1,724	5,225	33	6,982	8,570	20,183	11,256	40,009	46,991
South Dakota	611	2,827	121	3,559	3,729	10,440	1,853	16,022	19,581
Tennessee	3,653	10,187	81	13,921	18,436	45,553	13,748	77,737	91,658
Texas	6,855	24,695	255	31,805	210,248	237,309	65,495	513,052	544,857
Utah	1,010	4,731	39	5,780	9,199	10,419	761	20,379	26,159
Vermont	361	511	5	877	3,019	6,471	1,296	10,786	11,663
Virginia	2,765	9,414	249	12,428	32,006	26,469	14,928	73,403	85,831
Washington	3,046	13,371	201	16,618	15,704	26,508	5,625	47,837	64,455
West Virginia	956	2,131	46	3,133	15,000	29,073	2,302	46,375	49,508
Wisconsin	1,203	5,075	24	6,302	13,951	38,916	4,533	57,400	63,702
Wyoming	421	3,087	11	3,519	4,433	9,051	1,725	15,209	18,728
Total	115,888	377,051	5,054	497,993	1,239,605	1,680,092	416,633	3,336,330	3,834,323

(1) Vehicles of the civilian branches of the Federal government are given in this table. Vehicles of the military services are not included. Distribution by State is estimated by the Federal Highway Administration.
(2) This information, compiled chiefly from reports of State authorities, is incomplete in many cases. Some States give State-owned vehicles only; others excludes from registration certain classes, such as fire apparatus and police vehicles. For the states not reporting state, county and municipal vehicles separately from private and commercial vehicles and those reporting unsegregated totals only, classification by vehicle type has been approximately on the basis of other available data.
SOURCE: U.S. Department of Transportation, Federal Highway Administration.

Passenger Cars in Operation by Model Year and Average Age of Cars in Use

CARS IN OPERATION BY MODEL YEAR, 1987-2000 (as of July 1 of each year)

Units in Thousands

Model Year	1987	1988	1989	1990	1991	1992	1993	1994	1995	1996	1997	1998	1999	2000
2001	—	—	—	—	—	—	—	—	—	—	—	—	—	62
2000	—	—	—	—	—	—	—	—	—	—	—	—	102	6,603
1999	—	—	—	—	—	—	—	—	—	—	—	65	6,117	8,177
1998	—	—	—	—	—	—	—	—	—	—	76	5,554	7,714	7,655
1997	—	—	—	—	—	—	—	—	—	143	5,546	8,049	7,971	7,906
1996	—	—	—	—	—	—	—	—	8	6,011	7,696	7,564	7,488	7,413
1995	—	—	—	—	—	—	—	96	6,030	9,179	8,968	8,926	8,811	8,675
1994	—	—	—	—	—	—	11	5,540	8,150	7,973	7,938	7,878	7,771	7,628
1993	—	—	—	—	—	29	5,259	8,201	8,218	8,040	8,013	7,953	7,826	7,650
1992	—	—	—	—	60	5,227	7,739	7,718	7,651	7,474	7,430	7,320	7,204	7,021
1991	—	—	—	103	5,703	8,100	8,176	7,995	7,941	7,753	7,665	7,536	7,354	7,109
1990	—	—	—	5,958	8,696	8,372	8,362	8,225	8,151	7,932	7,821	7,620	7,387	7,071
1989	—	—	6,467	9,729	9,713	9,309	9,253	9,126	8,957	8,692	8,479	8,187	7,797	7,338
1988	—	6,830	10,304	10,245	10,124	9,761	9,686	9,410	9,146	8,803	8,463	8,008	7,475	6,876
1987	7,019	10,380	10,304	10,140	10,049	9,640	9,471	9,205	8,839	8,431	7,944	7,439	6,780	6,084
1986	10,694	10,635	10,489	10,366	10,214	9,752	9,501	9,134	8,665	8,134	7,504	6,870	6,089	5,334
1985	10,430	10,276	10,162	9,989	9,732	9,214	8,863	8,419	7,822	7,191	6,469	5,774	4,987	—
1984	10,131	10,036	9,870	9,549	9,208	8,567	8,068	7,510	6,843	6,106	5,342	4,636	—	—
1983	7,504	7,394	7,178	6,884	6,543	5,998	5,543	5,082	4,527	3,945	3,365	—	—	—
1982	7,083	6,864	6,592	6,188	5,721	5,077	4,507	3,988	3,429	2,871	—	—	—	—
1981	7,632	7,317	6,901	6,323	5,673	4,887	4,192	3,613	3,024	—	—	—	—	—
1980	7,886	7,423	6,843	6,111	5,326	4,448	3,709	3,138	—	—	—	—	—	—
1979	8,848	8,251	7,508	6,624	5,743	4,808	4,020	—	—	—	—	—	—	—
1978	8,432	7,673	6,761	5,791	4,891	4,024	—	—	—	—	—	—	—	—
1977	7,382	6,479	5,492	4,569	3,759	—	—	—	—	—	—	—	—	—
1976	5,555	4,620	3,733	2,981	—	—	—	—	—	—	—	—	—	—
1975	3,450	2,782	2,193	—	—	—	—	—	—	—	—	—	—	—
1974	3,440	2,722	2,120	—	—	—	—	—	—	—	—	—	—	—
1973	3,161	2,500	—	—	—	—	—	—	—	—	—	—	—	—
1972	2,431	—	—	—	—	—	—	—	—	—	—	—	—	—
Prior Years ...	8,764	9,331	9,835	11,720	12,167	13,073	14,636	15,572	15,805	15,935	15,954	16,587	17,996	19,119
Year Not Given	7	7	6	6	6	61	59	25	36	*	*	*	*	*
Total	119,849	121,520	122,758	123,276	123,328	120,347	121,055	121,997	123,242	124,613	124,673	125,966	126,869	127,721

*Includes all earlier models.
Source: The Polk Company. Permission for further use must be obtained from The Polk Company.

AVERAGE AGE OF PASSENGER CARS IN USE IN THE U.S., 1941-2000 (Age in Years)

Year	Mean[1]	Median[2]	Year	Mean[1]	Median[2]
2000	9.0	8.3	1976	6.2	5.5
1999	8.9	8.3	1974	5.7	5.2
1998	8.8	8.3	1972	5.7	5.1
1997	8.6	8.1	1970	5.6	4.9
1996	8.5	7.9	1968	5.6	4.7
1995	8.4	7.7	1966	5.7	4.8
1994	8.3	7.5	1964	6.0	5.3
1993	8.1	7.3	1962	6.0	5.7
1992	7.9	7.0	1960	5.9	5.4
1991	7.8	6.7	1958	5.6	5.1
1990	7.6	6.5	1956	5.6	5.1
1988	7.6	6.8	1954	6.2	4.8
1986	7.6	7.0	1952	6.8	4.5
1984	7.5	6.7	1950	7.8	6.2
1982	7.2	6.2	1948	8.8	8.0
1980	6.6	6.0	1946	9.0	8.8
1978	6.3	5.7	1941	5.5	4.9

* Includes all earlier models.
(1) Mean-The sum of the products of units multiplied by age, divided by the total units.
(2) Median-A value in an ordered set of values below and above which there are an equal number of values.
SOURCE: The Polk Company. Permission for further use must be obtained from The Polk Company.

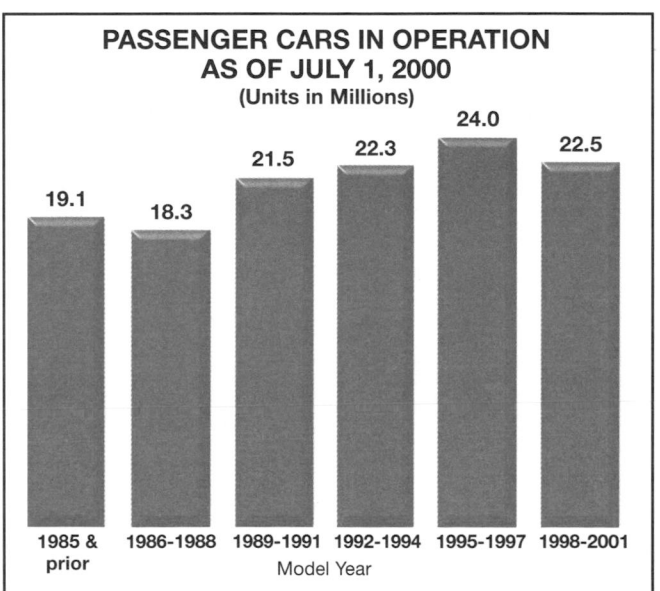

PASSENGER CARS IN OPERATION AS OF JULY 1, 2000
(Units in Millions)

1985 & prior	1986-1988	1989-1991	1992-1994	1995-1997	1998-2001
19.1	18.3	21.5	22.3	24.0	22.5

Model Year

Trucks in Operation by Model Year and Average Age of Trucks in Use

TRUCKS IN OPERATION BY MODEL YEAR, 1987-2000 (as of July 1 of each year)

Units in Thousands

Model Year	1987	1988	1989	1990	1991	1992	1993	1994	1995	1996	1997	1998	1999	2000
2001	—	—	—	—	—	—	—	—	—	—	—	—	—	285
2000	—	—	—	—	—	—	—	—	—	—	—	—	56	6,154
1999	—	—	—	—	—	—	—	—	—	—	—	206	5,897	7,726
1998	—	—	—	—	—	—	—	—	—	—	92	4,824	6,750	6,630
1997	—	—	—	—	—	—	—	—	—	234	4,532	6,550	6,507	6,313
1996	—	—	—	—	—	—	—	—	26	4,264	5,828	5,545	5,492	5,300
1995	—	—	—	—	—	—	—	29	4,068	6,448	6,362	6,165	6,063	5,818
1994	—	—	—	—	—	—	22	3,896	6,096	5,847	5,733	5,593	5,437	5,206
1993	—	—	—	—	—	23	3,371	5,181	5,176	4,976	4,838	4,711	4,539	4,335
1992	—	—	—	—	8	2,797	4,380	4,323	4,228	4,097	4,015	3,870	3,739	3,547
1991	—	—	—	153	2,911	4,254	4,305	4,223	4,136	4,020	3,912	3,800	3,626	3,411
1990	—	—	—	2,858	4,187	4,222	4,232	4,109	4,033	3,906	3,802	3,647	3,494	3,258
1989	—	—	3,133	4,872	4,913	4,864	4,859	4,753	4,620	4,498	4,340	4,171	3,940	3,665
1988	—	3,265	4,882	4,913	4,922	4,848	4,829	4,682	4,523	4,385	4,203	3,979	3,738	3,421
1987	2,954	4,450	4,441	4,435	4,414	4,333	4,298	4,160	3,972	3,844	3,633	3,418	3,145	2,860
1986	4,739	4,741	4,731	4,704	4,670	4,558	4,496	4,346	4,134	3,969	3,741	3,448	3,142	2,812
1985	4,179	4,166	4,139	4,097	4,041	3,915	3,858	3,712	3,509	3,360	3,111	2,855	2,560	—
1984	3,764	3,739	3,705	3,641	3,572	3,449	3,369	3,207	3,030	2,847	2,624	2,367	—	—
1983	2,439	2,419	2,388	2,332	2,279	2,173	2,111	1,996	1,873	1,748	1,596	—	—	—
1982	2,118	2,080	2,045	1,978	1,917	1,816	1,752	1,532	1,528	1,414	—	—	—	—
1981	1,979	1,939	1,891	1,813	1,708	1,650	1,580	1,447	1,344	—	—	—	—	—
1980	1,962	1,906	1,847	1,722	1,625	1,564	1,478	1,327	—	—	—	—	—	—
1979	3,452	3,332	3,178	3,020	2,854	2,726	2,569	—	—	—	—	—	—	—
1978	3,150	2,972	2,841	2,675	2,508	2,374	—	—	—	—	—	—	—	—
1977	2,708	2,559	2,425	2,255	2,094	—	—	—	—	—	—	—	—	—
1976	2,108	1,963	1,832	1,687	—	—	—	—	—	—	—	—	—	—
1975	1,436	1,320	1,223	—	—	—	—	—	—	—	—	—	—	—
1974	1,701	1,547	1,398	—	—	—	—	—	—	—	—	—	—	—
1973	1,610	1,456	—	—	—	—	—	—	—	—	—	—	—	—
1972	1,319	—	—	—	—	—	—	—	—	—	—	—	—	—
1971	—	—	—	—	—	—	—	—	—	—	—	—	—	—
1970	—	—	—	—	—	—	—	—	—	—	—	—	—	—
Prior Years	5,721	6,362	7,098	8,862	9,552	11,555	13,662	13,751	13,884	13,824	14,036	13,928	14,515	14,838
Year Not Given*	5	6	5	4	3	51	89	43	19	—	—	—	—	—
Total	47,344	50,222	53,202	56,021	58,178	61,172	65,260	66,717	70,199	73,681	76,398	79,077	82,640	85,579

*Includes all earlier models.
Source: The Polk Company. Permission for further use must be obtained from The Polk Company.

AVERAGE AGE OF TRUCKS IN USE IN THE U.S., 1941-2000 (Age in Years)

Year	Mean[1]	Median[2]	Year	Mean[1]	Median[2]
2000	8.0	6.9	1976	7.0	5.8
1999	8.2	7.2	1974	7.0	5.6
1998	8.3	7.5	1972	7.2	6.0
1997	8.3	7.8	1970	7.3	5.9
1996	8.3	7.7	1968	7.6	6.2
1995	8.4	7.6	1966	7.8	6.8
1994	8.4	7.5	1964	8.1	7.7
1993	8.6	7.5	1962	8.0	7.6
1992	8.4	7.2	1960	7.7	7.4
1991	8.1	6.8	1958	7.2	6.7
1990	8.0	6.5	1956	6.8	6.1
1988	7.9	7.1	1954	6.6	5.7
1986	8.0	7.7	1952	6.6	4.8
1984	8.2	7.4	1950	7.0	4.7
1982	7.8	6.8	1948	7.8	7.8
1980	7.1	6.3	1946	8.6	8.3
1978	6.9	5.8	1941	5.6	4.8

* Includes all earlier models.
(1) Mean-The sum of the products of units multiplied by age, divided by the total units.
(2) Median-A value in an ordered set of values below and above which there are an equal number of values.
SOURCE: The Polk Company. Permission for further use must be obtained from The Polk Company.

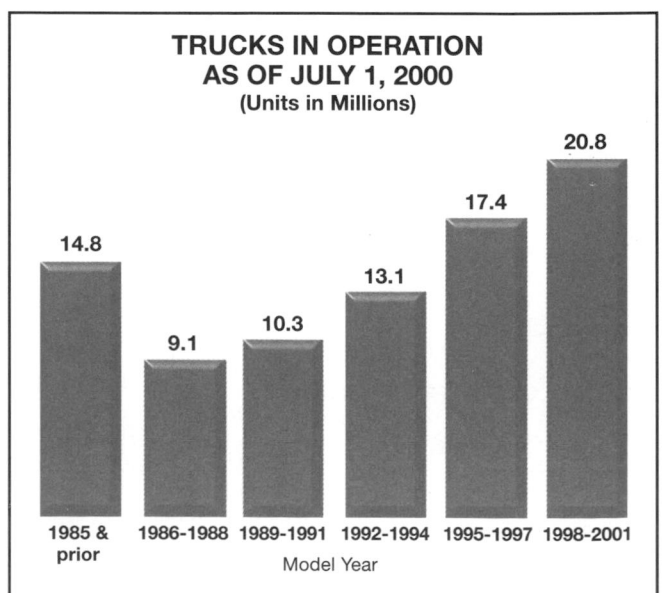

TRUCKS IN OPERATION AS OF JULY 1, 2000
(Units in Millions)

Model Year	Units
1985 & prior	14.8
1986-1988	9.1
1989-1991	10.3
1992-1994	13.1
1995-1997	17.4
1998-2001	20.8

Motor Vehicles in Operation by Year

MOTOR VEHICLES IN OPERATION, 1949-2000 (as of July 1 of each year)

Year	Passenger Cars	Trucks	Total	% Change	Truck % of Total
2000	127,720,809	85,578,504	213,299,313	1.8	40.1
1999	126,868,744	82,640,417	209,509,161	2.2	39.4
1998	125,965,709	79,076,930	205,042,639	2.0	38.6
1997	124,672,920	76,397,477	201,070,397	1.4	38.0
1996	124,612,787	73,680,672	198,293,459	2.5	37.2
1995	123,241,881	70,198,512	193,440,393	2.5	36.3
1994	121,996,580	66,717,417	188,713,997	1.3	35.4
1993	121,055,398	65,260,066	186,315,464	2.6	35.0
1992	120,346,746	61,172,404	181,519,150	0.0	33.7
1991	123,327,046	58,178,883	181,505,929	1.2	32.1
1990	123,276,268	56,022,934	179,299,202	1.9	31.2
1989	122,758,378	53,201,657	175,960,035	2.5	30.2
1968	121,519,074	50,221,502	171,740,576	2.7	29.2
1987	119,848,769	47,344,319	167,193,088	3.1	28.3
1986	117,268,071	44,825,523	162,093,594	3.2	27.7
1985	114,662,333	42,386,882	157,049,215	3.2	27.0
1984	112,018,640	40,142,872	152,161,512	3.4	26.4
1983	108,961,215	38,143,304	147,104,519	2.3	25.9
1982	106,867,108	36,986,537	143,853,645	1.4	25.7
1981	105,838,582	36,069,197	141,907,779	1.5	25.4
1980	104,563,781	35,267,535	139,831,316	1.9	25.2
1979	104,676,507	32,582,991	137,259,498	2.8	23.7
1978	102,956,713	30,564,701	133,521,414	4.2	22.9
1977	99,903,594	28,221,661	128,125,255	3.0	22.0
1976	97,818,221	26,560,296	124,378,517	3.6	21.4
1975	95,240,602	24,812,843	120,053,445	3.6	20.7
1974	92,607,551	23,312,245	115,919,796	4.2	20.1
1973	89,805,159	21,411,931	111,217,090	4.7	19.3
1972	86,438,957	19,772,938	106,211,895	4.5	18.6
1971	83,137,324	18,462,287	101,599,611	3.5	18.2
1970	80,448,463	17,687,505	98,135,968	3.2	18.0
1969	78,494,938	16,586,368	95,081,306	4.4	17.4
1968	75,358,034	15,684,917	91,042,951	3.5	17.2
1967	72,967,686	14,988,491	87,956,177	2.7	17.0
1966	71,263,738	14,356,591	85,620,329	4.3	16.8
1965	68,939,770	13,126,579	82,066,349	4.5	16.0
1964	66,051,415	12,444,964	78,496,379	4.1	15.9
1963	63,493,277	11,902,039	75,395,316	4.2	15.8
1962	60,919,579	11,463,381	72,382,960	3.6	15.8
1961	58,854,380	11,042,770	69,897,150	2.9	15.8
1960	57,102,676	10,802,959	67,905,635	3.5	15.9
1959	55,086,761	10,532,145	65,618,906	4.9	16.1
1958	52,492,509	10,056,567	62,549,076	2.2	16.1
1957	51,432,460	9,775,950	61,208,410	3.1	16.0
1956	49,803,977	9,544,082	59,348,059	5.0	16.1
1955	47,377,970	9,162,444	56,540,414	6.3	16.2
1954	44,387,113	8,800,408	53,187,521	4.5	16.5
1953	42,202,349	8,692,574	50,894,923	5.6	17.1
1952	39,769,741	8,419,855	48,189,596	3.5	17.5
1951	38,515,538	8,064,883	46,580,421	7.1	17.3
1950	35,923,583	7,577,037	43,500,620	9.2	17.4
1949	32,730,718	7,087,128	39,817,846	8.9	17.8

SOURCE: The Polk Company. Permission for further use must be obtained from the Polk Company.

Lease Penetration Rates and Used Vehicle Sales

LEASE PENETRATION RATES BY VEHICLE SEGMENT

Segment	1985	1990	1995	1996	1997	1998	1999	2000	2001	2002
PASSENGER CARS										
Budget	2.2	5.5	12.1	13.6	13.4	12.1	12	10.3	10	9.7
Small	1.8	5.3	18.9	18.5	15.4	14.8	14.4	14.2	12.1	10.4
Lower Middle	8.2	12.8	26.9	27.3	28.1	27.3	27.2	25.7	24.5	22.2
Core Middle	11.5	16.2	30.4	31.8	31.1	28.6	27.3	26.9	26.3	25.7
Upper Middle	11.5	14.7	26.2	27.3	28.1	29.1	29.4	29.2	30	31.9
Near Luxury	16.6	25.2	50.5	52.6	57.3	58.3	58.8	59.7	58.9	60.2
Luxury	39.6	52.6	62.0	64.2	65.9	65.2	57.8	51.3	55.5	58.8
Specialty	11.1	24.6	59.7	61.3	58.5	57.5	55.3	50.4	52.3	51.1
Sport	16.2	18.8	26.2	30.4	34.4	39.3	40.2	41.1	44.4	47.8
LIGHT TRUCKS										
Compact Pickup	1.3	4.4	14.6	15.2	16.3	15.7	15.6	15.7	15.8	16.1
Compact Sport Utility ..	5.2	9.6	34.3	36.7	38.4	39.7	41.2	40.7	42.2	44.7
Full Size Pickup	4.6	8.2	18.3	19.4	22.7	25.3	28.1	26.3	27.1	27.3
Full Size Sport Utility ...	4.2	9.3	36.9	38.2	42.1	42.7	44.4	46.5	45.9	46.7
Full Size Van	7.1	12.1	20.0	21.3	22.7	22.4	21.9	21.1	21	20.7
Minivan	4.2	8.4	25.8	28.1	32.8	33.5	35.7	32.3	36.6	37.3
Total	**3.5**	**7.3**	**24.2**	**27.2**	**29.3**	**31.5**	**29.1**	**28.7**	**29.2**	**31.5**

USED VEHICLE SALES (In Thousands)

	Franchised Dealers	Independent Dealers	Casual	Total
2000	$16,178	$13,559	$11,883	$41,620
1999	16,504	12,786	11,448	40,738
1998	15,684	13,182	11,976	40,842
1997	15,796	12,685	12,757	41,238
1996	15,713	13,247	11,871	40,831
1995	15,679	14,124	11,958	41,761
1994	15,047	14,548	10,541	40,136
1993	14,792	14,011	9,257	38,060
1992	14,619	11,681	10,646	36,946
1991	14,573	10,633	12,092	37,298
1990	14,222	10,678	12,632	37,532

AVERAGE USED VEHICLE TRANSACTION PRICES

	Franchised Dealers	Independent Dealers	Casual	Total
2000	$12,748	$7,613	$4,539	$8,896
1999	12,630	7,590	4,505	8,828
1998	12,165	7,172	4,190	8,341
1997	12,350	7,155	4,164	8,399
1996	12,256	7,076	4,283	8,257
1995	11,585	7,413	4,316	8,093
1994	11,150	7,209	3,762	7,781
1993	9,871	7,157	3,554	7,335
1992	8,895	6,934	3,405	6,693
1991	7,830	7,260	3,172	6,157
1990	7,410	7,125	2,956	6,830

SOURCE: CNW Marketing Research, Inc.

Passenger Car Fleet Registrations and Fleets by State

FLEETS AND VEHICLES BY STATE, 1999

	Fleets (10+Vehicles)	Automobiles	Trucks Class 1-2	Trucks Class 3-5	Trucks Class 6-8	Total Vehicles
Alabama	2,085	69,444	55,265	27,331	54,432	206,472
Alaska	397	8,978	7,430	7,463	7,120	30,991
Arizona	1,523	55,228	44,806	41,847	31,713	173,594
Arkansas	1,385	26,160	32,577	16,680	36,089	111,506
California	12,005	474,627	443,869	205,883	321,332	1,445,711
Colorado	2,068	58,043	52,587	36,963	45,210	192,803
Connecticut	2,349	65,794	57,905	28,365	59,073	211,137
Delaware	462	11,366	12,453	7,991	17,299	49,109
District of Columbia	267	14,135	12,663	5,348	12,087	44,233
Florida	5,986	233,209	208,919	88,230	199,408	729,766
Georgia	3,524	104,932	92,191	31,597	105,199	333,919
Hawaii	492	11,205	12,159	8,883	9,129	41,376
Idaho	844	17,326	18,802	13,737	14,117	63,982
Illinois	5,653	178,939	149,886	76,441	179,770	585,036
Indiana	2,968	83,745	69,457	23,615	93,565	270,382
Iowa	2,173	48,558	45,948	31,955	53,525	179,786
Kansas	1,849	32,925	39,217	17,666	41,999	131,807
Kentucky	1,915	54,451	53,820	24,528	42,521	175,320
Louisiana	2,217	56,263	56,322	27,425	61,167	201,177
Maine	916	19,625	17,664	15,223	16,710	69,222
Maryland	2,720	80,899	81,163	34,735	74,225	271,022
Massachusetts	3,294	80,942	81,643	41,344	82,222	286,151
Michigan	3,945	149,536	103,684	53,670	104,373	411,263
Minnesota	2,698	64,876	60,209	33,554	78,812	237,451
Mississippi	1,253	37,801	32,887	18,281	25,553	114,522
Missouri	2,751	69,035	66,236	36,164	84,360	255,795
Montana	698	12,294	15,337	12,928	11,641	52,200
Nebraska	1,302	24,727	27,199	16,823	37,824	106,573
Nevada	685	18,006	20,236	14,438	11,433	64,113
New Hampshire	849	18,778	15,484	13,079	11,195	58,536
New Jersey	3,919	139,327	121,717	35,172	119,839	416,055
New Mexico	802	25,864	23,830	8,348	18,187	76,229
New York	6,706	227,144	191,415	78,215	182,015	678,789
North Carolina	3,821	102,047	109,667	38,342	142,354	392,410
North Dakota	691	10,144	11,915	11,073	11,819	44,951
Ohio	5,418	177,830	130,846	60,350	163,627	532,653
Oklahoma	1,728	44,528	44,480	11,798	53,681	154,487
Oregon	1,780	51,856	42,639	29,964	45,074	169,533
Pennsylvania	5,973	166,880	148,086	52,840	179,086	546,892
Rhode Island	548	13,800	13,206	5,000	13,359	45,365
South Carolina	1,772	48,934	49,119	19,241	59,580	176,874
South Dakota	433	11,056	13,156	5,340	11,396	40,948
Tennessee	2,510	93,915	72,339	26,757	84,598	277,609
Texas	8,851	260,885	262,270	107,599	247,960	878,714
Utah	818	22,461	24,419	14,995	24,259	86,134
Vermont	446	8,507	9,295	7,469	7,349	32,620
Virginia	3,025	108,230	90,087	32,083	99,310	329,710
Washington	2,496	79,272	61,298	30,208	59,724	230,502
West Virginia	912	24,476	26,847	18,492	16,594	86,409
Wisconsin	3,261	64,291	73,938	54,762	80,964	273,955
Wyoming	408	5,907	7,624	4,345	6,611	24,487
Total	**127,591**	**3,869,201**	**3,516,211**	**1,664,580**	**3,550,489**	**12,600,281**

SOURCE: Bobit Publishing Company, Automotive Fleet Magazine.

Total Motor Vehicle Registrations by Country

MOTOR VEHICLE REGISTRATIONS BY COUNTRY, 1998-1999

Country	1998 Passenger Cars	1998 Commercial Vehicles	1998 Total	1999 Passenger Cars	1999 Commercial Vehicles	1999 Total	Population (000)	Persons Per Car
AFRICA								
Algeria	320,100	432,500	752,600	330,000	435,000	765,000	29,950	90.8
Angola	28,200	30,600	58,800	30,200	35,700	65,900	12,357	409.2
Benin	7,300	6,200	13,500	7,500	6,500	14,000	6,114	815.2
Botswana	83,800	77,700	161,500	105,000	80,000	185,000	1,588	15.1
Burkina Faso	35,500	19,500	55,000	32,000	24,000	56,000	10,996	343.6
Burundi	8,200	11,800	20,000	8,000	11,500	19,500	6,678	834.8
Cameroon	50,400	47,700	98,100	50,700	48,000	98,700	14,691	289.8
Central African Republic ...	400	400	800	550	400	950	3,540	6,436.4
Congo	29,000	16,600	45,600	26,200	20,400	46,600	2,859	109.1
Congo, Dem. Rep.	141,000	129,000	270,000	145,000	132,000	277,000	49,776	343.3
Cote d'Ivoire	78,100	36,300	114,400	18,600	93,600	112,200	15,545	835.8
Ethipoia	55,644	43,797	99,441	57,500	45,000	102,500	62,782	1,091.9
Ghana	32,600	38,400	71,000	32,900	38,300	71,200	18,785	571.0
Kenya	16,301	11,634	27,935	16,037	12,784	28,821	29,410	1,833.9
Liberia	17,400	10,700	28,100	16,200	12,500	28,700	3,044	187.9
Libya	305,900	180,900	486,800	315,000	181,000	496,000	5,419	17.2
Madagascar	65,000	48,700	113,700	67,000	50,000	117,000	15,051	224.6
Malawi	9,000	12,300	21,300	9,500	12,500	22,000	10,788	1,135.6
Mali	6,300	7,600	13,900	6,000	7,300	13,300	10,584	1,764.0
Mauritania	5,400	6,600	12,000	8,900	5,700	14,600	2,598	291.9
Mauritius	80,578	12,117	92,695	85,154	12,482	97,636	1,174	13.8
Morocco	1,035,000	348,000	1,383,000	1,014,000	348,000	1,362,000	28,238	27.8
Mozambique	27,200	14,500	41,700	27,500	15,000	42,500	17,299	629.1
Niger	18,000	16,000	34,000	18,200	18,100	36,300	10,496	576.7
Nigeria	589,600	363,900	953,500	610,000	385,000	995,000	123,897	203.1
Reunion	190,400	65,500	255,900	184,200	62,850	247,050	691	3.8
Sierra Leone	32,400	11,900	44,300	36,200	12,300	48,500	4,949	136.7
South Africa	3,905,761	2,537,227	6,442,988	3,966,252	2,590,606	6,556,858	42,106	10.6
Sudan	126,800	60,000	186,800	124,200	58,200	182,400	28,993	233.4
Tanzania	13,800	42,500	56,300	14,750	44,600	59,350	32,923	2,232.1
Togo	74,700	34,600	109,300	82,000	38,750	120,750	4,567	55.7
Tunisia	137,876	107,620	245,496	145,000	117,000	262,000	9,457	65.2
Uganda	28,000	40,000	68,000	28,500	44,000	72,500	21,479	753.6
Zambia	96,000	66,000	162,000	100,000	68,000	168,000	9,881	98.8
Zimbabwe	325,000	77,500	402,500	386,000	89,000	475,000	11,904	30.8
Total	**7,976,660**	**4,966,295**	**12,942,955**	**8,104,743**	**5,156,072**	**13,260,815**	**660,609**	**81.5**

Total Motor Vehicle Registrations by Country

MOTOR VEHICLE REGISTRATIONS BY COUNTRY, 1998-1999 — continued

Country	1998 Passenger Cars	1998 Commercial Vehicles	1998 Total	1999 Passenger Cars	1999 Commercial Vehicles	1999 Total	Population (000)	Persons Per Car
AMERICA, Caribbean								
Bahamas	67,400	16,800	84,200	69,000	18,645	87,645	298	4.3
Barbados	56,868	6,361	63,229	60,000	7,350	67,350	267	4.5
Bermuda	19,900	4,300	24,200	22,500	4,500	27,000	64	2.8
Cuba	10,600	11,100	21,700	13,000	13,000	26,000	11,178	859.8
Dominican Republic	255,000	180,000	435,000	236,800	171,500	408,300	8,404	35.5
Haiti	20,200	23,100	43,300	32,000	21,000	53,000	7,803	243.8
Jamaica	104,000	48,000	152,000	109,500	52,300	161,800	2,598	23.7
Netherlands Antilles	72,563	26,722	99,285	74,000	24,000	98,000	215	2.9
Puerto Rico	746,608	247,847	994,455	878,000	190,000	1,068,000	3,890	4.4
Trinidad and Tobago	61,900	20,500	82,400	66,000	20,500	86,500	1,293	19.6
Total	**1,415,039**	**584,730**	**1,999,769**	**1,560,800**	**522,795**	**2,083,595**	**36,010**	**23.1**
AMERICA, Central & South								
Argentina	4,950,000	1,485,000	6,435,000	5,056,146	1,550,836	6,606,982	36,580	7.2
Belize	9,929	12,043	21,972	10,230	12,290	22,520	247	24.1
Bolivia	37,000	82,000	119,000	39,000	86,000	125,000	8,138	208.7
Brazil	14,700,000	3,602,000	18,302,000	14,805,000	3,880,000	18,685,000	167,967	11.3
Chile	1,020,516	679,897	1,700,413	1,061,109	558,888	1,619,997	15,018	14.2
Colombia	725,384	420,898	1,146,282	762,000	440,000	1,202,000	41,539	54.5
Costa Rica	316,844	198,158	515,002	334,000	206,000	540,000	3,589	10.7
Ecuador	186,050	280,000	466,050	212,507	312,192	524,699	12,412	58.4
El Salvador	49,016	56,738	105,754	56,000	65,000	121,000	6,154	109.9
French Guiana	28,200	9,900	38,100	29,850	11,210	41,060	168	5.6
Guatemala	90,203	97,163	187,366	102,000	97,000	199,000	11,088	108.7
Guyana	9,500	3,200	12,700	10,200	3,100	13,300	856	83.9
Honduras	17,242	53,947	71,189	18,300	58,000	76,300	6,318	345.2
Nicaragua	31,176	50,459	81,635	34,000	53,000	87,000	4,919	144.7
Panama	169,217	104,037	273,254	178,500	60,600	239,100	2,811	15.7
Paraguay	75,746	75,750	151,496	82,000	84,300	166,300	5,359	65.4
Peru	598,000	385,000	983,000	602,500	390,600	993,100	25,230	41.9
Suriname	52,000	17,000	69,000	55,350	20,817	76,167	413	7.5
Uruguay	546,000	68,500	614,500	571,583	53,876	625,459	3,313	5.8
Venezuela	1,615,000	489,000	2,104,000	1,845,000	594,000	2,439,000	23,707	12.8
Total	**25,227,023**	**8,170,690**	**33,397,713**	**25,865,275**	**8,537,709**	**34,402,984**	**375,826**	**14.5**
AMERICA, Central & South								
Canada	13,887,270	3,694,077	17,581,347	14,142,761	3,119,597	17,262,358	30,491	2.2
Mexico	4,950,000	2,800,000	7,750,000	5,000,000	2,850,000	7,850,000	96,586	19.3
United States	131,838,538	79,062,475	210,901,013	126,868,700	86,640,400	213,509,100	278,230	2.2
Total	**150,675,808**	**85,556,552**	**236,232,360**	**146,011,461**	**92,609,997**	**238,621,458**	**405,307**	**2.8**

Total Motor Vehicle Registrations by Country

MOTOR VEHICLE REGISTRATIONS BY COUNTRY, 1998-1999 — continued

Country	1998			1999			Population (000)	Persons Per Car
	Passenger Cars	Commercial Vehicles	Total	Passenger Cars	Commercial Vehicles	Total		
ASIA, Far East								
Afghanistan	29,000	22,000	51,000	33,500	26,500	60,000	25,869	772.2
Bangladesh	57,068	75,599	132,667	57,000	77,000	134,000	127,669	2,239.8
Brunei	94,136	14,766	108,902	104,000	17,700	121,700	322	3.1
Hong Kong	715,377	262,037	977,414	760,000	273,000	1,033,000	6,721	8.8
India	4,820,000	2,610,000	7,430,000	5,200,000	3,000,000	8,200,000	997,515	191.8
Indonesia	491,457	2,097,674	2,589,131	580,000	2,305,000	2,885,000	207,022	356.9
Japan	49,895,735	20,918,819	70,814,554	51,164,204	20,558,558	71,722,762	126,570	2.5
South Korea	7,580,926	2,888,672	10,469,598	7,837,251	3,267,068	11,104,319	46,858	6.0
Malaysia	3,517,484	931,690	4,449,174	3,852,693	994,785	4,847,478	22,710	5.9
Myanmar	5,100	11,500	16,600	5,300	12,000	17,300	45,029	8,496.0
Pakistan	322,513	227,198	549,711	340,000	236,000	576,000	134,790	396.4
Peoples Republic of China . .	2,940,243	8,313,493	11,253,736	3,400,000	9,400,000	12,800,000	1,253,595	368.7
Philippines	749,204	579,244	1,328,448	745,144	650,000	1,395,144	74,259	99.7
Singapore	393,103	142,615	535,718	403,165	151,300	554,465	3,952	9.8
Sri Lanka	210,600	319,700	530,300	268,500	198,900	467,400	18,985	70.7
Taiwan	4,545,488	179,110	4,724,598	4,509,430	176,676	4,686,106	22,191	4.9
Thailand	1,712,900	3,442,500	5,155,400	2,044,565	4,075,537	6,120,102	60,246	29.5
Vietnam	76,500	103,385	179,885	81,000	114,000	195,000	77,515	957.0
Total	**78,156,834**	**43,140,002**	**121,296,836**	**81,385,752**	**45,534,024**	**126,919,776**	**3,251,818**	**40.0**
ASIA, Middle East								
Bahrain	157,208	39,515	196,723	159,266	34,526	193,792	666	4.2
Cyprus	249,225	110,845	360,070	256,989	112,949	369,938	760	3.0
Egypt	1,764,337	545,152	2,309,489	1,869,253	577,230	2,446,483	62,655	33.5
Iran	684,500	355,100	1,039,600	770,000	364,000	1,134,000	62,977	81.8
Iraq	680,000	335,000	1,015,000	685,000	375,000	1,060,000	22,797	33.3
Israel	1,297,965	301,803	1,599,768	1,341,339	312,775	1,654,114	6,105	4.6
Jordan	180,000	77,552	257,552	182,200	89,800	272,000	4,740	26.0
Kuwait	538,000	155,000	693,000	641,000	153,000	794,000	1,924	3.0
Lebanon	385,961	171,005	556,966	390,000	170,000	560,000	4,271	11.0
Oman	205,577	102,000	307,577	253,043	110,717	363,760	2,348	9.3
Qatar	126,000	67,638	193,638	138,900	67,200	206,100	565	4.1
Saudi Arabia	1,032,071	1,005,006	2,037,077	1,080,000	1,100,000	2,180,000	20,198	18.7
Syria	138,624	174,550	313,174	169,700	226,500	396,200	15,711	92.6
Turkey	3,838,631	1,317,349	5,155,980	4,072,326	1,405,158	5,477,484	64,385	15.8
United Arab Emirates	742,874	419,650	1,162,524	780,000	450,000	1,230,000	2,815	3.6
Yemen	264,000	321,700	585,700	258,900	306,700	565,600	17,048	65.8
Total	**12,284,973**	**5,498,865**	**17,783,838**	**13,047,916**	**5,855,555**	**18,903,471**	**289,965**	**22.2**

Total Motor Vehicle Registrations by Country

MOTOR VEHICLE REGISTRATIONS BY COUNTRY, 1998-1999 — continued

Country	1998 Passenger Cars	1998 Commercial Vehicles	1998 Total	1999 Passenger Cars	1999 Commercial Vehicles	1999 Total	Population (000)	Persons Per Car
EUROPE, East								
Bulgaria	1,809,350	283,755	2,093,105	1,703,000	261,000	1,964,000	8,208	4.8
Czech Republic	3,687,451	332,909	4,020,360	3,431,481	287,110	3,718,591	10,278	3.0
Hungary	2,365,000	370,686	2,735,686	2,255,500	340,068	2,595,568	10,068	4.5
Poland	5,603,398	939,608	6,543,006	7,526,000	1,448,000	8,974,000	38,654	5.1
Romania	2,822,254	578,337	3,400,591	2,980,014	620,271	3,600,285	22,458	7.5
Slovak Republic	1,150,000	146,200	1,296,200	1,246,959	160,495	1,407,454	5,396	4.3
Ukraine	426,414	79,455	505,869	304,338	81,134	385,472	49,950	164.1
Yugoslavia (former)	1,312,000	343,800	1,655,800	1,812,000	358,000	2,170,000	10,616	5.9
Total	**19,175,867**	**3,074,750**	**22,250,617**	**21,259,292**	**3,556,078**	**24,815,370**	**155,628**	**7.3**
EUROPE, West								
Austria	3,887,174	335,010	4,222,184	4,009,604	345,606	4,355,210	8,092	2.0
Belgium	4,458,010	542,651	5,000,661	4,547,236	571,705	5,118,941	10,226	2.2
Denmark	1,877,117	311,442	2,188,559	1,853,770	383,572	2,237,342	5,326	2.9
Finland	2,021,116	289,650	2,310,766	2,069,222	317,612	2,386,834	5,166	2.5
France	26,800,000	5,500,000	32,300,000	27,480,000	5,609,000	33,089,000	58,620	2.1
Germany	41,673,781	4,356,511	46,030,292	42,423,254	3,370,011	45,793,265	82,100	1.9
Gibraltar	21,900	12,400	34,300	22,450	1,786	24,236	28	1.2
Greece	2,675,676	1,013,677	3,689,353	2,605,000	902,200	3,507,200	10,538	4.0
Iceland	140,372	18,094	158,466	151,409	19,428	170,837	278	1.8
Ireland	1,196,901	188,219	1,385,120	1,269,245	208,567	1,477,812	3,752	3.0
Italy	31,370,765	3,336,733	34,707,498	31,953,732	3,409,399	35,363,131	57,646	1.8
Latvia	482,670	96,450	579,120	525,572	101,776	627,348	2,431	4.6
Luxembourg	244,130	27,321	271,451	253,406	28,840	282,246	432	1.7
Malta	175,020	43,957	218,977	206,500	45,300	251,800	379	1.8
Netherlands	5,931,000	709,000	6,640,000	6,120,000	774,000	6,894,000	15,805	2.6
Norway	1,786,404	427,047	2,213,451	1,813,642	327,696	2,141,338	4,460	2.5
Portugal	3,150,000	1,085,200	4,235,200	3,350,000	1,176,600	4,526,600	9,989	3.0
Spain	16,050,057	3,561,556	19,611,613	16,847,397	3,788,728	20,636,125	39,410	2.3
Sweden	3,792,056	353,215	4,145,271	3,889,902	369,125	4,259,027	8,857	2.3
Switzerland	3,383,273	282,841	3,666,114	3,467,275	313,646	3,780,921	7,136	2.1
United Kingdom	22,115,000	3,168,900	25,283,900	27,539,160	3,392,031	30,931,191	59,501	2.2
Total	**173,232,422**	**25,659,874**	**198,892,296**	**182,397,776**	**25,456,628**	**207,854,404**	**390,172**	**2.1**
PACIFIC								
Australia	8,400,102	2,266,098	10,666,200	9,750,000	2,382,000	12,132,000	18,967	1.9
Fiji	54,723	41,387	96,110	58,007	42,369	100,376	801	13.8
French Polynesia	38,700	22,700	61,400	41,500	16,200	57,700	231	5.6
Guam	125,100	43,500	168,600	126,000	43,000	169,000	152	1.2
New Caledonia	60,600	25,100	85,700	42,707	34,301	77,008	209	4.9
New Zealand	1,824,600	378,650	2,203,250	1,901,061	386,093	2,287,154	3,811	2.0
Papua New Guinea	21,700	89,700	111,400	36,000	60,000	96,000	4,705	130.7
Samoa (American)	5,400	5,500	10,900	5,500	5,700	11,200	169	30.7
Vanuatu	2,700	3,800	6,500	4,000	2,500	6,500	193	48.3
Total	**10,533,625**	**2,876,435**	**13,410,060**	**11,964,775**	**2,972,163**	**14,936,938**	**29,238**	**2.4**
WORLD TOTAL	**478,678,251**	**179,528,193**	**658,206,444**	**491,597,790**	**190,201,021**	**681,798,811**	**5,594,573**	**11.4**

SOURCE: Collected from various sources.

U.S. Motor Vehicle Exports by Country of Destination and Vehicle Type

U.S. EXPORTS BY COUNTRY OF DESTINATION AND VEHICLE TYPE, 2000

COUNTRY	Passenger Cars Units	Passenger Cars Value ($000)	Trucks Units	Trucks Value ($000)	Buses Units	Buses Value ($000)	Total Units	Total Value ($000)
Albania	2	55	3	372	0	0	5	427
Algeria	15	263	21	2,738	0	0	36	3,001
Angola	65	981	15	892	9	394	89	2,267
Anguilla	33	476	0	0	0	0	33	476
Antigua	25	427	15	574	1	30	41	1,031
Argentina	2,964	30,685	135	7,175	19	202	3,118	38,062
Armenia	5	150	0	0	0	0	5	150
Aruba	210	3,185	69	2,009	14	157	293	5,351
Australia	9,046	187,002	2,887	52,641	0	0	11,933	239,643
Austria	1,104	17,410	63	3,872	25	284	1,192	21,566
Azerbaijan	4	143	1	31	0	0	5	174
Bahamas	1,578	22,683	1,412	20,675	43	1,176	3,033	44,534
Bahrain	343	7,110	83	2,111	4	74	430	9,295
Bangladesh	5	130	19	1,398	0	0	24	1,528
Barbados	34	983	21	749	0	0	55	1,732
Belgium	2,800	50,600	7,951	121,909	26	595	10,777	173,104
Belize	108	1,526	153	2,734	55	465	316	4,725
Benin	17	368	2	100	0	0	19	468
Bermuda	9	146	42	1,587	1	8	52	1,741
Bolivia	70	1,433	22	602	0	0	92	2,035
Bosnia-Hercegov	13	436	0	0	1	13	14	449
Botswana	1	7	25	1,650	0	0	26	1,657
Br Virgin Isls.	100	1,711	13	225	8	189	121	2,125
Brazil	1,003	14,772	208	1,984	40	369	1,251	17,125
Brunei	0	0	7	1,262	0	0	7	1,262
Bulgaria	44	982	2	306	0	0	46	1,288
Cambodia	39	627	3	638	7	81	49	1,346
Cameroon	8	107	0	0	0	0	8	107
Canada	599,199	8,754,744	241,857	5,374,872	3,921	152,844	844,977	14,282,460
Cayman	570	9,662	80	2,479	4	47	654	12,188
Chile	3,002	42,027	2,047	46,213	5	125	5,054	88,365
China	173	3,663	637	24,820	12	136	822	28,619
Colombia	361	5,124	350	6,347	68	586	779	12,057
Congo(ROC)	1	28	5	135	0	0	6	163
Costa Rica	657	9,701	551	8,176	79	881	1,287	18,758
Cote d'Ivoire	22	461	5	50	0	0	27	511
Croatia	27	827	96	8,664	0	0	123	9,491
Cyprus	64	1,462	7	139	0	0	71	1,601
Czech Republic	162	3,744	2	26	0	0	164	3,770
Denmark	260	4,284	33	395	0	0	293	4,679
Dominica Is.	2	71	4	193	2	64	8	328
Dominican Rep.	2,248	38,226	637	25,984	69	1,101	2,954	65,311
Ecuador	83	1,692	87	4,116	10	586	180	6,394

U.S. Motor Vehicle Exports by Country of Destination and Vehicle Type

U.S. EXPORTS BY COUNTRY OF DESTINATION AND VEHICLE TYPE, 2000 — continued

COUNTRY	Passenger Cars Units	Passenger Cars Value ($000)	Trucks Units	Trucks Value ($000)	Buses Units	Buses Value ($000)	Total Units	Total Value ($000)
Egypt	747	12,923	258	13,868	2	54	1,007	26,845
El Salvador	220	3,762	743	9,632	130	857	1,093	14,251
Eq. Guinea	7	266	0	0	1	8	8	274
Estonia	23	541	0	0	0	0	23	541
F St. Micronesia	0	0	12	361	2	21	14	382
Finland	74	1,683	48	709	22	579	144	2,971
Fr. Polynesia	13	275	6	220	0	0	19	495
France	2,652	56,244	293	5,516	221	1,384	3,166	63,144
Gabon	10	385	12	280	0	0	22	665
Georgia	28	649	1	9	0	0	29	658
Germany	47,456	1,049,418	601	15,176	1,578	9,150	49,635	1,073,744
Ghana	57	941	41	1,202	8	111	106	2,254
Gibraltar	41	370	0	0	0	0	41	370
Greece	1,228	20,066	36	7,392	10	8	1,274	27,466
Grenada	9	129	15	946	1	60	25	1,135
Guadeloupe	136	2,198	3	42	0	0	139	2,240
Guatemala	658	11,353	1,407	15,456	241	1,333	2,306	28,142
Guinea	3	41	3	18	6	171	12	230
Guyana	33	457	22	328	3	30	58	815
Haiti	32	504	812	11,941	16	182	860	12,627
Honduras	504	9,536	563	8,480	197	1,459	1,264	19,475
Hong Kong	1,173	16,987	50	406	0	0	1,223	17,393
Hungary	52	1,056	4	235	161	1,394	217	2,685
Iceland	106	1,174	4	76	14	175	124	1,425
India	10	173	8	1,030	0	0	18	1,203
Indonesia	431	9,089	158	4,612	0	0	589	13,701
Ireland	215	3,910	16	264	0	0	231	4,174
Israel	3,253	47,029	1,771	73,864	81	1,674	5,105	122,567
Italy	2,605	51,083	68	920	28	321	2,701	52,324
Jamaica	194	4,307	282	9,309	5	210	481	13,826
Japan	31,448	621,485	3,322	200,898	39	763	34,809	823,146
Jordan	150	1,879	6	109	3	30	159	2,018
Kazakhstan	2	60	3	162	1	34	6	256
Kenya	9	104	1	6	0	0	10	110
Korea	1,110	21,244	75	1,234	3	59	1,188	22,537
Kuwait	3,032	51,528	1,398	30,706	2	108	4,432	82,342
Kyrgystan	6	207	0	0	0	0	6	207
Laos	0	0	17	1,754	0	0	17	1,754
Latvia	20	582	0	0	0	0	20	582
Lebanon	672	11,992	74	2,119	0	0	746	14,111
Liberia	2	25	18	275	6	49	26	349
Lithuania	10	156	1	10	0	0	11	166
Luxembourg	95	3,097	7	1,299	2	106	104	4,502

U.S. Motor Vehicle Exports by Country of Destination and Vehicle Type

U.S. EXPORTS BY COUNTRY OF DESTINATION AND VEHICLE TYPE, 2000 — continued

COUNTRY	Passenger Cars Units	Value ($000)	Trucks Units	Value ($000)	Buses Units	Value ($000)	Total Units	Value ($000)
Macedonia	298	5,843	7	445	0	0	305	6,288
Malawi	1	30	4	899	0	0	5	929
Malaysia	28	791	2	20	2	512	32	1,323
Malta & Gozo	7	220	5	214	0	0	12	434
Marshall Isl.	14	156	15	343	2	63	31	562
Mauritania	0	0	1	150	0	0	1	150
Mauritius	12	347	3	20	0	0	15	367
Mexico	161,206	2,117,311	51,159	906,853	2,521	35,715	214,886	3,059,879
Moldova	5	150	2	58	0	0	7	208
Monaco	0	0	1	60	0	0	1	60
Mongolia	3	61	0	0	0	0	3	61
Morocco	48	1,259	23	712	0	0	71	1,971
Mozambique	0	0	10	84	0	0	10	84
Namibia	3	106	28	844	0	0	31	950
Netherlands	3,326	52,933	384	7,812	5	80	3,715	60,825
Netherlands Ant.	437	7,473	131	4,275	9	121	577	11,869
New Caledonia	30	711	0	0	0	0	30	711
New Zealand	730	13,916	155	7,888	2	16	887	21,820
Nicaragua	165	2,786	197	2,569	52	262	414	5,617
Niger	3	22	3	36	0	0	6	58
Nigeria	359	5,402	363	6,061	11	261	733	11,724
Norway	759	11,940	127	1,981	3	48	889	13,969
Oman	706	11,990	121	3,813	0	0	827	15,803
Pakistan	39	1,260	6	379	0	0	45	1,639
Palau	0	0	2	167	0	0	2	167
Panama	1,132	17,952	348	7,198	68	545	1,548	25,695
Paraguay	12	249	1	11	25	66	38	326
Peru	139	2,879	136	10,515	25	227	300	13,621
Philippines	3,730	58,501	221	6,870	1	7	3,952	65,378
Poland	231	5,309	6	145	5	108	242	5,562
Portugal	70	1,804	10	1,997	0	0	80	3,801
Qatar	585	13,046	289	10,882	1	3	875	23,931
Romania	128	3,022	2	150	0	0	130	3,172
Russia	327	8,959	32	2,026	0	0	359	10,985
Saudi Arabia	8,916	149,228	5,607	145,239	239	2,143	14,762	296,610
Senegal	14	247	0	0	0	0	14	247
Sierra Leone	3	90	1	96	0	0	4	186
Singapore	105	1,199	59	1,293	0	0	164	2,492
Slovakia	76	2,542	0	0	0	0	76	2,542
Slovenia	21	572	0	0	0	0	21	572
South Africa	2,748	33,632	1,459	43,665	6	6	4,213	77,303
Spain	6,543	80,476	121	1,704	4	86	6,668	82,266
St Kitts-Nevis	9	20	5	390	0	12	14	422

U.S. Motor Vehicle Exports by Country of Destination and Vehicle Type

U.S. EXPORTS BY COUNTRY OF DESTINATION AND VEHICLE TYPE, 2000 — continued

COUNTRY	Passenger Cars Units	Passenger Cars Value ($000)	Trucks Units	Trucks Value ($000)	Buses Units	Buses Value ($000)	Total Units	Total Value ($000)
St Lucia	17	220	13	1,200	0	0	30	1,420
St Vinc & Grenada	11	424	1	6	0	0	12	430
Sudan	0	113	0	0	0	0	0	113
Suriname	72	1,345	28	1,646	1	12	101	3,003
Sweden	1,315	31,197	79	3,512	6	99	1,400	34,808
Switzerland	2,155	52,778	144	1,463	1	128	2,300	54,369
Syria	37	512	2	40	0	0	39	552
Taiwan	10,751	147,178	310	13,215	65	1,280	11,126	161,673
Thailand	162	1,893	119	7,559	1	5	282	9,457
Trin & Tobago	60	1,203	49	1,538	0	0	109	2,741
Tunisia	18	544	25	1,500	0	0	43	2,044
Turkey	519	13,208	75	5,215	4	67	598	18,490
Turkmenistan	9	266	0	0	0	0	9	266
Turks & Caic	175	2,381	188	2,206	2	17	365	4,604
Uganda	4	120	1	6	0	0	5	126
Ukraine	42	1,240	82	2,294	0	0	124	3,534
UAE	2,043	40,611	969	31,930	20	1,079	3,032	73,620
United Kingdom	14,528	236,232	984	25,543	46	1,349	15,558	263,124
Uruguay	12	292	11	364	0	0	23	656
Uzbekistan	7	244	0	0	0	0	7	244
Venezuela	1,344	24,753	440	17,006	187	4,023	1,971	45,782
Vietnam	5	60	52	706	2	27	59	793
Western Samoa	2	85	1	8	5	21	8	114
Yemen	6	159	7	1,612	0	0	13	1,771
Yugoslavia	5	116	0	0	0	0	5	116
Zambia	7	210	1	5	0	0	8	215
Zimbabwe	8	225	8	183	0	0	16	408
Total	**951,284**	**14,411,065**	**336,364**	**7,448,328**	**10,527**	**229,125**	**1,298,175**	**22,088,518**

U.S. EXPORTS OF PASSENGER CARS BY COUNTRY OF DESTINATION, 1988-2000

Year	Canada	France	Germany	Japan	Kuwait	Mexico	Saudi Arabia	Taiwan	Other Countries	Total Exports
2000	599,199	2,652	47,456	31,448	3,032	161,206	8,916	10,751	86,624	951,284
1999	583,999	2,782	42,415	36,602	1,650	117,018	5,076	8,054	107,814	905,410
1998	566,481	2,675	44,611	43,580	2,519	70,130	11,956	9,604	147,080	898,636
1997	626,629	2,514	57,426	71,789	2,565	62,911	10,146	24,697	216,626	1,075,303
1996	502,652	3,802	59,462	109,917	7,708	46,562	18,253	35,141	190,137	973,634
1995	492,107	2,538	26,690	130,524	6,661	18,649	12,523	61,002	238,673	989,367
1994	559,513	6,083	39,568	100,400	9,246	36,569	18,587	72,491	176,801	1,019,258
1993	480,909	2,942	44,038	56,741	7,923	4,036	32,827	71,332	163,490	864,238
1992	459,910	8,704	56,615	40,598	15,208	4,261	35,502	90,231	140,045	851,074
1991	495,373	5,563	38,285	28,160	16,312	10,592	28,270	44,934	87,461	754,950
1990	505,352	10,475	34,485	39,188	2,919	12,827	23,288	66,609	98,614	793,757
1989	569,039	13,215	19,732	21,966	13,179	1,080	16,995	58,362	64,805	778,373
1988	618,647	5,713	19,110	21,725	10,522	692	19,670	46,622	38,470	781,171

Source: Compiled from official statistics of the U.S. Department of Commerce.

U.S. Motor Vehicle Imports by Country of Origin and Vehicle Type

U.S. IMPORTS BY COUNTRY OF ORIGIN AND VEHICLE TYPE, 2000

Country of Origin	Passenger Cars Units	Passenger Cars Value ($000)	Trucks Units	Trucks Value ($000)	Buses Units	Buses Value ($000)	Total Units	Total Value ($000)
Australia	13,192	236,255	1	15	1	5	13,194	236,275
Austria	1,481	58,737	27	178	159	428	1,667	59,343
Belgium	40,361	909,291	30	1,275	594	165,680	40,985	1,076,246
Brazil	12,231	166,144	42	887	3	238	12,276	167,269
Canada	2,076,181	33,252,486	491,399	10,832,873	8,666	675,048	2,576,246	44,760,407
Finland	12,419	465,133	14	930	0	0	12,433	466,063
France	52	605	1,057	31,274	0	0	1,109	31,879
Germany	489,086	14,523,268	1,186	25,347	86	16,825	490,358	14,565,440
Hungary	7,393	200,979	0	0	633	39,479	8,026	240,458
Italy	2,059	159,680	111	865	1	200	2,171	160,745
Japan	1,661,906	31,429,027	27,395	537,649	21	919	1,689,322	31,967,595
Korea	560,728	4,824,055	1,303	29,428	2	100	562,033	4,853,583
Mexico	927,574	15,645,520	282,589	5,102,887	2,525	129,751	1,212,688	20,878,158
Netherlands	34,429	655,969	21	731	15	2,765	34,465	659,465
Norway	62	1,950	0	0	0		62	1,950
South Africa	1,191	23,317	0	0	0		1,191	23,317
Spain	3	29	32	586	0	0	35	615
Sweden	85,713	2,163,618	6	289	1	172	85,720	2,164,079
Switzerland	7	61	41	248	17	67	65	376
Taiwan	127	949	283	1,639	0	410	2,588	
United Kingdom	79,639	2,754,630	193	6,476	64	4,869	79,896	2,765,975
Other	63	922	68	987	2	151	133	2060
Total	6,005,834	107,471,703	805,732	16,573,592	12,788	1,036,546	6,824,354	125,081,841

U.S. IMPORTS OF NEW ASSEMBLED PASSENGER CARS BY COUNTRY OF ORIGIN, 1965-2000*

Year	Canada	Germany	Japan	South Korea	Mexico	Sweden	United Kingdom	Other	Total Imports
2000	2,076,181	489,086	1,661,906	560,728	927,574	85,713	79,639	125,007	6,005,834
1999	2,125,876	456,246	1,560,857	369,264	637,486	82,808	67,689	99,590	5,399,816
1998	1,817,836	372,632	1,317,702	207,165	586,973	84,404	49,037	65,690	4,501,439
1997	1,722,199	298,032	1,383,519	222,535	539,384	79,725	43,726	68,100	4,357,220
1996	1,688,123	234,480	1,190,581	225,613	550,622	86,595	43,616	44,817	4,064,447
1995	1,678,276	206,892	1,387,193	216,618	463,305	82,634	42,176	36,823	4,113,917
1994	1,591,326	187,999	1,593,169	217,962	360,370	63,867	28,239	54,082	4,097,014
1993	1,468,272	184,356	1,597,391	126,576	299,634	58,742	20,048	53,441	3,808,460
1992	1,200,358	206,124	1,637,066	133,244	266,149	76,832	11,007	43,942	3,574,722
1990	1,220,221	245,286	1,867,794	201,475	215,986	93,084	27,271	73,485	3,944,602
1985	1,144,805	473,110	2,527,467	N.A.	13,647	142,640	24,474	71,536	4,397,679
1980	594,770	338,711	1,991,502	N.A.	1	61,496	32,517	97,451	3,116,448
1975	733,766	370,012	695,573	N.A.	0	51,993	67,106	156,203	2,074,653
1970	692,783	674,945	381,338	N.A.	N.A.	57,844	76,257	130,253	2,013,420
1965	33,378	376,950	25,538	N.A.	N.A.	26,010	66,565	35,232	563,673

N.A. - Not available.
*Data include imports into Puerto Rico; data do not include automobiles assembled in U.S. foreign trade zones.
Source: Compiled from official statistics of the U.S. Department of Commerce.

World Trade in Motor Vehicles

EXPORTS AND IMPORTS OF MOTOR VEHICLES FOR SELECTED COUNTRIES, 1999

Country	Exports Passenger Cars	Exports Commercial Vehicles	Exports Total	Imports Passenger Cars	Imports Commercial Vehicles	Imports Total
Argentina	63,323	35,039	98,362	134,739	24,810	159,549
Austria	119,345	14,706	134,051	331,905	38,065	369,970
Belgium	889,838	93,198	983,036	771,325	103,191	874,516
Brazil	200,404	67,965	268,369	129,119	49,551	178,670
Canada	1,936,800	395,000	2,331,800	1,005,784	243,272	1,249,056
Czech Republic	288,708	23,699	312,407	225,335	15,294	240,629
Finland	30,000	19	30,019	148,537	20,806	169,343
France	2,890,368	365,090	3,255,458	1,576,096	250,152	1,826,248
Germany	3,438,019	237,737	3,675,756	2,087,510	220,344	2,307,854
Italy	595,547	202,240	797,787	1,893,227	153,754	2,046,981
Japan	3,757,450	651,493	4,408,943	268,795	2,168	270,963
Korea, South	1,390,072	119,588	1,509,660	2,922	2,753	5,675
Mexico	673,682	403,739	1,077,421	135,069	119,489	254,558
Norway	0	0	0	145,338	30,336	175,674
Portugal	181,151	44,524	225,675	330,584	77,065	407,649
Spain	1,799,214	514,897	2,314,111	1,091,039	112,038	1,203,077
Sweden	204,098	16,884	220,982	280,634	25,408	306,042
Switzerland	0	0	0	328,225	24,481	352,706
Turkey	77,459	8,350	85,809	131,215	41,728	172,943
United Kingdom	1,138,477	75,004	1,213,481	1,690,922	137,407	1,828,329
United States	951,284	346,891	1,298,175	6,005,834	818,520	6,824,354
Total	20,625,239	3,616,063	24,241,302	18,714,154	2,510,632	21,224,786

WORLD MOTOR VEHICLE EXPORTS, 1975-1999

Motor Vehicle Exports by Country of Origin (In Thousands)

Year	World Total[1]	Belgium	Canada	France	Germany	Italy	Japan	Sweden	United Kingdom	United States
1999	24,241.3	983.0	2,331.8	3,255.5	3,675.8	797.8	4,408.9	221.0	1,213.5	1,298.2
1998	24,145.6	1,026.3	2,220.5	3,122.8	3,510.9	812.4	4,528.9	425.9	1,123.6	1,247.8
1997	23,620.8	1,050.8	2,220.5	2,822.5	3,035.6	739.3	4,553.2	416.6	1,065.3	1,591.0
1996	21,691.1	1,192.7	2,134.8	2,272.0	2,841.8	799.2	3,711.7	194.5	1,073.3	1,289.6
1995	20,142.7	1,218.8	1,908.6	2,261.2	2,639.5	806.5	3,790.8	206.3	837.0	1,243.6
1994	19,795.6	1,215.7	1,852.0	2,428.5	2,410.3	669.6	4,460.3	192.8	718.2	1,293.2
1993	19,095.9	1,097.8	2,023.8	2,263.0	2,176.1	504.0	5,017.8	194.4	632.0	1,045.3
1992	20,250.5	1,130.6	1,765.4	2,295.8	2,729.9	697.6	5,667.7	210.8	708.4	1,012.5
1991	19,598.6	1,127.8	1,639.1	2,420.6	2,346.7	806.2	5,753.4	203.4	701.0	962.9
1990	18,315.8	1,225.9	1,699.4	2,315.9	2,765.6	900.9	5,831.2	205.2	510.3	953.1
1989	19,498.8	1,203.0	1,664.2	2,379.1	2,897.7	846.6	5,883.9	205.4	431.3	975.8
1988	19,322.6	1,188.7	1,643.3	2,279.2	2,676.9	827.3	6,104.2	214.6	331.9	1,016.7
1987	18,653.3	1,166.8	1,364.8	2,103.0	2,607.3	766.0	6,304.9	273.4	299.6	861.0
1985	17,810.5	979.8	1,612.1	1,892.8	2,745.9	565.7	6,730.5	260.1	291.8	890.6
1980	15,161.7	883.8	938.5	2,218.9	2,084.3	591.6	5,967.0	192.9	481.0	807.2
1975	10,807.2	792.1	1,005.6	1,938.3	1,653.5	710.5	2,677.6	195.3	695.9	864.1

Percent of World Motor Vehicle Exports

Year		Belgium	Canada	France	Germany	Italy	Japan	Sweden	United Kingdom	United States
1999	100.0	4.1	9.6	13.4	15.2	3.3	18.2	1.0	5.0	5.4
1998	100.0	4.3	9.2	12.9	14.5	3.4	18.8	1.8	4.7	5.2
1997	100.0	4.4	9.4	11.9	12.9	3.1	19.3	1.8	4.5	6.7
1996	100.0	5.5	9.8	10.5	13.1	3.7	17.1	0.9	4.9	5.9
1995	100.0	6.1	9.5	11.2	13.1	4.0	18.8	1.0	4.2	6.2
1994	100.0	6.1	9.4	12.3	12.2	3.4	22.5	0.0	3.6	6.5
1993	100.0	5.7	10.6	11.9	11.4	2.6	26.3	1.0	3.3	5.5
1992	100.0	5.6	8.7	11.3	13.5	3.4	27.0	1.0	3.5	4.0
1991	100.0	5.8	8.4	12.4	11.0	4.1	29.4	1.0	3.6	4.9
1990	100.0	6.7	9.3	12.6	15.1	4.9	31.8	1.1	2.8	5.2
1989	100.0	6.2	8.5	12.2	14.9	4.3	30.2	1.1	2.2	5.0
1988	100.0	6.2	8.5	11.8	13.9	4.3	31.6	1.1	1.7	5.3
1987	100.0	6.3	7.3	11.3	13.0	4.1	33.8	1.5	1.6	4.6
1985	100.0	5.5	9.1	10.6	15.4	3.2	37.8	1.5	1.6	5.0
1980	100.0	5.8	6.2	14.6	13.7	3.9	39.4	1.3	3.2	5.3
1975	100.0	7.3	9.3	17.9	15.3	6.6	24.8	1.8	6.4	7.0

(1) World total includes countries with vehicle exports not shown separately.
SOURCE: Compiled by Ward's Communications from various sources.

Material Usage by the Automotive Industry

AUTOMOTIVE CONSUMPTION OF MATERIALS BY TYPE, 1996-2000

Material	U.S. Total Consumption	Automotive Consumption	Automotive Percentage	Material/Year	U.S. Total Consumption	Automotive Consumption	Automotive Percentage
ALUMINUM (Thousands of Pounds)				PLASTIC (Thousands of Pounds)			
2000	24,486,000	7,963,000	32.5	2000	N.A.	N.A.	N.A.
1999*	24,674,000	7,938,000	32.2	1999	100,281,000	3,910,959	3.9
1998	20,405,000	6,305,000	30.9	1998	94,101,000	3,666,390	3.8
1997	19,580,000	5,626,000	28.7	1997	82,714,959	3,199,348	3.9
1996	18,354,000	5,188,000	28.3	1996	78,747,672	3,091,535	3.9
COPPER AND COPPER ALLOY (Thousands of Pounds)				NATURAL RUBBER (Metric Tons)			
2000	9,569,000	1,097,000	11.5	2000	1,194,786	947,465	79.3
1999*	9,189,000	1,085,000	11.8	1999	1,116,299	798,154	71.5
1998	8,636,000	1,122,000	13.0	1998	1,309,000	1,001,000	76.5
1997	8,300,000	1,060,000	12.8	1997	1,056,000	803,000	76.0
1996	7,591,000	919,000	12.1	1996	1,001,726	775,661	77.4
GRAY IRON (Tons)				SYNTHETIC RUBBER (Metric Tons)			
2000	5,648,000	1,707,000	30.2	2000	2,143,590	1,202,554	56.1
1999	5,769,000	1,752,000	30.4	1999	2,080,962	1,338,059	64.3
1998	5,950,000	1,870,000	31.4	1998	2,203,000	1,256,000	57.0
1997	6,039,000	2,115,000	35.6	1997	2,305,000	1,269,000	55.1
1996	5,747,000	2,117,000	36.8	1996	2,186,602	1,232,202	56.4
DUCTILE IRON (Tons)				ALLOY STEEL (Tons)			
2000	3,992,000	1,286,000	32.2	2000	5,378,889	561,346	10.4
1999	3,964,000	1,257,000	31.7	1999	5,420,669	552,908	10.2
1998	3,837,000	1,174,000	30.6	1998	5,768,641	577,048	10.0
1997	3,986,000	1,165,000	29.2	1997	6,449,181	594,735	9.2
1996	3,746,000	1,131,000	30.2	1996	5,561,920	605,442	10.9
MALLEABLE IRON (Tons)				STAINLESS STEEL (Tons)			
2000	160,000	82,000	51.2	2000	2,102,962	494,531	23.5
1999	177,000	92,000	52.0	1999	2,086,495	465,288	22.3
1998	194,000	101,000	52.1	1998	2,026,483	431,132	21.3
1997	201,000	115,000	57.2	1997	2,057,002	428,848	20.8
1996	232,000	157,000	67.7	1996	1,942,776	448,822	23.1
TOTAL IRON (Tons)				TOTAL STEEL (Tons)			
2000	9,800,000	3,075,000	31.4	2000	109,050,451	14,889,854	13.7
1999	9,910,000	3,101,000	31.3	1999	106,201,045	16,771,000	15.8
1998	9,981,000	3,145,000	31.5	1998	102,420,000	15,842,000	15.5
1997	10,226,000	3,395,000	33.2	1997	105,858,000	14,253,667	13.5
1996	9,725,000	3,405,000	35.0	1996	100,877,829	14,664,738	14.5
LEAD (Metric Tons)				ZINC (Tons)			
2000	1,680,000	1,293,600	77.0	2000	1,320,000	303,600	23.0
1999	1,660,000	1,258,400	75.8	1999	1,340,000	308,200	23.0
1998	1,630,000	1,260,100	77.3	1998	1,290,000	296,700	23.0
1997	1,620,000	1,225,050	75.6	1997	1,260,000	289,800	23.0
1996	1,610,000	1,132,800	70.4	1996	1,212,000	278,760	23.0

NOTE: For most materials listed, automotive consumption includes materials used for cars, trucks, buses and replacement parts. *Revised figures.
SOURCE: Ward's Communications from various sources.

Material Usage, Vehicles Retired From Use and Vehicle Recycling

POUNDS OF MATERIAL IN A TYPICAL FAMILY VEHICLE, 1978 - 2001

Material	1978 Pounds	1978 Percent	1985 Pounds	1985 Percent	1990 Pounds	1990 Percent	2001 Pounds	2001 Percent
Regular Steel, Sheet, Strip, Bar and Rod	1,915.0	53.6	1,481.5	46.5	1,405.0	44.7	1,349.0	40.8
High and Medium Strength Steel	133.0	3.7	217.5	6.8	238.0	7.6	351.5	10.6
Stainless Steel	26.0	0.7	29.0	0.9	34.0	1.1	54.5	1.6
Other Steels	55.0	1.5	54.5	1.7	39.5	1.3	25.5	0.8
Iron	512.0	14.3	468.0	14.7	454.0	14.5	345.0	10.4
Plastics and Plastic Composites	180.0	5.0	211.5	6.6	229.0	7.3	253.0	7.6
Aluminum	112.5	3.2	138.0	4.3	158.5	5.0	256.5	7.8
Copper and Brass	37.0	1.0	44.0	1.4	48.5	1.5	46.0	1.4
Powder Metal Parts	15.5	0.4	19.0	0.6	24.0	0.8	37.5	1.1
Zinc Die Castings	31.0	0.9	18.0	0.6	18.5	0.6	11.0	0.3
Magnesium Castings	1.0	0.0	2.5	0.1	3.0	0.1	8.5	0.3
Fluids and Lubricants	198.0	5.5	184.0	5.8	182.0	5.8	196.0	5.9
Rubber	146.5	4.1	136.0	4.3	130.5	4.3	145.5	4.4
Glass	86.5	2.4	85.0	2.7	86.5	2.8	98.5	3.0
Other Materials	120.5	3.4	99.0	3.1	83.5	2.7	131.0	4.0
Total	3,569.5	100.0	3,187.5	100.0	3,140.5	100.0	3,309.0	100.0

SOURCE: American Metal Market from Industry Reports. Copywrite 2001, Cahners Business Information.

MOTOR VEHICLES RETIRED FROM USE, 1957-2000 (In Thousands)

Year Ending June 30	Passenger Cars	Trucks & Buses	Total
2000	8,085	6,214	14,299
1999	7,216	4,447	11,663
1998	6,819	4,846	11,665
1997	8,244	4,265	12,509
1996	7,527	3,284	10,811
1995	7,414	2,918	10,332
1994	7,824	4,545	12,369
1993	7,366	1,048	8,414
1992	11,194	1,587	12,781
1991	8,565	2,284	10,849
1990	8,897	2,177	11,074
1989	8,981	2,189	11,170
1988	8,754	2,251	11,005
1987	8,103	2,364	10,467
1985	7,729	2,100	9,829
1983	6,243	1,491	7,734
1981	7,542	1,519	9,061
1979	9,312	1,916	11,228
1977	8,234	1,668	9,902
1975	5,669	908	6,577
1973	7,987	1,208	9,195
1971	6,021	1,044	7,065
1969	6,348	966	7,314
1967	6,984	947	7,931
1965	5,704	736	6,440
1963	4,741	720	5,461
1961	4,294	647	4,941
1959	2,982	372	3,354
1957	4,309	630	4,939

NOTE: Figures represent vehicles which are not re-registered.
SOURCE: The Polk Company. Permission for further use must be obtained from The Polk Company.

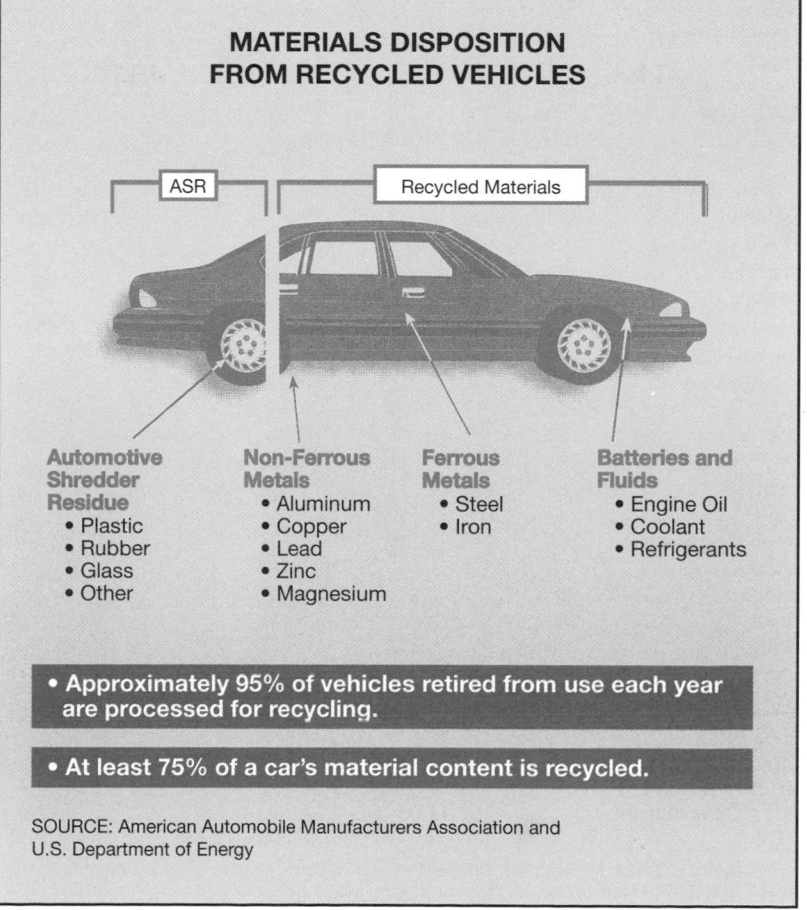

MATERIALS DISPOSITION FROM RECYCLED VEHICLES

ASR

Recycled Materials

Automotive Shredder Residue
- Plastic
- Rubber
- Glass
- Other

Non-Ferrous Metals
- Aluminum
- Copper
- Lead
- Zinc
- Magnesium

Ferrous Metals
- Steel
- Iron

Batteries and Fluids
- Engine Oil
- Coolant
- Refrigerants

- **Approximately 95% of vehicles retired from use each year are processed for recycling.**

- **At least 75% of a car's material content is recycled.**

SOURCE: American Automobile Manufacturers Association and U.S. Department of Energy

Licensed Drivers by Age Group, Sex and State

LICENSED DRIVERS BY STATE, 2000

State	Male (000)	Female (000)	Total (000)
Alabama	1,717	1,728	3,445
Alaska	246	212	458
Arizona	1,672	1,624	3,296
Arkansas	965	960	1,925
California	10,832	9,998	20,830
Colorado	1,518	1,472	2,990
Connecticut	1,183	1,190	2,373
Delaware	271	280	551
Dist. of Columbia	179	169	348
Florida	6,225	6,174	12,399
Georgia	2,685	2,785	5,470
Hawaii	397	355	752
Idaho	441	431	872
Illinois	3,956	3,968	7,924
Indiana	1,977	1,878	3,855
Iowa	953	982	1,935
Kansas	942	949	1,891
Kentucky	1,324	1,335	2,659
Louisiana	1,349	1,413	2,762
Maine	452	459	911
Maryland	1,494	1,700	3,194
Massachusetts	2,215	2,205	4,420
Michigan	3,406	3,456	6,862
Minnesota	1,476	1,430	2,906
Mississippi	871	917	1,788
Missouri	1,899	1,940	3,839
Montana	335	324	659
Nebraska	602	599	1,201
Nevada	691	630	1,321
New Hampshire	463	455	918
New Jersey	2,757	2,793	5,550
New Mexico	609	611	1,220
New York	5,577	5,049	10,626
North Carolina	2,720	2,771	5,491
North Dakota	231	226	457
Ohio	3,958	4,087	8,045
Oklahoma	1,126	1,186	2,312
Oregon	1,238	1,222	2,460
Pennsylvania	4,281	4,196	8,477
Rhode Island	340	348	688
South Carolina	1,363	1,446	2,809
South Dakota	271	272	543
Tennessee	2,050	2,125	4,175
Texas	6,784	6,575	13,359
Utah	725	714	1,439
Vermont	250	245	495
Virginia	2,327	2,401	4,728
Washington	2,097	2,031	4,128
West Virginia	642	631	1,273
Wisconsin	1,875	1,857	3,732
Wyoming	185	177	362
Total	94,166	93,004	187,170

SOURCE: U.S. Department of Transportation, Federal Highway Administration

DRIVERS BY AGE GROUP AND SEX, 2000

Age (In Years)	Male (000)	Female (000)	Total (000)
Under 16	17	15	32
16	753	704	1,457
17	1,200	1,130	2,330
18	1,434	1,332	2,766
19	1,563	1,457	3,020
20	1,559	1,482	3,041
21	1,561	1,490	3,051
22	1,600	1,536	3,136
23	1,587	1,520	3,107
24	1,631	1,559	3,190
25-29	9,067	8,670	17,737
30-34	9,633	9,279	18,912
35-39	10,635	10,464	21,099
40-44	10,376	10,345	20,721
45-49	9,328	9,288	18,616
50-54	8,096	8,037	16,133
55-59	6,200	6,147	12,347
60-64	4,859	4,804	9,663
65-69	4,163	4,167	8,330
70-74	3,645	3,807	7,452
75-79	2,777	3,011	5,788
80-84	1,582	1,748	3,330
85 AND OVER	889	1,004	1,893
Total	94,166	93,004	187,170

DRIVERS BY SEX, 1968-2000

Year	Male (000)	Percent Male	Female (000)	Percent Female	Total (000)
2000	94,166	74.32	93,004	69.87	187,170
1998	93,105	50.33	91,875	49.67	184,980
1997	91,905	50.30	90,804	49.70	182,709
1996	90,519	50.42	89,021	49.58	179,539
1995	89,214	50.51	87,414	49.49	176,628
1994	89,194	50.85	86,209	49.15	175,403
1993	87,993	50.82	85,156	49.18	173,149
1992	88,387	51.05	84,738	48.95	173,125
1991	86,665	51.28	82,330	48.72	168,995
1990	85,792	51.37	81,223	48.63	167,015
1989	85,378	51.57	80,177	48.43	165,555
1988	85,230	51.91	78,967	48.09	164,197
1987	84,084	51.91	77,891	48.09	161,975
1986	82,494	52.02	76,100	47.98	158,594
1985	81,592	52.01	75,276	47.99	156,868
1984	80,977	52.10	74,447	47.90	155,424
1983	80,894	52.40	73,495	47.60	154,389
1982	78,553	52.29	71,681	47.71	150,234
1981	77,888	52.96	69,187	47.04	147,075
1980	77,187	53.12	68,108	46.88	145,295
1979	76,531	53.41	66,753	46.59	143,284
1978	75,594	53.67	65,249	46.33	140,844
1977	74,467	53.91	63,654	46.09	138,121
1976	72,523	54.11	61,513	45.89	134,036
1975	70,505	54.32	59,286	45.68	129,791
1974	68,574	54.67	56,853	45.33	125,427
1973	67,115	55.22	54,431	44.78	121,546
1972	66,027	55.76	52,387	44.24	118,414
1971	64,291	56.19	50,135	43.81	114,426
1970	63,302	56.75	48,241	43.25	111,543
1969	62,346	57.56	45,960	42.44	108,306
1968	61,204	58.06	44,206	41.94	105,410

Demographics of New Car Buyers and Initial Vehicle Quality

DEMOGRAPHICS OF NEW VEHICLE BUYERS AND INITIAL VEHICLE QUALITY, 2001 MODEL YEAR

NEW PASSENGER CAR BUYERS					NEW LIGHT TRUCK BUYERS				
Characteristic	Domestic[1]	European[2]	Asian[2]	Total	Characteristic	Domestic[1]	European[2]	Asian[2]	Total
Gender					**Gender**				
Male	53.9%	57.0%	49.1%	52.4%	Male	69.6%	61.9%	56.2%	65.5%
Female	40.8	38.2	45.4	42.3	Female	25.5	32.4	38.9	29.6
No Answer	5.3	4.8	5.5	5.3	No Answer	4.9	5.7	4.9	4.9
Total	**100.0**	**100.0**	**100.0**	**100.0**	**Total**	**100.0**	**100.0**	**100.0**	**100.0**
Age of Principal Purchaser (In Years)					**Age of Principal Purchaser (In Years)**				
Under 25	5.0%	4.4%	6.0%	5.3%	Under 25	2.4%	0.5%	2.8%	2.4%
25-29	4.4	9.3	8.3	6.0	25-29	5.4	2.4	5.9	5.4
30-34	5.0	10.5	7.5	7.1	30-34	8.6	11.4	10.8	9.3
35-39	5.3	10.6	6.7	6.9	35-39	10.4	13.3	12.8	11.2
40-44	7.6	10.4	8.7	8.6	40-44	12.1	12.5	12.8	12.3
45-49	9.8	11.2	10.6	10.4	45-49	11.9	12.4	11.6	11.8
50-54	11.2	11.7	11.2	11.3	50-54	12.0	14.8	11.8	12.0
55-59	9.4	8.8	8.1	8.8	55-59	9.6	9.6	8.0	9.2
60-64	7.5	5.7	6.6	6.8	60-64	7.5	7.0	5.7	6.9
65 and over	23.5	8.1	15.3	17.1	65 and over	10.9	5.6	8.7	10.1
No Answer	11.3	9.5	11.1	10.9	No Answer	9.4	10.7	9.2	9.4
Total	**100.0**	**100.0**	**100.0**	**100.0**	**Total**	**100.0**	**100.0**	**100.0**	**100.0**
Highest Education Level					**Highest Education Level**				
8th Grade or Less	0.8%	0.2%	0.6%	0.6%	8th Grade or Less	1.0%	0.2%	0.6%	0.9%
Some High School	2.8	0.4	1.5	1.8	Some High School	2.5	0.2	1.7	2.2
High School Graduate	20.0	4.8	11.3	13.4	High School Graduate	19.6	3.7	11.3	16.8
Technical/Trade School	6.8	2.8	4.4	5.0	Trade/Technical	8.5	3.5	5.8	7.6
Some College	26.3	18.9	24.5	24.2	Some College	25.6	17.4	23.6	24.8
College Graduate	17.7	29.2	23.9	22.5	College Graduate	19.9	28.9	23.1	21.0
Post Graduate	6.5	9.9	7.7	7.7	Post Graduate	5.8	9.5	7.8	6.4
Advanced Degree	12.7	18.6	20.0	18.8	Advanced Degree	11.8	30.3	20.6	14.8
No Answer	6.4	5.2	6.1	6.0	No Answer	5.5	6.3	5.6	5.5
Total	**100.0**	**100.0**	**100.0**	**100.0**	**Total**	**100.0**	**100.0**	**100.0**	**100.0**
Census Region					**Census Region**				
Northeast	21.7%	23.9%	21.9%	22.2%	Northeast	15.5%	24.3%	17.7%	16.4%
North Central	33.4	16.3	18.3	23.7	North Central	29.3	19.1	16.4	25.3
South	29.1	25.6	30.2	28.9	South	33.8	23.0	35.0	33.9
West	15.8	34.2	29.7	25.2	West	21.4	33.6	30.8	24.4
Total	**100.0**	**100.0**	**100.0**	**100.0**	**Total**	**100.0**	**100.0**	**100.0**	**100.0**
Race					**Race**				
White/Caucasian	83.8%	79.6%	72.9%	78.3%	White/Caucasian	85.7%	75.0%	76.3%	82.7%
Black/African-American	3.9	3.0	5.2	4.3	Black/African-American	2.1	3.9	3.9	2.7
Asian	0.9	5.6	8.0	4.9	Asian	0.8	9.7	6.8	2.7
Hispanic	2.3	3.0	4.3	3.3	Hispanic	3.4	1.6	4.4	3.6
Other	1.0	1.5	1.3	1.2	Other	1.2	1.8	1.3	1.2
No Answer	8.0	7.3	8.3	8.0	No Answer	6.8	8.0	7.3	7.1
Total	**100.0**	**100.0**	**100.0**	**100.0**	**Total**	**100.0**	**100.0**	**100.0**	**100.0**
How Many Children in Household					**How Many Children in Household**				
None	57.3%	55.1%	57.0%	56.7%	None	49.5%	38.5%	45.5%	48.1%
One	12.1	13.8	14.3	13.4	One	14.1	20.5	17.0	15.1
Two	9.7	14.0	10.4	10.8	Two	15.7	20.5	18.3	16.6
Three	2.8	3.4	3.0	3.0	Three	5.2	5.0	5.5	5.3
Four	0.6	0.6	0.6	0.6	Four	1.5	1.2	1.0	1.4
Five or More	0.4	0.2	0.4	0.3	Five or More	0.6	0.3	0.6	0.6
No Answer	17.1	12.9	14.3	15.1	No Answer	13.4	13.9	12.0	13.0
Total	**100.0**	**100.0**	**100.0**	**100.0**	**Total**	**100.0**	**100.0**	**100.0**	**100.0**
Median Household					**Median Household**				
Income	$61,784	$115,447	$68,146	$71,654	Income	$74,635	$177,658	$78,234	$76,438
Initial Quality					**Initial Quality**				
Study 2 Results	**140.5**	**136.9**	**133.0**	**136.6**	**Study 2 Results**	**160.7**	**180.2**	**150.8**	**158.2**
(Problems per 100 passenger cars)					(Problems per 100 passenger cars)				

NOTE: Study conducted among personal use buyers of 2001 model year vehicles.
(1) Domestic figures include captive import buyers.
(2) Import figures include North American assembled vehicle buyers.
SOURCE: J.D. Power and Associates, 2001 Vehicle Quality Survey

Passenger Car Operating Costs

PASSENGER CAR OPERATING COSTS, 1950-2001 MODEL YEARS

| | Variable Cost in Cents Per Mile | | | | Cost Per 10,000 Miles | | | |
Model Year	Gas & Oil	Maintenance	Tires	Total	Variable Cost	Fixed Cost	Total Cost	Total Cost Per Mile
2001	7.90¢	3.90¢	1.80¢	13.60¢	$1,360	$4,621	$5,981	59.81¢
2000	6.90	3.60	1.70	12.60	1,220	4,724	5,944	59.44
1999	5.60	3.30	1.70	10.60	1,060	4,660	5,720	57.20
1998	6.20	3.10	1.40	10.70	1,060	4,528	5,588	55.88
1997	6.60	2.80	1.40	10.80	1,090	4,348	5,438	54.38
1996	5.60	2.80	1.20	9.60	960	4,193	5,153	51.53
1995	5.80	2.60	1.20	9.60	960	4,005	4,965	49.65
1994	5.60	2.50	1.00	9.10	910	3,836	4,746	47.46
1993	5.90	2.40	0.90	9.20	920	3,722	4,642	46.42
1992	5.90	2.20	0.90	9.00	900	3,784	4,684	46.84
1991	6.60	2.20	0.90	9.70	970	3,566	4,536	45.36
1990	5.40	2.10	0.90	8.40	840	3,256	4,096	40.96
1989	5.30	1.90	0.80	7.00	800	2,920	3,720	37.20
1987	4.40	1.50	0.80	6.70	670	2,328	2,998	29.98
1985	5.57	1.20	0.65	7.42	742	2,061	2,803	28.03
1983	6.13	0.98	0.69	7.80	780	2,084	2,864	28.64
1981	6.27	1.18	0.72	8.17	817	2,375	3,192	31.92
1980	5.86	1.12	0.64	7.62	762	2,033	2,795	27.95
1979	4.11	1.10	0.65	5.86	586	1,811	2,397	23.97
1977	4.11	1.03	0.66	5.80	580	1,439	2,019	20.19
1975	4.82	0.97	0.66	6.45	645	1,186	1,831	18.31
1971	2.96	0.73	0.56	4.25	425	1,125	1,550	15.50
1969	2.76	0.68	0.51	3.95	395	1,053	1,448	14.48
1965	2.58	0.68	0.44	3.70	370	807	1,177	11.77
1960	2.62	0.79	0.49	3.90	390	808	1,198	11.98
1950	2.14	0.68	0.46	3.28	328	533	861	8.61

ANNUAL FIXED COST OF OPERATING A PASSENGER CAR, 1950-2001 MODEL YEARS

| | Insurance | | | | | | | |
Model Year	Fire & Theft[1]	Collision[2]	Property Damage & Liability[3]	License, Registration & Taxes	Depreciation	Finance Charge	Total	Average Fixed Cost Per Day
2001	$167	$345	$479	$208	$3,548	$866	$5,613	$15.38
2000	163	326	481	223	3,492	849	5,534	15.16
1999	162	324	484	226	3,436	828	5,460	14.96
1998	134	287	479	226	3,364	813	5,303	14.53
1997	120	326	401	216	3,272	768	5,103	13.98
1996	144	275	426	215	3,170	718	4,948	13.56
1995	121	252	410	203	3,073	686	4,745	13.00
1994	123	246	400	194	2,940	648	4,551	12.47
1993	116	243	385	178	2,830	670	4,422	12.12
1992	128	286	373	174	2,717	796	4,474	12.26
1991	108	247	353	168	2,504	266	3,646	9.99
1990	110	245	318	165	2,357	680	3,875	10.62
1989	102	234	309	144	2,018	588	3,395	9.30
1987	87	196	252	128	1,494	526	2,683	7.35
1985	75	177	213	110	1,262	534	2,371	6.50
1983	67	181	222	97	1,298	529	2,394	6.56
1981	76	180	254	88	1,287	490	2,375	6.51
1980	70	172	248	82	1,038	423	2,033	5.57
1979	74	168	241	90	942	296	1,811	4.96
1977	80	188	250	74	847	—	1,439	3.94
1975	53	141	189	30	773	—	1,186	3.25
1971	62	125	175	25	738	—	1,125	3.08
1969	44	102	154	24	729	—	1,053	2.88
1965	31	—	126	24	626	—	807	2.21
1960	30	—	110	22	646	—	808	2.21
1950	16	—	60	15	442	—	533	1.46

(1) No deductible prior to 1973; $50 deductible 1973-1977; $100 deductible 1978-1992; $250 deductible 1993-2001.
(2) $100 deductible 1967-1977; $250 deductible 1978-1992; $500 deductible 1993-2001.
(3) Coverage: 1949 to 1955-$15,000/$30,000; 1957 to 1965-$25,000/$50,000; 1967 to 2001-$100,000/$300,000
NOTE: Beginning in 1985 ownership costs are based on a six year /60,000 mile retention cycle rather than four year/60,000 miles.
SOURCE: American Automobile Association.

Light Truck Operating Costs

LIGHT TRUCK OPERATING COSTS, 1992-2001 MODEL YEARS

| Model Year | Variable Cost in Cents Per Mile | | | | Cost Per 10,000 Miles | | | |
	Gas & Oil	Maintenance	Tires	Total	Variable Cost	Fixed Cost	Total Cost	Total Cost Per Mile
2001	8.05¢	4.00¢	1.60¢	13.65¢	$1,310	$5,197	$6,507	65.07¢
2000	7.55	3.90	1.55	13.00	1,300	4,379	5,679	56.79
1999	6.15	3.60	1.35	11.10	1,110	5,312	6,422	64.22
1998	7.00	3.30	1.35	11.65	1,165	5,208	6,373	63.73
1997	7.40	3.00	1.35	11.75	1,185	5,028	6,213	62.13
1996	6.30	3.00	1.35	10.65	1,065	4,831	5,896	58.96
1995	5.95	2.65	1.30	9.90	990	3,854	4,844	48.44
1994	6.00	2.60	1.00	9.60	688	3,676	4,364	43.64
1993	6.05	2.25	0.90	9.20	920	3,663	4,583	45.83
1992	6.00	2.10	0.90	9.00	900	3,551	4,451	44.51

ANNUAL FIXED COST OF OPERATING A LIGHT TRUCK, 1992-2001 MODEL YEARS

| Model Year | Insurance | | Property Damage & Liability | License, Registration & Taxes | Depreciation | Finance Charge | Total | Average Fixed Cost Per Day |
	Fire & Theft	Collision						
2001	$182	$423	$389	$285	$3,720	$980	$5,979	$16.38
2000	202	491	481	355	2,940	638	5,107	13.99
1999	205	455	484	401	3,558	924	6,027	16.51
1998	205	447	479	388	3,483	907	5,909	16.19
1997	209	435	401	357	3,426	890	5,718	15.67
1996	138	311	426	356	3,378	885	5,494	15.05
1995	104	241	410	277	2,857	671	4,560	12.49
1994	91	206	400	288	2,745	637	4,367	11.96
1993	107	226	385	306	2,634	688	4,346	11.91
1992	108	259	373	180	2,476	806	4,202	11.51

NOTE: Ownership costs are based on a six year /60,000 mile retention cycle rather than four year/60,000 miles.
SOURCE: American Automobile Association.

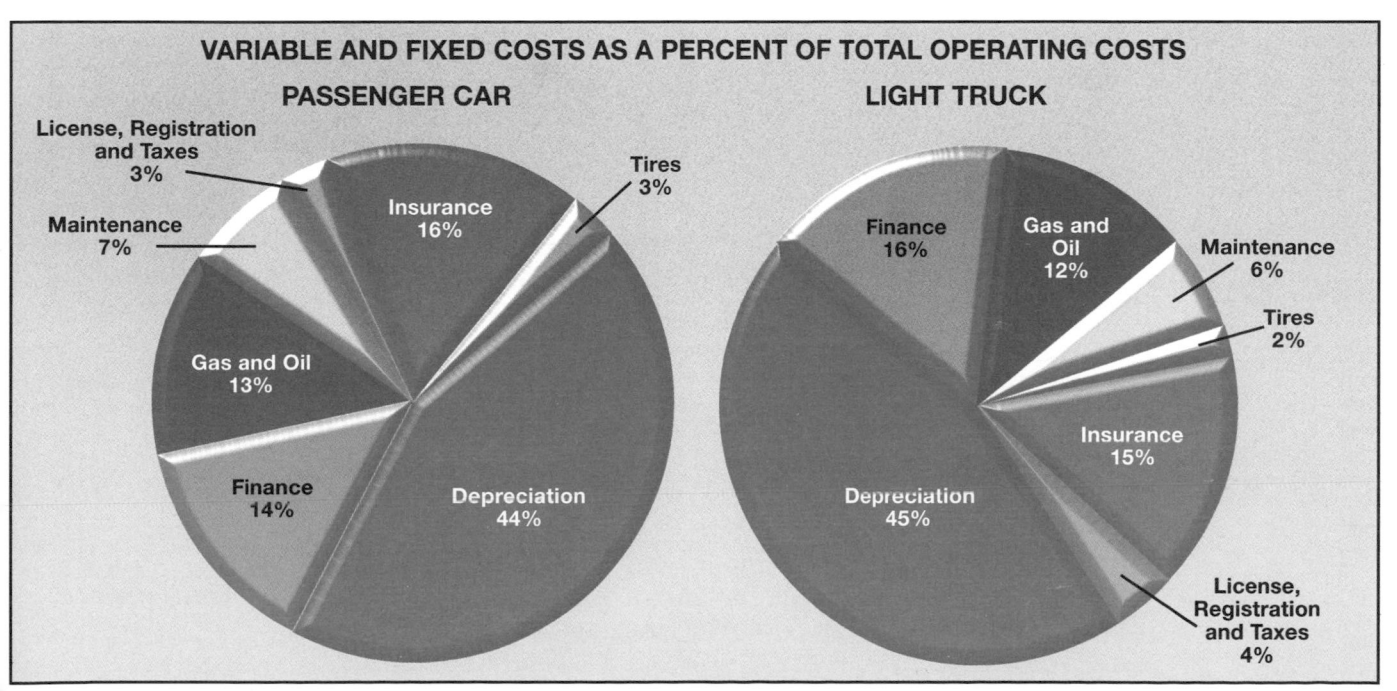

VARIABLE AND FIXED COSTS AS A PERCENT OF TOTAL OPERATING COSTS

PASSENGER CAR

- License, Registration and Taxes 3%
- Maintenance 7%
- Gas and Oil 13%
- Finance 14%
- Insurance 16%
- Tires 3%
- Depreciation 44%

LIGHT TRUCK

- Finance 16%
- Gas and Oil 12%
- Maintenance 6%
- Tires 2%
- Insurance 15%
- Depreciation 45%
- License, Registration and Taxes 4%

Automobile Financing

NEW AND USED CAR FINANCING WITH FINANCE COMPANIES, 1980-2000

Year	Average Interest Rate	Average Maturity (Months)	Average Amount Financed	Average Monthly Payment
NEW CARS				
2000	6.3%	55.9	$21,080	$436.12
1999	6.75	2.7	19,880	436.49
1998	6.35	2.1	19,083	419.60
1997	7.15	4.1	18,077	391.45
1996	9.85	1.6	16,987	404.75
1995	11.25	4.1	16,210	382.98
1994	9.85	4.0	15,375	353.25
1993	9.55	4.5	14,332	324.79
1992	9.85	4.0	13,607	313.01
1990	12.65	4.6	12,071	291.31
1988	12.65	6.2	11,663	275.95
1986	9.45	0.0	10,665	258.74
1984	14.64	8.3	9,337	256.90
1982	15.94	6.0	8,178	238.16
1980	14.8	45.0	6,322	183.91
USED CARS				
2000	13.7%	57.1	$14,152	$338.71
1999	12.65	5.9	13,642	324.15
1998	12.65	3.5	12,691	311.51
1997	13.35	1.0	12,281	316.54
1996	13.55	1.4	12,182	313.39
1995	14.55	2.2	11,590	300.66
1994	13.55	0.2	10,709	280.37
1993	12.84	8.8	9,875	260.63
1992	13.74	7.9	9,211	250.70
1990	16.04	6.1	8,289	249.35
1988	15.14	6.7	7,824	222.68
1986	16.04	2.6	6,555	202.52
1984	17.93	9.7	5,691	190.92
1982	20.83	7.0	4,746	174.84
1980	19.1	34.8	3,810	143.44

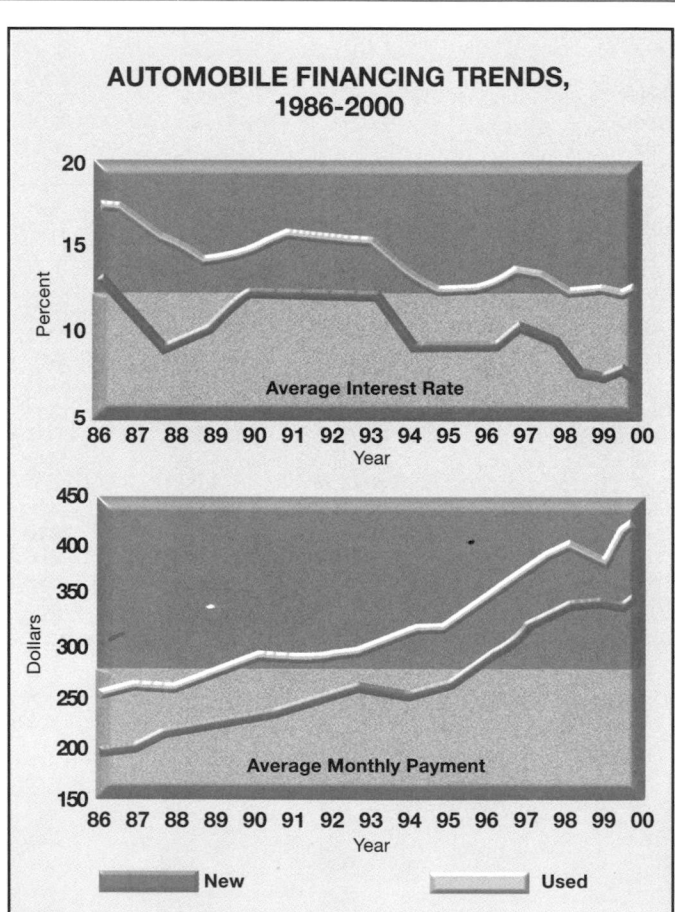

AUTOMOBILE FINANCING TRENDS, 1986-2000

CONSUMER CREDIT OUTSTANDING BY HOLDER, 1980-2000 (In Millions)

Year	Commercial Banks	Finance Companies	Credit Unions	Savings Institutions	Nonfinancial Business	Other	Total
2000	1,468,565	512,411	191,457	176,542	61,410	73,896	2,484,281
1999	1,352,749	487,496	172,556	160,466	57,265	69,364	2,299,895
1998	1,267,858	497,506	159,111	152,971	49,020	68,409	2,194,874
1997	1,213,714	511,229	155,847	147,773	46,796	70,173	2,145,532
1996	1,150,416	506,041	153,545	137,238	42,709	73,362	2,063,311
1995	1,034,389	475,268	142,137	125,638	38,882	80,081	1,896,395
1994	900,762	420,029	124,884	109,061	37,906	74,961	1,667,604
1993	805,872	372,133	112,361	95,944	37,253	66,627	1,490,191
1992	776,986	358,547	118,022	89,889	38,384	62,293	1,444,121
1991	783,293	369,452	126,454	88,934	46,156	62,983	1,477,272
1990	787,212	377,178	136,436	90,972	56,172	64,843	1,512,813
1985	558,189	278,092	100,391	71,114	51,186	57,406	1,116,377
1980	347,673	180,672	60,295	44,252	20,908	41,546	695,346

Personal Consumption Expenditures for Transportation

AVERAGE EXPENDITURE PER NEW CAR, 1967-2000

	Average Expenditure Per New Car[1]			Estimated Average New Car Price for a 1967 "Comparable Car"		Annual Median Family Earnings[4]	Average New Car Expend-iture[5]	Weeks of Median Family Earnings to Equal Cost of "Comparable Car"	
Year	Domestic*	Import	Average	With Added Safety & Emissions Equipment[2]	Without Added Safety & Emissions Equipment[3]			With Added Safety & Emissions Equipment[6]	Without Added Safety & Emissions Equipment[7]
2000	18,684	25,971	20,355	13,178	9,157	53,983	19.6	12.7	8.8
1999	18,630	28,931	20,658	13,163	9,157	50,784	21.2	13.5	9.4
1998	18,479	29,614	20,364	13,205	9,233	48,000	22.1	14.3	10.0
1997	17,907	27,722	19,531	13,240	9,297	45,326	22.4	15.2	10.7
1996	17,468	26,205	18,777	13,184	9,281	42,789	22.8	16.0	11.3
1995	16,864	23,202	17,959	12,857	9,115	40,572	23.0	16.5	11.7
1994	16,930	21,989	17,903	12,429	8,925	38,178	24.4	16.9	12.2
1993	15,976	20,261	16,871	11,808	8,631	36,764	23.9	16.7	12.2
1992	15,644	18,593	16,636	11,488	8,424	35,672	24.3	16.7	12.3
1991	15,192	16,327	15,475	11,187	8,224	34,775	23.1	16.7	12.3
1989	13,936	15,510	14,371	10,282	7,825	32,448	23.0	16.5	12.5
1987	12,922	14,470	13,386	9,775	7,518	29,744	23.4	17.1	13.1
1985	11,589	12,853	11,838	9,014	6,958	27,144	22.7	17.3	13.3
1983	10,516	10,868	10,606	8,415	6,544	24,580	22.4	17.8	13.8
1981	8,912	8,806	8,010	7,720	6,115	22,388	20.7	17.9	14.2
1979	6,889	6,704	6,847	6,198	5,337	19,661	18.1	16.4	14.1
1977	5,985	5,072	5,814	5,292	4,593	16,009	18.9	17.2	14.9
1975	5,084	4,384	4,950	4,689	4,103	13,719	18.8	17.8	15.6
1973	4,181	3,344	4,052	3,903	3,572	12,051	17.5	16.8	15.4
1971	3,919	2,769	3,742	3,777	3,601	10,285	18.9	19.1	18.2
1969	3,697	2,496	3,557	3,464	3,357	9,433	19.6	19.1	18.5
1967	3,313	2,276	3,216	3,196	3,185	7,933	21.1	20.9	20.9

* Includes transplants
(1) U.S. Departments of Commerce, Bureau of Economic Analysis (BEA), "Average Transaction Price Per New Car." Includes purchases by business, government, and consumers.
(2) 1967 "Average Transaction Price" plus the value of added safety and emissions equipment as determined by the U.S. Bureau of Labor Statistics (BLS), all inflated to current dollars using the BLS, "New Car Consumer Price Index - All Urban Consumers." For example, 1969 is equal to the 1968 value plus the BLS stated value of added safety and emissions equipment for the 1969 model year multiplied by 1968-1969 monthly changes in the New Car Consumer Price Index. The cost to improve fuel economy, which prior to 1980 was included with "Other Quality Adjustments," has since been included by the BLS with the cost of emissions improvements.
(3) 1967 "Average Transaction Price" inflated to current dollars.
(4) BLS, "Median Family Earnings."
(5) "Average Expenditure," as reported by the BEA, divided by "Annual Median Family Earnings," multiplied by 52 weeks. This index is not a good reflection car prices because it includes upgrading - the purchase of more expensive types of vehicles with more options - and downgrading.
(6) "Estimated Average New Car Price of Comparable Cars With New Safety and Emissions Equipment Added," divided by "Annual Median Family Earnings," multiplied by 52 weeks. This index is a good reflection of price as seen by car purchasers who would not otherwise buy safety / emissions equipment.
(7) "Estimated Average New Car Price of Comparable Cars Without New Safety and Emissions Equipment" divided by "Annual Median Family Earnings," multiplied by 52 weeks. This index is a good reflection of price as seen by purchasers who place full value on new safety/emissions equipment.

INDICES OF CONSUMER COSTS, 1980-2000

	Consumer Price Index - All Urban Consumers (1982-4 = 100)							Calculated New Car Index With Added Safety & Emissions*
Year	All Items	Housing	Medical Care	Public Transportation	Gasoline	Used Cars	New Cars	
2000	172.2	169.6	260.8	209.6	128.6	155.8	139.6	156.7
1999	166.6	163.9	250.6	197.7	100.1	152.0	139.6	156.5
1998	163.0	160.4	242.1	190.3	91.6	150.6	140.7	157.0
1997	160.5	156.8	234.6	186.7	105.8	151.1	141.7	157.4
1996	156.9	152.8	228.2	181.9	105.9	157.1	141.5	156.7
1995	152.4	148.5	220.5	175.9	99.8	156.5	139.0	152.9
1994	148.2	144.8	211.0	172.0	98.2	141.7	136.0	147.8
1993	144.5	141.2	201.4	167.0	97.7	133.9	131.5	140.4
1992	140.3	137.5	190.1	151.4	99.0	123.2	128.4	136.6
1991	136.2	133.6	177.0	148.9	99.2	118.1	125.3	133.0
1990	130.7	128.5	162.8	142.6	101.0	117.6	121.0	126.2
1986	109.6	110.9	122.0	117.0	77.0	108.8	110.6	112.1
1984	103.9	103.6	106.8	105.7	97.8	112.5	102.8	103.6
1982	96.5	96.9	92.5	94.9	102.8	88.8	97.4	96.4
1980	82.4	81.1	74.9	69.0	97.5	62.3	88.4	81.9

*Calculated by Ward's Communications. SOURCE: U.S. Department of Labor, Bureau of Labor Statistics.

Personal Consumption Expenditures for Transportation

PERSONAL CONSUMPTION EXPENDITURES FOR TRANSPORTATION, 1988-2000 (In Millions)

	1988	1990	1992	1994	1996	1998	1999	2000
User-Operated Transportation								
New Autos	$101,041	$96,692	$78,016	$86,478	$81,872	$87,771	$97,349	$101,895
Net Purchases of Used Autos	30,532	33,663	31,176	43,001	51,436	55,313	58,738	59,556
Other Motor Vehicles*	45,577	49,586	60,523	77,682	84,349	104,048	119,859	130,526
Tires, Tubes, Accessories and Parts	20,685	22,483	30,523	35,165	38,654	41,709	44,779	47,754
Repair, Greasing, Washing, Parking, Storage and Rental	73,531	82,538	90,293	109,980	134,175	153,119	162,115	173,090
Gasoline and Oil	86,899	108,471	104,880	108,955	124,160	115,238	128,336	162,444
Bridge, Tunnel, Ferry and Road Tolls	1,774	2,024	2,839	3,255	3,726	4,176	4,351	4,717
Insurance Premiums, Less Claims Paid	16,842	18,066	25,728	27,767	31,781	38,002	39,066	40,141
Total User-Operated Transportation	**$376,881**	**$413,523**	**$423,978**	**$492,283**	**$550,153**	**$599,376**	**$654,593**	**$720,123**
Purchased Local Transportation								
Transit Systems	$5,377	$5,707	$6,463	$7,091	$7,691	$8,010	$8,239	$9,035
Taxicabs	2,935	3,209	2,586	2,953	3,530	4,053	4,025	3,927
Total Purchased Local Transportation	**$8,312**	**$8,916**	**$9,049**	**$10,044**	**$11,221**	**$12,063**	**$12,264**	**$12,962**
Purchased Intercity Transportation								
Railway Excluding Commutation	$588	$708	$647	$603	$642	$712	$747	$838
Bus	2,181	1,396	1,595	1,518	1,769	2,087	2,174	2,337
Airline	22,993	26,467	21,281	23,665	26,183	29,511	30,717	34,230
Other	2,229	2,644	3,592	4,025	4,677	4,858	5,053	5,359
Total Purchased Intercity Transportation	**$27,991**	**$31,215**	**$27,115**	**$29,811**	**$33,271**	**$37,168**	**$38,691**	**$42,764**
Total Transportation Expenditures	**$413,184**	**$453,654**	**$460,142**	**$532,138**	**$594,645**	**$648,607**	**$705,548**	**$775,849**
Total Personal Consumption Expenditures	**$3,296,126**	**$3,748,417**	**$4,209,653**	**$4,716,394**	**$5,237,499**	**$5,850,863**	**$6,268,650**	**$6,757,276**

*New and used trucks, recreation vehicles, etc.
SOURCE: U.S. Department of Commerce, Bureau of Economic Analysis.

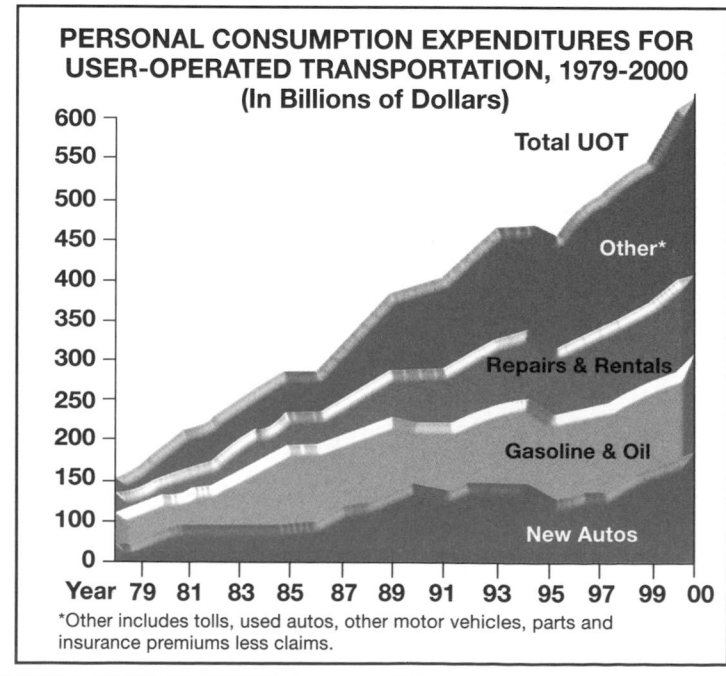

PERSONAL CONSUMPTION EXPENDITURES FOR USER-OPERATED TRANSPORTATION, 1979-2000 (In Billions of Dollars)

*Other includes tolls, used autos, other motor vehicles, parts and insurance premiums less claims.

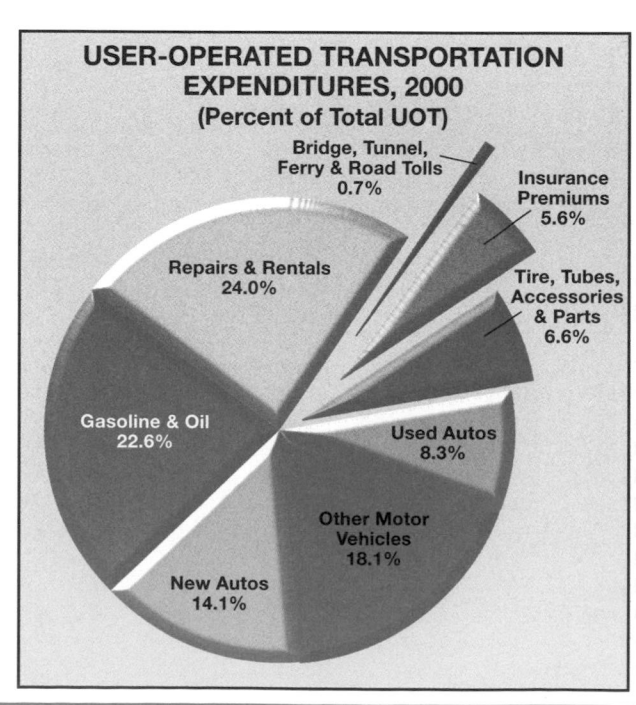

USER-OPERATED TRANSPORTATION EXPENDITURES, 2000 (Percent of Total UOT)

- Bridge, Tunnel, Ferry & Road Tolls 0.7%
- Insurance Premiums 5.6%
- Tire, Tubes, Accessories & Parts 6.6%
- Repairs & Rentals 24.0%
- Gasoline & Oil 22.6%
- Used Autos 8.3%
- Other Motor Vehicles 18.1%
- New Autos 14.1%

U.S. Motor Vehicle Thefts by State, Area and Year

MOTOR VEHICLE THEFTS BY STATE, 1998-1999

State	1998	1999	Percent Change	State	1998	1999	Percent Change
Alabama	14,871	13,134	-11.68	Montana	2,014	1,896	-5.86
Alaska	2,607	2,658	1.96	Nebraska	5,788	5,440	-6.01
Arizona	40,391	38,247	-5.31	Nevada	13,766	13,094	-4.88
Arkansas	7,187	6,664	-7.28	New Hampshire	1,474	1,354	-8.14
California	195,517	168,480	-13.83	New Jersey	35,185	35,357	0.49
Colorado	16,087	14,795	-8.03	New Mexico	10,767	8,126	-24.53
Connecticut	12,705	11,297	-11.08	New York	68,171	58,261	-14.54
Delaware	3,186	3,043	-4.49	North Carolina	24,616	25,577	3.90
Dist. of Columbia	6,501	6,652	2.32	North Dakota	1,127	1,036	-8.07
Florida	104,250	93,191	-10.61	Ohio	43,021	39,192	-8.90
Georgia	42,538	40,120	-5.68	Oklahoma	13,565	13,132	-3.19
Hawaii	5,594	4,660	-16.70	Oregon	17,262	13,633	-21.02
Idaho	2,282	1,898	-16.83	Pennsylvania	42,668	39,234	-8.05
Illinois	52,932	52,114	-1.55	Rhode Island	3,829	4,032	5.30
Indiana	21,187	20,290	-4.23	South Carolina	15,948	14,445	-9.42
Iowa	5,974	5,135	-14.04	South Dakota	763	861	12.84
Kansas	5,988	6,048	1.00	Tennessee	28,099	25,255	-10.12
Kentucky	8,573	8,631	0.68	Texas	96,646	92,037	-4.77
Louisiana	23,661	21,695	-8.31	Utah	7,700	7,382	-4.13
Maine	1,509	1,694	12.26	Vermont	874	912	4.35
Maryland	28,212	25,447	-9.80	Virginia	18,355	17,953	-2.19
Massachusetts	26,403	25,628	-2.94	Washington	35,200	33,807	-3.96
Michigan	58,338	56,800	-2.64	West Virginia	3,390	3,762	10.97
Minnesota	15,366	13,275	-13.61	Wisconsin	14,210	13,819	-2.75
Mississippi	9,322	13,532	45.16	Wyoming	669	596	-10.91
Missouri	24,466	22,984	-6.06	Total	1,317,324	1,148,305	-12.83

SOURCE: Federal Bureau of Investigation.

MOTOR VEHICLE THEFTS, 1970-1999

Year	Thefts*	Motor Vehicle Registrations	Ratio of Vehicles Stolen/Registered	Year	Thefts*	Motor Vehicle Registrations	Ratio of Vehicles Stolen/Registered
1999	1,148,305	209,509,161	1 in 182	1980	1,114,651	139,831,316	1 in 125
1998	1,317,324	205,042,639	1 in 156	1975	1,000,500	120,053,445	1 in 120
1997	1,353,707	201,070,397	1 in 149	1970	921,400	98,135,968	1 in 107
1996	1,394,238	198,293,459	1 in 142				
1995	1,472,441	193,440,393	1 in 131				
1994	1,539,287	188,713,997	1 in 123				
1993	1,563,060	186,315,464	1 in 119				
1991	1,661,738	181,505,929	1 in 109				
1990	1,635,907	179,299,202	1 in 109				
1989	1,564,800	175,960,035	1 in 112				
1988	1,432,916	171,740,576	1 in 120				
1987	1,288,674	167,193,088	1 in 130				
1986	1,224,137	162,093,594	1 in 132				
1985	1,102,862	157,049,215	1 in 142				
1984	1,032,165	152,161,512	1 in 147				
1983	1,007,933	147,104,519	1 in 146				

* Includes cars, motorcycles, trucks and buses.

TOP TEN AUTO THEFT AREAS, 1999

1	Miami, Florida
2	Detroit, Michigan
3	Phoenix, Arizona
4	Jersey City, New Jersey
5	Seattle, Washington
6	Albuquerque, New Mexico
7	Fresno, California
8	Jackson, Mississippi
9	Las Vegas, Nevada
10	New Orleans, Louisiana

SOURCE: National Insurance Crime Bureau

Vehicle Miles of Travel and Fuel Consumption

VEHICLE MILES OF TRAVEL AND FUEL CONSUMPTION, 1960-1999

	Passenger Vehicles				Trucks			All Motor Vehicles
	Passenger Cars	Light Trucks	Buses	Total	Single Unit Trucks	Combination Trucks	Total	
VEHICLE MILES OF TRAVEL (In Millions)								
1999	1,569,270	901,121	7,663	2,478,054	70,311	132,386	202,697	2,680,751
1998	1,549,577	868,275	7,007	2,424,859	68,021	128,359	196,380	2,621,239
1997	1,502,556	850,739	6,842	2,360,137	66,893	124,584	191,477	2,551,614
1996	1,469,854	816,540	6,563	2,292,957	64,072	118,899	182,971	2,475,928
1994	1,416,329	764,634	6,409	2,187,372	61,284	108,932	170,216	2,357,588
1990	1,417,823	574,571	5,726	1,998,120	51,901	94,341	146,242	2,144,362
1985	1,255,884	390,961	4,478	1,651,323	45,441	78,063	123,504	1,774,827
1980	1,121,810	290,935	6,059	1,418,804	39,813	68,678	108,491	1,527,295
1970	919,679	123,286	4,544	1,047,509	27,081	35,134	62,215	1,109,724
1960	587,012	N.A.	4,346	N.A.	N.A.	28,854	28,854	718,762
AVERAGE ANNUAL MILES TRAVELED PER VEHICLE								
1999	11,850	11,958	10,515	34,323	12,201	65,261	77,462	21,208
1998	11,754	12,173	9,793	33,720	11,861	64,265	76,126	12,211
1997	11,581	12,115	9,809	11,768	12,637	69,601	27,032	12,107
1996	11,330	11,811	9,446	11,497	12,167	68,075	26,092	11,813
1994	10,759	12,156	9,560	11,205	12,491	64,783	25,838	11,683
1990	10,277	11,902	9,133	10,693	11,567	55,206	23,603	11,107
1985	9,419	10,506	7,545	9,649	9,893	55,629	20,597	10,020
1980	8,813	10,437	11,458	9,112	9,103	48,472	18,736	9,458
1970	9,989	8,676	12,035	9,821	7,356	38,819	13,565	9,976
1960	9,518	N.A.	15,970	N.A.	N.A.	N.A.	10,693	9,732
FUEL CONSUMED (Millions of Gallons)								
1999	73,160	52,771	1,146	127,077	7,122	26,240	33,362	160,652
1998	71,695	50,462	1,040	123,197	6,817	25,157	31,974	155,379
1997	69,892	49,388	1,027	119,280	9,576	20,302	29,878	150,386
1996	69,221	47,354	990	116,575	9,408	20,193	29,601	147,365
1994	68,079	44,112	964	113,155	9,032	18,653	27,685	140,839
1990	69,759	35,611	895	106,266	8,357	16,133	24,490	130,755
1985	71,700	27,363	834	99,897	7,399	14,005	21,404	121,301
1980	70,186	23,796	1,018	95,000	6,923	13,037	19,960	114,960
1970	67,879	12,313	820	81,013	3,968	7,348	11,316	92,329
1960	41,171	N.A.	827	N.A.	N.A.	N.A.	15,882	57,880
AVERAGE ANNUAL FUEL CONSUMPTION PER VEHICLE (Gallons)								
1999	552	700	1,573	2,825	1,236	12,935	14,171	729
1998	544	707	1,454	2,705	1,189	12,596	13,785	721
1997	539	703	1,472	596	1,809	11,342	4,218	711
1996	534	685	1,425	586	1,787	11,561	4,221	700
1994	517	701	1,438	580	1,841	11,093	4,202	698
1990	506	738	1,428	569	1,862	9,441	3,953	677
1985	538	735	1,405	584	1,611	9,980	3,570	685
1980	551	854	1,926	610	1,583	9,201	3,447	712
1970	737	866	2,172	760	1,078	8,119	2,467	830
1960	668	N.A.	3,039	N.A.	N.A.	N.A.	1,333	784

*Passenger cars include motorcycles through 1994.
N.A.-Not available.
SOURCE: U.S. Department of Transportation, Federal Highway Administration.

Annual Motor Vehicle Miles of Travel

VEHICLE MILES OF TRAVEL, 1999 (In Millions)

	Rural Interstate	Total Rural	Urban Interstate	Total Urban	Total
Alabama	6,029	28,799	5,788	27,366	56,165
Alaska	827	2,373	556	2,172	4,545
Arizona	6,765	16,723	4,343	30,106	46,829
Arkansas	3,807	18,982	2,550	10,265	29,247
California	15,198	58,470	60,435	241,596	300,066
Colorado	4,777	16,218	4,772	24,514	40,732
Connecticut	1,703	7,434	7,982	22,492	29,926
Delaware	0	3,518	1,402	5,024	8,542
Dist. of Columbia	0	0	481	3,462	3,462
Florida	11,755	37,377	17,252	104,526	141,903
Georgia	10,344	42,904	16,057	55,955	98,859
Hawaii	88	2,427	1,684	5,689	8,116
Idaho	2,082	8,979	1,040	4,997	13,976
Illinoio	10,288	31,243	18,596	71,151	102,394
Indiana	8,520	35,967	7,444	34,074	70,041
Iowa	4,440	18,739	2,056	10,399	29,138
Kansas	3,380	14,578	3,076	13,121	27,699
Kentucky	6,147	27,461	5,828	20,355	47,816
Louisiana	5,462	22,700	4,978	18,505	41,205
Maine	2,302	10,454	631	3,689	14,143
Maryland	3,710	15,487	10,789	33,639	49,126
Massachusetts	2,504	8,712	12,627	43,108	51,820
Michigan	7,179	37,039	13,814	58,605	95,644
Minnesota	4,211	25,061	7,200	26,349	51,410
Mississippi	4,127	24,102	2,013	10,778	34,880
Missouri	6,840	30,167	10,835	36,568	66,735
Montana	2,163	7,602	256	2,233	9,835
Nebraska	2,689	11,225	931	6,786	18,011
Nevada	1,910	6,148	2,072	11,243	17,391
New Hampshire	1,693	7,006	943	4,888	11,894
New Jersey	2,485	12,811	10,207	52,729	65,540
New Mexico	4,569	14,054	1,831	8,308	22,362
New York	7,184	36,549	17,076	89,942	126,491
North Carolina	8,202	43,519	8,897	44,240	87,759
North Dakota	1,241	5,441	249	1,821	7,262
Ohio	10,037	41,503	19,570	63,984	105,487
Oklahoma	4,762	21,302	4,073	21,267	42,569
Oregon	4,378	18,421	3,916	16,259	34,680
Pennsylvania	10,982	45,614	11,355	56,400	102,014
Rhode Island	375	1,103	1,787	7,180	8,283
South Carolina	8,081	27,862	3,344	16,284	44,146
South Dakota	1,886	6,374	341	1,870	8,244
Tennessee	9,133	29,436	8,761	35,319	64,755
Texas	15,668	70,374	31,641	140,500	210,874
Utah	3,291	8,331	4,110	13,713	22,044
Vermont	1,204	4,578	360	2,289	6,867
Virginia	9,338	31,343	11,466	42,561	73,904
Washington	4,478	16,887	10,085	35,827	52,714
West Virginia	3,657	13,778	1,389	5,255	19,033
Wisconsin	6,040	30,697	3,785	26,263	56,960
Wyoming	2,273	5,758	312	2,039	7,797
U.S. Total	**260,204**	**1,063,630**	**382,986**	**1,627,705**	**2,691,335**

NOTE: Includes travel by motorcycle.
SOURCE: U.S. Department of Transportation, Federal Highway Administration.

TOTAL VEHICLE MILES TRAVELED, 1938-1999 (In Billions)

Year	Rural	Urban	Total	% Change
1999	1,063	1,628	2,691	2.5
1998	1,033	1,592	2,625	3.5
1997	985	1,547	2,532	2.0
1996	960	1,522	2,482	2.5
1995	933	1,489	2,422	2.7
1994	909	1,449	2,358	2.7
1993	887	1,410	2,297	2.2
1992	884	1,363	2,247	3.4
1991	884	1,289	2,173	1.2
1990	870	1,277	2,147	1.9
1989	849	1,258	2,107	4.0
1988	818	1,208	2,026	5.5
1987	780	1,141	1,921	4.7
1986	748	1,087	1,835	3.4
1985	730	1,044	1,774	3.1
1984	718	1,002	1,720	4.1
1983	701	952	1,653	3.6
1982	689	906	1,595	2.7
1981	686	867	1,553	1.7
1980	672	855	1,527	-0.2
1979	676	854	1,530	-0.9
1978	682	862	1,544	5.2
1977	651	816	1,467	4.6
1976	625	777	1,402	5.6
1975	602	726	1,328	3.8
1973	606	707	1,313	4.2
1972	590	670	1,260	6.9
1971	573	606	1,179	6.3
1970	539	570	1,109	4.5
1969	524	537	1,061	4.4
1968	506	510	1,016	5.4
1967	481	483	964	4.1
1966	476	450	926	4.3
1965	464	424	888	5.0
1964	441	405	846	5.1
1963	420	385	805	5.0
1962	399	368	767	3.9
1961	398	340	738	2.6
1960	387	332	719	2.6
1959	377	324	701	5.4
1958	358	307	665	2.8
1957	350	297	647	2.5
1956	344	287	631	4.1
1955	331	275	606	7.8
1954	314	248	562	3.3
1953	308	236	544	6.0
1952	289	224	513	4.5
1951	268	223	491	7.2
1950	240	218	458	8.0
1949	219	205	424	6.5
1948	199	199	398	7.3
1947	187	184	371	8.8
1946	171	170	341	36.4
1944	102	111	213	2.4
1942	130	138	268	-19.8
1940	152	150	302	6.0
1938	135	136	271	0.4

Selected Travel Data by State

TRAVEL DATA BY STATE, 1999

State	Resident Population in Thousands	Population Per Vehicle	Annual Miles Traveled Per Vehicle	Annual Miles Traveled Per Licensed Driver	Public Road and Street Mileage Rural	Public Road and Street Mileage Urban	Public Road and Street Mileage Total	State Gasoline Tax Rate
Alabama	4,370	1.27	14,224	16,303	73,589	20,657	94,246	18.0¢
Alaska	620	1.35	7,986	9,923	10,858	1,808	12,666	8.0
Arizona	4,778	1.45	13,002	14,207	37,178	17,278	54,456	18.0
Arkansas	2,551	1.33	16,146	15,193	86,957	10,602	97,559	18.6
California	33,145	1.59	11,403	14,405	83,185	83,787	166,972	18.0
Colorado	4,056	1.36	10,573	13,622	70,902	14,247	85,149	22.0
Connecticut	3,282	1.38	10,858	12,611	9,014	11,774	20,788	32.0
Delaware	754	1.37	13,920	15,503	3,779	1,969	5,748	23.0
District of Columbia	519	1.49	14,865	9,948	0	1,426	1,426	20.0
Florida	15,111	1.22	12,507	11,445	67,636	48,321	115,957	13.1
Georgia	7,788	1.42	14,214	18,072	86,434	27,458	113,892	7.5
Hawaii	1,185	1.58	11,368	10,793	2,362	1,895	4,257	16.0
Idaho	1,252	1.44	12,411	16,028	41,798	4,004	45,802	25.0
Illinois	12,128	1.53	10,967	12,922	102,053	36,192	138,245	19.0
Indiana	5,943	1.54	12,809	18,169	73,664	19,942	93,606	15.0
Iowa	2,869	1.48	9,579	15,058	103,385	9,519	112,904	20.0
Kansas	2,654	1.40	12,474	14,648	123,791	10,171	133,962	18.0
Kentucky	3,961	1.49	18,047	17,983	63,041	11,079	74,120	16.4
Louisiana	4,372	1.58	11,829	14,919	46,886	13,942	60,828	20.0
Maine	1,253	1.38	15,499	15,524	20,033	2,632	22,665	19.0
Maryland	5,172	1.62	12,646	15,381	16,000	14,321	30,321	23.5
Massachusetts	6,175	1.40	9,738	11,724	12,202	23,063	35,265	21.0
Michigan	9,864	1.44	11,573	13,938	91,791	29,931	121,722	19.0
Minnesota	4,776	1.64	12,868	17,691	116,044	15,955	131,999	20.0
Mississippi	2,769	1.55	15,124	19,508	65,386	7,933	73,319	18.4
Missouri	5,468	1.42	15,199	17,383	106,460	16,369	122,829	17.0
Montana	883	1.34	9,883	14,924	67,078	2,585	69,663	27.0
Nebraska	1,666	1.39	11,518	14,997	87,622	5,175	92,797	22.8
Nevada	1,809	1.37	14,984	13,165	30,082	5,788	35,870	24.75
New Hampshire	1,201	1.31	11,336	12,956	12,244	2,931	15,175	19.5
New Jersey	8,143	1.47	10,776	11,809	11,778	24,166	35,944	10.5
New Meico	1,740	1.43	14,216	18,329	53,839	6,074	59,913	18.5
New York	18,197	1.71	11,816	11,904	71,746	40,915	112,661	22.05
North Carolina	7,651	1.39	15,504	15,982	75,906	23,395	99,301	21.2
North Dakota	633	1.39	10,343	15,890	84,781	1,835	86,616	20.0
Ohio	11,257	1.40	10,343	13,112	82,874	33,494	116,368	22.0
Oklahoma	3,358	1.45	14,602	18,412	99,225	13,285	112,510	17.0
Oregon	3,316	1.35	11,559	14,097	55,977	10,902	66,879	12.0
Pennsylvania	11,994	1.41	11,368	12,034	85,096	34,285	119,381	7.0
Rhode Island	991	1.44	11,116	12,039	1,333	4,719	6,052	2.0
South Carolina	3,886	1.38	14,664	15,716	54,283	10,621	64,904	3.0
South Dakota	733	1.35	10,579	15,182	81,431	1,981	83,412	8.0
Tennessee	5,483	1.31	14,686	15,510	69,536	17,723	87,259	20.0
Teas	20,044	1.50	15,077	15,785	218,537	81,970	300,507	20.0
Utah	2,130	1.48	13,987	15,319	34,142	7,316	41,458	24.5
Vermont	594	1.20	13,316	13,873	12,890	1,376	14,266	20.0
Virginia	6,873	1.45	12,626	15,631	51,325	19,000	70,325	17.5
Washington	5,756	1.39	108,621	12,770	62,062	18,194	80,256	23.0
West Virginia	1,807	1.42	13,832	14,951	33,116	3,224	36,340	25.35
Wisconsin	5,250	1.41	13,394	15,262	95,366	16,540	111,906	25.4
Wyoming	480	1.33	14,838	21,539	24,484	2,295	26,779	14.0
Total	**272,690**	**1.46**	**12,484**	**14,379**	**3,071,181**	**846,064**	**3,917,245**	

SOURCE: U.S. Department of Commerce, Bureau of the Census, and U.S. Department of Transportation.

State Highway Agency
Capital Outlay and Maintenance

STATE HIGHWAY AGENCY CAPITAL OUTLAY AND MAINTENANCE, 1998-1999 (In Thousands)

	Capital Outlay		Maintenance		Total		Percent Change
	1998	1999	1998	1999	1998	1999	
Alabama	$535,282	$554,576	$156,151	$140,112	$691,433	$694,688	0.5
Alaska	224,607	243,317	38,600	28,840	263,207	272,157	3.4
Arizona	649,427	943,562	61,684	57,860	711,111	1,001,422	40.8
Arkansas	491,817	407,752	110,496	109,992	602,313	517,744	-14.0
California	2,669,580	2,812,093	421,279	492,588	3,090,859	3,304,681	6.9
Colorado	609,823	690,817	122,558	154,261	732,381	845,078	15.4
Connecticut	502,141	514,861	64,831	63,919	566,972	578,780	2.1
Delaware	248,521	242,346	41,722	30,312	290,243	272,658	-6.1
District of Columbia	115,387	127,604	18,971	43,912	134,358	171,516	27.7
Florida	2,448,044	2,522,813	305,411	338,124	2,753,455	2,860,937	3.9
Georgia	1,111,114	1,247,005	114,047	121,894	1,225,161	1,369,799	11.8
Hawaii	194,746	184,955	21,958	7,298	216,704	192,253	-11.3
Idaho	209,119	235,891	19,591	16,727	228,710	252,618	10.5
Illinois	1,472,402	1,385,520	246,118	265,407	1,718,520	1,650,927	-3.9
Indiana	785,505	755,078	277,513	176,465	1,063,018	931,543	-12.4
Iowa	505,566	529,904	64,752	62,288	570,318	592,192	3.8
Kansas	637,165	695,583	97,955	100,264	735,120	795,847	8.3
Kentucky	777,719	885,990	173,109	185,138	950,828	1,071,128	12.7
Louisiana	643,033	704,414	115,656	114,808	758,689	819,222	8.0
Maine	187,691	205,640	71,902	88,360	259,593	294,000	13.3
Maryland	588,224	598,666	91,314	124,597	679,538	723,263	6.4
Massachusetts	1,853,968	2,767,089	63,280	56,968	1,917,248	2,824,057	47.3
Michigan	965,723	1,158,367	146,161	155,934	1,111,884	1,314,301	18.2
Minnesota	561,994	613,962	168,688	172,314	730,682	786,276	7.6
Mississippi	564,335	698,228	57,605	54,220	621,940	752,448	21.0
Missouri	791,672	865,389	216,997	269,197	1,008,669	1,134,586	12.5
Montana	211,567	245,013	52,625	51,751	264,192	296,764	12.3
Nebraska	271,469	327,044	38,247	67,865	309,716	394,909	27.5
Nevada	218,907	330,095	60,099	48,969	279,006	379,064	35.9
New Hampshire	168,936	175,086	57,500	68,908	226,436	243,994	7.8
New Jersey	775,648	1,190,238	183,675	174,908	959,323	1,365,146	42.3
New Mexico	269,662	507,705	44,447	50,990	314,109	558,695	77.9
New York	2,551,865	2,666,234	361,628	371,814	2,913,493	3,038,048	4.3
North Carolina	1,355,164	1,535,277	521,001	467,989	1,876,165	2,003,266	6.8
North Dakota	189,898	227,500	20,139	76,895	210,037	304,395	44.9
Ohio	1,464,561	1,452,394	194,925	201,831	1,659,486	1,654,225	-0.3
Oklahoma	459,816	732,712	125,657	139,845	585,473	872,557	49.0
Oregon	450,821	389,821	154,756	161,008	605,577	550,829	-9.0
Pennsylvania	1,546,071	1,904,337	893,197	799,390	2,439,268	2,703,727	10.8
Rhode Island	180,173	170,966	27,780	36,969	207,953	207,935	0.0
South Carolina	465,434	509,081	130,578	146,364	596,012	655,445	10.0
South Dakota	203,678	256,622	27,452	27,342	231,130	283,964	22.9
Tennessee	772,521	722,717	213,654	225,533	986,175	948,250	-3.8
Texas	2,368,058	2,866,376	769,766	789,518	3,137,824	3,655,894	16.5
Utah	820,138	788,433	69,718	72,400	889,856	860,833	-3.3
Vermont	99,873	124,787	27,115	16,568	126,988	141,355	11.3
Virginia	1,244,314	1,389,482	589,488	636,336	1,833,802	2,025,818	10.5
Washington	692,370	697,724	95,906	105,806	788,276	803,530	1.9
West Virginia	499,433	517,001	249,047	261,290	748,480	778,291	4.0
Wisconsin	709,128	775,042	84,921	88,590	794,049	863,632	8.8
Wyoming	200,559	255,354	65,574	70,844	266,133	326,198	22.6
Total	$38,534,669	$43,349,363	$8,347,244	$8,591,522	$46,881,913	$51,940,885	10.8

SOURCE: U.S. Department of Transportation, Federal Highway Administration.

Motor Vehicle and Equipment Manufacturing Employment by State

MOTOR VEHICLE AND EQUIPMENT MANUFACTURING EMPLOYMENT BY STATE, 1998

State	Vehicle Manufacturing	Motor Vehicle Body & Trailer	Engine & Engine Parts	Electrical Components	Suspension, Brake & Powertrain	Other Motor Vehicle Parts Manufacturing
Alabama	1,250	4,030	275	3,368	3,000	3,335
Alaska	*	45	*	*	*	
Arizona	250	742	502	1,690	400	4,991
Arkansas	130	2,334	1,250	1,081	1,525	3,114
California	6,756	10,144	4,422	8,551	2,803	24,900
Colorado	260	773	125	125	175	2,391
Connecticut	*	50	1,069	1,837	525	1,772
Delaware	5,000	*	*	*	*	*
District of Columbia		*	*	*	*	*
Florida	175	5,170	1,000	2,073	350	2,160
Georgia	6,250	4,313	1,258	1,200	1,661	2,929
Hawaii	*	*	*	*	*	*
Idaho	*	1,226	*	*	*	*
Illinois	10,000	4,141	2,831	7,555	3,642	8,971
Indiana	7,140	24,985	9,583	13,661	40,947	22,500
Iowa	100	7,849	1,648	1,427	1,372	3,015
Kansas	2,499	2,840	250	1,250	125	1,412
Kentucky	17,100	1,201	2,600	3,292	5,724	8,419
Louisiana	2,500	325	*	600	75	*
Maine	*	*	*	150	250	*
Maryland	2,600	750	*	650	*	450
Massachusetts	125	319	100	734	434	3,000
Michigan	54,748	3,320	29,540	9,949	44,113	53,129
Minnesota	1,250	1,592	932	702	1,197	1,084
Mississippi	*	1,149	1,450	6,000	2,750	1,851
Missouri	12,500	2,590	1,112	1,326	5,951	7,500
Montana	*	325	*	*	*	*
Nebraska	*	1,589	1,222	45	600	2,266
Nevada	*	*	325	125	41	*
New Hampshire	*	*	*	107	500	*
New Jersey	3,000	750	364	486	350	
New Mexico	1,240	125	75	45	*	*
New York	625	928	10,938	5,747	8,416	7,706
North Carolina	5,100	4,116	2,415	2,455	6,555	7,000
North Dakota	750	403	*	750	*	*
Ohio	32,000	4,765	9,949	16,791	28,505	25,468
Oklahoma	3,500	3,391	1,128	1,887	2,298	1,060
Oregon	2,300	4,432	69	568	626	1,070
Pennsylvania	1,875	7,585	892	3,877	2,823	6,800
Rhode Island	*	*	30	*	*	*
South Carolina	4,200	730	2,071	1,500	6,706	2,602
South Dakota	125	983	100	125	200	402
Tennessee	16,000	2,307	4,569	1,622	9,518	13,036
Texas	3,000	6,531	1,333	5,951	1,437	7,200
Utah	*	1,250	325	650	200	3,000
Vermont	*	*	*	*	250	*
Virginia	1,500	1,250	2,178	1,500	2,739	1,858
Washington	1,560	1,337	596	650	200	1,414
West Virginia	*	325	*	325	70	*
Wisconsin	7,415	5,374	4,716	2,681	2,520	9,441
Wyoming	*	125	75	*	*	*
Total	235,483	128,687	104,197	118,129	205,762	247,313

Note: In some cases, an average was taken based on the Bureau of the Census employment range.
* Omission of data for individual states is due to either the absences of such business from the state or the necessity of withholding the data to avoid disclosure of individual firm's data.
SOURCE: U.S. Department of Commerce, Bureau of the Census.

Motor Vehicle and Equipment Manufacturing Employment by State

MOTOR VEHICLE AND EQUIPMENT MANUFACTURING EMPLOYMENT BY STATE, 1998 — continued

State	Vehicle Metal Stamping	Tires & Inner Tubes	Storage Batteries	Total Motor Vehicle & Equipment Manufacturing	Motor Vehicle and Equipment Total State Manufacturing Employment	% of Total State Manufacturing Employment
Alabama	357	8,124	*	23,739	352,422	6.7
Alaska	*	*	*	45	12,117	0.4
Arizona	196	*	*	8,771	212,284	4.1
Arkansas	*	2,225	100	11,759	232,671	5.1
California	1,772	926	1,550	61,824	1,827,350	3.4
Colorado	*	75	365	4,289	173,403	2.5
Connecticut	447	*	254	5,954	246,125	2.4
Delaware	*	*	345	5,345	43,511	12.3
District of Columbia	*	*	*	*	2,991	-
Florida	855	75	1,300	13,158	428,642	3.1
Georgia	1,446	1,844	1,400	22,301	535,051	4.2
Hawaii	*	*	*	*	14,535	-
Idaho	*	*	*	1,226	66,719	1.8
Illinois	5,135	6,176	1,044	49,495	883,472	5.6
Indiana	12,360	1,750	358	133,284	635,658	20.0
Iowa	1,300	2,825	1,250	20,786	245,282	8.5
Kansas	*	1,700	2,017	12,093	196,519	6.2
Kentucky	3,961	1,500	750	44,547	290,665	15.3
Louisiana	*	*	300	3,800	171,549	2.2
Maine	*	155	*	555	80,640	0.7
Maryland	550	*	*	5,000	163,123	3.1
Massachusetts	400	150	*	5,262	409,938	1.3
Michigan	52,114	*	*	246,913	828,751	29.8
Minnesota	250	*	75	7,082	378,392	1.9
Mississippi	130	1,500	325	15,155	230,175	6.6
Missouri	1,176	502	1,700	34,357	382,003	8.0
Montana	*	*	*	325	20,686	1.6
Nebraska	125	*	*	5,847	109,645	5.3
Nevada	*	*	*	491	39,029	1.3
New Hampshire	75	*	*	682	101,513	0.7
New Jersey	75	*	750	5,775	405,275	1.4
New Mexico	*	*	*	1,485	40,561	3.7
New York	1,300	1,500	365	37,525	752,511	4.0
North Carolina	325	8,640	1,750	38,356	771,282	4.0
North Dakota	*	*	*	1,903	23,209	8.2
Ohio	29,995	2,913	760	151,146	994,788	15.2
Oklahoma	120	6,602	80	20,066	168,140	11.9
Oregon	70	75	165	9,375	211,636	4.4
Pennsylvania	2,472	1,226	3,250	30,800	818,215	3.8
Rhode Island	*	*	*	30	74,181	-
South Carolina	1,505	2,700	365	22,379	343,295	6.5
South Dakota	*	*	*	1,935	48,082	4.0
Tennessee	2,211	6,247	365	55,875	482,811	11.6
Texas	315	1,767	350	27,884	986,892	2.8
Utah	*	75	*	5,500	124,504	4.4
Vermont	150	*	*	400	44,836	0.9
Virginia	*	2,650	*	13,675	368,397	3.7
Washington	127	*	80	5,964	335,467	1.8
West Virginia	750	80	*	1,550	74,424	2.1
Wisconsin	2,455	*	355	34,957	566,219	6.2
Wyoming	*	*	*	200	8,916	2.2
Total	126,060	65,298	22,745	1,253,674	16,958,502	7.4

* Omission of data for individual states is due to either the absence of such business from the state or the necessity of withholding the data to avoid disclosure of individual firm's data.
SOURCE: U.S. Department of Commerce, Bureau of the Census.

U.S. Motor Vehicle and Related Industries Employment

U.S. EMPLOYMENT IN MOTOR VEHICLE AND RELATED INDUSTRIES 1998

Industry	Establishments	Employees	Payrolls(000)
Motor Vehicle and Equipment Manufacturing			
Light vehicle manufacturing	324	204,054	$11,956,677
Heavy truck manufacturing	87	31,429	1,420,477
Motor Vehicle body & trailer	2,116	128,687	3,815,998
Motor Vehicle engine and engine parts	1,048	104,197	4,491,238
Motor vehicle electrical & electrical equipment	1,135	118,129	4,094,164
Motor vehicle suspension, brake and power trains	1,043	205,762	9,786,270
Other motor vehicle parts manufacturing	1,916	247,313	8,802,877
Motor vehicle metal stamping	789	126,060	5,549,720
Tires and Inner Tubes	160	65,298	2,822,163
Storage Batteries	132	22,745	792,005
Sub-total	**8,750**	**1,253,674**	**$53,531,589**
Motor Freight Transportation and Related Services			
Trucking and courier services, except by air or by the U.S. Postal Service	119,572	1,866,637	56,307,059
Road transporation support activities	705	9,471	232,196
Arrangement of transportation of freight and cargo	15,798	148,393	5,445,735
Miscellaneous services incidental to transportation	1,046	20,744	681,635
Sub-total	**137,121**	**2,045,245**	**$62,666,625**
Petroleum Refining and Wholesale Distribution			
Petroleum Refining	304	69,491	4,202,766
Asphalt paving mixtures and blocks	1,202	13,612	642,887
Lubricating oils and greases	382	10,720	457,619
Petroleum bulk stations and terminals	7,503	99,466	3,305,423
Petroleum and petroleum products wholesalers, except bulk stations and terminals	3,747	34,598	1,452,019
Sub-total	**13,138**	**227,887**	**$10,060,714**
Passenger Transportation			
Local and suburban transportation	6,889	188,843	3,767,020
Taxi & Limousine service	6,619	60,473	1,017,861
Intercity and rural bus transportation	415	23,374	650,834
Bus charter service	1,531	32,327	594,383
School and Employee bus transportation	4,400	152,621	1,950,914
Arrangement of passenger transportation	36,190	310,522	8,016,274
Passenger car rental	4,212	111,980	2,519,646
Passenger car leasing	853	8,028	327,986
Truck,utility trailer and RV rental	5,768	51,133	1,602,214
Automobile parking	9,612	78,538	1,081,254
Recreational vehicle parks and campsites	3,987	17,156	315,277
Sub-total	**80,476**	**1,034,995**	**$21,843,663**
Automotive Sales and Servicing			
Retail automotive dealers (New and Used)	26,216	1,049,618	38,856,462
Retail automotive dealers (used only)	23,651	101,761	2,577,914
Auto parts, accessories and tire stores	59,631	498,754	11,145,837
Gasoline service stations *	123,894	946,405	12,329,772
Recreational vehicle dealers	3,012	30,999	962,766
Wholesale trade in motor vehicles	28,701	384,187	12,657,112
Automotive repair shops	142,231	629,798	15,764,758
Automotive services, except repair	30,597	236,033	3,416,030
Sub-total	**437,933**	**3,877,555**	**97,710,651**
Total of Motor Vehicle and Related Industries	**677,418**	**8,439,356**	**245,813,242**
U.S. Total	**6,941,822**	**108,117,731**	**$3,309,405,533**
Motor Vehicle Percent of U.S. Total	**9.8%**	**7.8%**	**7.4%**

SOURCE: U.S. Department of Commerce, Bureau of the Census. * Includes truck stops and stations with and without convienience stores.
The U.S. Census Bureau is currently in the process of changing over from the SIC coding system to the new NAICS, it will not be fully converted and implemented until 2004. Please note figures may reflect these modifications and are subject to change.

New-Car Dealerships

FRANCHISED NEW-CAR DEALERSHIPS BY STATE, 2000

State	Establish-ments*	Sales (Millions)	Paid Employees	Payrolls (Millions)	State	Establish-ments*	Sales (Millions)	Paid Employees	Payrolls (Millions)
Alabama	356	$8,883	15,692	$582	Nebraska	241	$3,573	7,102	$255
Alaska	44	1,126	2,253	102	Nevada	104	5,021	8,132	404
Arizona	216	13,387	22,997	996	New Hampshire	175	3,620	6,666	282
Arkansas	292	5,069	8,668	296	New Jersey	636	23,290	32,246	1,550
California	1634	78,615	127,602	6,082	New Meico	133	3,319	6,865	251
Colorado	267	11,258	18,700	820	New York	1,269	30,853	50,288	2,150
Connecticut	350	8,164	14,510	674	North Carolina	701	18,320	32,261	1,288
Delaware	69	1,791	3,714	146	North Dakota	116	1,526	3,236	104
Florida	988	44,099	68,324	2,930	Ohio	1,061	26,630	48,063	1,819
Georgia	609	21,155	34,089	1,425	Oklahoma	312	7,340	13,564	472
Hawaii	61	2,104	3,977	165	Oregon	279	7,339	14,498	594
Idaho	127	2,842	5,432	202	Pennsylvania	1,292	28,663	53,712	1,979
Illinois	1093	25,028	45,294	1,933	Rhode Island	73	1,952	3,331	136
Indiana	594	14,854	24,880	950	South Carolina	323	8,268	15,160	576
Iowa	438	6,193	13,047	455	South Dakota	136	1,719	3,588	123
Kansas	297	5,728	11,264	422	Tennessee	427	12,285	22,493	925
Kentucky	338	6,801	14,204	494	Texas	1,360	55,089	86,466	3,705
Louisiana	337	8,885	17,346	633	Utah	143	4,691	8,415	316
Maine	165	2,527	5,289	187	Vermont	99	1,372	2,784	99
Maryland	363	12,961	23,718	994	Virginia	555	16,639	31,564	1,262
Massachussetts	527	14,998	24,376	1,059	Washington	384	11,923	22,215	960
Michigan	826	26,861	41,407	1,892	West Virginia	197	3,268	6,874	212
Minnesota	493	13,510	21,953	852	Wisconsin	647	12,550	24,139	855
Mississippi	255	4,818	9,142	335	Wyoming	76	904	2,138	74
Missouri	533	13,109	23,047	922	Dist. of Columbia	4	132	259	10
Montana	141	1,725	3,717	118	**Total**	**22,150**	**646,774**	**1,110,700**	**46,072**

*Establishment data are NADA estimates for January 1, 2001.

DEALERSHIPS' TOTAL SERVICE AND PARTS SALES
(Billions of Dollars)

	Amount	% Change
2000	73.43	8.5
1999	67.84	6.7
1998	63.56	1.7
1997	62.93	3.6
1996	60.76	7.4
1995	56.57	2.6
1994	55.12	7.4
1993	51.31	4.6
1992	49.07	4.4
1991	47.00	-2.8
1990	48.34	6.3
1989	45.50	4.9

DEALERSHIPS' SERVICE AND PARTS SALES, 1999-2000
(Billions of Dollars)

	1999	2000	Percent Change
Service Labor Sale			
Customer mechanical	12.27	13.51	10.10
Customer body	3.93	4.15	5.41
Warranty	5.40	5.73	6.05
Sublet	2.82	3.07	8.87
Internal	3.72	4.11	10.48
Other	1.89	1.00	5.54
Total Service Labor	**30.04**	**32.56**	**8.40**

	1999	2000	Percent Change
Parts Sales			
Customer mechanical	9.80	10.50	7.14
Customer body	3.15	3.36	6.67
Wholesale	11.23	12.18	8.46
Counter	2.12	2.26	6.61
Warranty	6.90	7.65	10.87
Internal	2.90	3.14	8.28
Other	1.53	1.79	
Total Parts	**37.63**	**40.88**	**8.64**

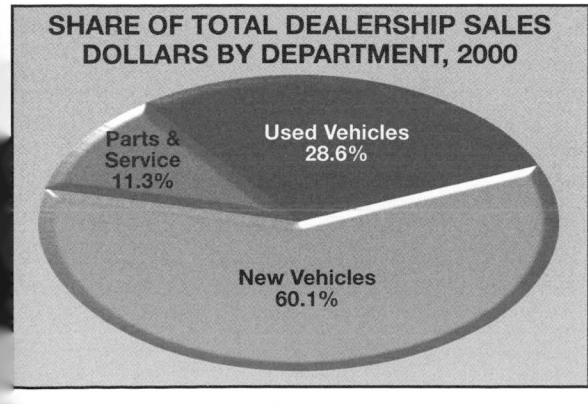

SHARE OF TOTAL DEALERSHIP SALES DOLLARS BY DEPARTMENT, 2000

Parts & Service 11.3%
Used Vehicles 28.6%
New Vehicles 60.1%

PROFILE OF THE FRANCHISED DEALERSHIP'S SERVICE AND PARTS OPERATION, 2000

	Average Dealership	All Dealers
Total service and parts sales	$3,315,077	$73.4 Billion
Total gross profit as percent of service and parts sales	44.5%	—
Total net profit as percent of service and parts sales	5.6%	—
Total number of repair orders written	10,320	229 Million
Total service and parts sales per customer repair order	$186	—
Total service and parts sales per warranty repair order	$207	—
Number of technicians	11.1	245,865
Number of service bays (excluding body)	17.5	387,625
Total parts inventory	$236,400	$5.2 Billion
Average customer mechanical labor rate	$60	—

SOURCE: National Automobile Dealers Association.

Personal Income of Motor Vehicle and Equipment Manufacturing Employees by State

PERSONAL INCOME OF MOTOR VEHICLE AND EQUIPMENT MANUFACTURING EMPLOYEES, 1997-1999[1]

	Personal Income (In Millions)						1999 Motor Vehicle & Equipment Percent of Total Manufacturing
	Motor Vehicle and Equipment Manufacturing Employees			All Manufacturing Employees			
	1997	1998	1999	1997	1998	1999	
Alabama	$614	$719	$773	$13,489	$13,754	$13,634	5.7%
Alaska	*	*	*	598	566	558	*
Arizona	249	282	247	9,733	10,710	10,763	2.3
Arkansas	293	317	297	7,790	8,114	8,266	3.6
California	1,623	1,703	1,642	96,313	102,939	111,257	1.5
Colorado	113	118	113	9,276	9,915	10,196	1.1
Connecticut	204	217	219	16,448	17,311	17,787	1.2
Delaware	353	420	483	4,320	3,843	3,794	12.7
District of Columbia	6	*	*	965	942	1,030	*
Florida	284	298	279	19,557	20,490	20,443	1.4
Georgia	885	977	1,004	21,963	23,645	24,450	4.1
Hawaii	*	2	2	799	716	658	0.3
Idaho	36	38	45	3,111	3,242	3,516	1.3
Illinois	1,834	1,959	1,807	47,783	48,996	49,141	3.7
Indiana	4,832	5,403	5,692	30,921	31,921	32,654	17.4
Iowa	472	504	520	9,967	10,357	10,264	5.1
Kansas	426	421	424	8,263	8,676	8,750	4.8
Kentucky	1,848	2,107	2,249	12,444	12,938	13,251	16.0
Louisiana	176	*	*	8,564	9,191	8,973	*
Maine	16	17	18	3,364	3,481	3,422	0.5
Maryland	284	259	259	8,428	8,617	8,751	2.0
Massachusetts	76	78	63	23,910	24,678	25,595	0.2
Michigan	21,206	23,699	23,559	54,899	59,880	60,621	38.9
Minnesota	332	362	373	19,961	20,818	21,173	1.8
Mississippi	178	211	182	7,256	7,610	7,682	2.4
Missouri	1,826	1,872	1,919	18,068	18,045	17,750	10.8
Montana	7	8	8	863	950	920	0.9
Nebraska	139	145	141	4,135	4,260	4,327	3.3
Nevada	12	19	21	1,577	1,735	1,792	1.2
New Hampshire	36	56	107	4,895	5,180	5,142	2.1
New Jersey	405	437	449	26,798	28,890	28,450	1.6
New Mexico	51	52	51	1,857	1,852	1,734	2.9
New York	1,977	2,038	1,349	48,272	50,072	50,321	2.7
North Carolina	1,161	1,353	1,345	30,426	31,220	31,398	4.3
North Dakota	51	57	60	756	816	826	7.3
Ohio	6,732	6,917	7,104	52,317	53,091	53,487	13.3
Oklahoma	592	537	573	7,322	8,152	8,316	6.9
Oregon	395	480	517	10,899	11,152	11,383	4.5
Pennsylvania	866	879	878	43,457	45,775	47,508	1.8
Rhode Island	31	26	21	3,069	3,154	3,088	0.7
South Carolina	634	742	800	13,415	13,813	13,392	5.0
South Dakota	51	59	60	1,536	1,695	1,762	3.4
Tennessee	2,109	2,128	2,189	19,567	20,153	20,342	10.8
Texas	733	842	880	56,712	54,748	55,562	1.6
Utah	288	300	289	4,837	4,955	4,988	5.8
Vermont	24	24	24	1,897	2,019	2,085	1.2
Virginia	608	665	728	16,117	16,446	16,072	4.5
Washington	256	310	314	18,117	18,811	18,857	1.7
West Virginia	15	27	47	3,337	3,394	3,381	1.4
Wisconsin	1,297	1,396	1,309	25,157	26,116	26,415	4.0
Wyoming	3	2	3	402	445	435	0.7
Total	56,639	61,482	61,436	855,927	890,289	906,362	6.8

* Withheld to avoid disclosure; estimates are included in the U.S. total.
(1) Personal Income is measured as the sum of wage and salary disbursements, other labor income, proprietors' income, rental income, personal dividend income and personal interest income.
SOURCE: U.S. Department of Commerce, Bureau of Economic Analysis.

Automotive Employment and Compensation

HOURLY COMPENSATION OF AUTOMOTIVE PRODUCTION EMPLOYEES IN SELECTED COUNTRIES, 1995-1998

Country	National Currency	Exchange Rate National Currency Per U.S. Dollar	Hourly Compensation National Currency 1997	1998	U.S. Currency 1997	1998	1998 Percent of U.S. Earnings
Canada	Dollar	1.484	29.20	29.63	21.08	19.97	69
France	Franc	5.900	111.35	114.34	19.07	19.38	67
Germany	Mark	1.760	66.28	66.84	38.20	37.98	132
Ireland	Pound	0.702	10.68	11.18	16.20	15.93	55
Italy	Lira	1,737.000	31,728	31,509	18.62	18.14	63
Japan	Yen	131.000	2,910	2,948	24.03	22.50	78
Korea	Won	1,400.000	11,209	11,326	11.79	8.09	28
Mexico	Peso	9.152	27.00	27.91	2.95	3.05	11
Spain	Peseta	149.400	2,336	2,339	15.79	15.66	54
Taiwan	Dollar	33.550	198.58	207.00	6.90	6.17	21
United Kingdom	Pound	0.603	11.33	11.89	18.56	19.72	69
United States	Dollar	1.000	28.14	28.74	28.14	28.74	100

Hourly compensation estimated on annual total production figures

U.S. MOTOR VEHICLE AND EQUIPMENT MANUFACTURING EMPLOYMENT, 1970-2000

Year	All Employees (000)	Production Workers Number (000)	Percent of Total Employees	Average Hourly Earnings
2000	1,010.6	769.8	76.2	$19.59
1999	1,000.1	762.4	76.2	18.41
1998	989.8	760.3	76.8	17.86
1997	985.6	779.1	79.1	18.04
1996	962.5	760.3	79.0	17.75
1995	933.1	758.9	81.3	17.36
1994	898.6	703.9	78.3	17.02
1993	836.6	642.0	76.7	16.10
1992	812.5	621.9	76.5	15.45
1991	788.8	601.5	76.3	15.23
1990	812.1	617.1	76.0	14.56
1989	858.5	663.8	77.3	14.25
1988	856.4	667.4	77.9	13.99
1987	865.9	673.1	77.7	13.53
1986	871.8	670.2	76.9	13.45
1985	883.1	684.5	77.5	13.39
1984	861.5	663.9	77.1	12.73
1982	699.3	511.9	73.2	11.62
1980	788.8	575.4	72.9	9.85
1978	1,004.9	781.7	77.8	8.50
1976	881.0	682.4	77.5	7.09
1974	907.7	687.5	75.7	5.87
1972	874.8	676.0	77.3	5.13
1970	799.0	605.3	75.8	4.22

NOTE: These figures are annual averages for the Motor Vehicle and Equipment Manufacturing Industry (SIC 371) as defined by the Standard Industrial Classification System. Many others are employed in manufacturing automotive components which are classified in other industries. SOURCE: U.S. Department of Labor, Bureau of Labor Statistics.

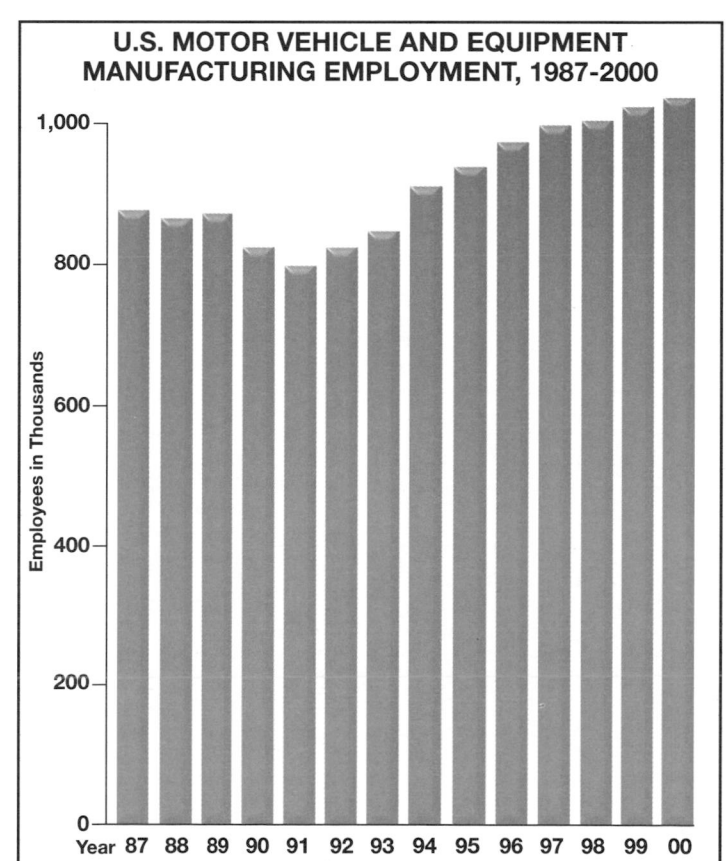

U.S. MOTOR VEHICLE AND EQUIPMENT MANUFACTURING EMPLOYMENT, 1987-2000

Industrial Production and Capacity Utilization

INDUSTRIAL PRODUCTION INDEX FOR MOTOR VEHICLE AND PARTS MANUFACTURERS, 1989-2000

	Industrial Production Index			
	Total		Motor Vehicle and Parts	
Year	Index	Percent Change	Index	Percent Change
2000	153.6	7.9	170.5	12.9
1999	142.3	4.3	151.0	6.6
1998	136.4	4.8	141.7	0.8
1997	130.1	8.9	140.6	6.0
1996	119.5	4.5	132.6	3.2
1995	114.4	4.9	128.5	-0.9
1994	109.1	5.4	129.7	14.1
1993	103.5	3.5	113.7	13.7
1992	100.0	3.1	100.0	13.0
1991	97.0	-1.9	88.5	-7.1
1990	98.9	-0.2	95.3	-5.8
1989	99.1	1.7	101.2	0.0

NOTE: "Industrial Production" is an index benchmarked to 1992=100.
SOURCE: Board of Governors of the Federal Reserve System.

CAPACITY UTILIZATION FOR MOTOR VEHICLE AND PARTS MANUFACTURING, 1989-2000

Year	All Manufac- turing	Percent Change	Vehicle & Parts Mfg.	Percent Change
2000	81.3	1.9	81.3	-0.9
1999	79.8	-1.4	82.0	6.1
1998	80.9	-1.8	77.3	-2.8
1997	82.4	1.2	79.5	4.2
1996	81.4	-1.6	76.3	-0.8
1995	82.7	0.2	76.9	-7.9
1994	82.5	2.5	83.5	8.0
1993	80.5	1.3	77.3	10.6
1992	79.5	2.1	69.9	9.2
1991	77.9	-4.3	64.0	-10.6
1990	81.4	-2.6	71.6	-9.9
1989	83.6	-0.2	79.5	-2.1

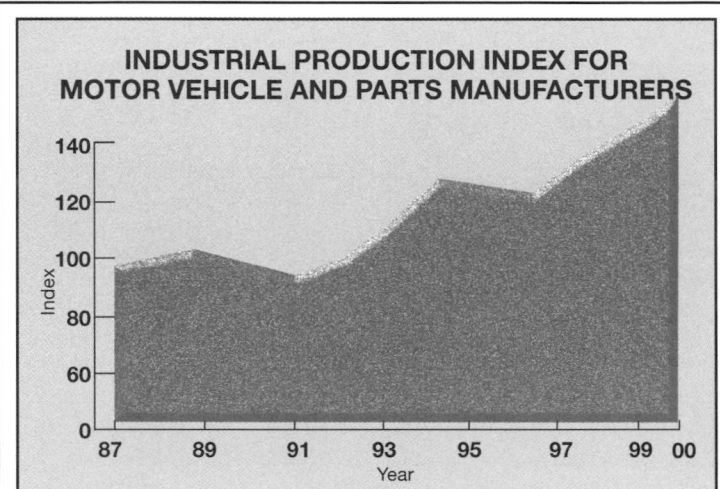

INDUSTRIAL PRODUCTION INDEX FOR MOTOR VEHICLE AND PARTS MANUFACTURERS

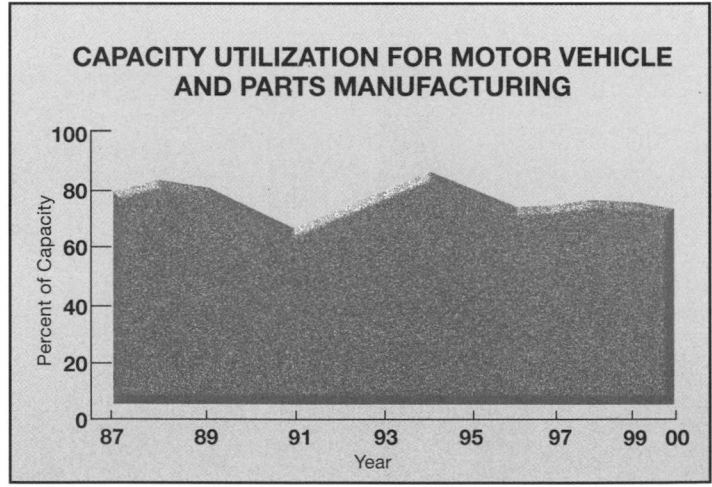

CAPACITY UTILIZATION FOR MOTOR VEHICLE AND PARTS MANUFACTURING

NOTE: "Capacity Utilization" is a percent of capacity.
SOURCE: Board of Governors of the Federal Reserve System.

AUTO AND TRUCK OUTPUT, 1988-2000 (Dollars in Billions)

Year	Auto Output	Auto Percent of GDP	Truck Output	Truck Percent of GDP	Total Motor Vehicle Output	Percent of GDP	Gross Domestic Product (GDP)
2000	$117.9	1.2%	$224.8	2.3%	$342.7	3.4%	$9,965.7
1999	126.1	1.4	220.5	2.4	346.6	3.7	9,256.1
1998	127.3	1.5	187.5	2.1	314.8	3.6	8,759.9
1997	126.7	1.5	167.0	2.0	293.7	3.5	8,300.8
1996	126.1	1.6	149.5	1.9	275.6	3.5	7,813.2
1995	130.5	1.8	139.8	1.9	270.3	3.7	7,400.5
1994	133.3	1.9	129.0	1.8	262.3	3.7	7,054.3
1993	121.9	1.8	105.0	1.6	226.9	3.4	6,642.3
1992	111.7	1.8	89.2	1.4	200.9	3.2	6,318.9
1991	102.3	1.7	72.4	1.2	174.7	2.9	5,986.2
1990	113.1	1.9	77.0	1.3	190.1	3.3	5,803.5
1989	121.8	2.2	81.8	1.5	203.6	3.7	5,489.1
1988	121.6	2.4	75.4	1.5	197.0	3.9	5,108.3

SOURCE: U.S. Department of Commerce, Bureau of Economic Analysis.

Corporate Profits and Research and Development Spending

SELECTED AUTOMOBILE MANUFACTURERS' REVENUES/NET INCOME, 1955-2000 (U.S. Dollars in Millions)

Year	DaimlerChrysler*		Ford		General Motors		Toyota		Volkswagen	
	Revenues	Net Income	Revenues	Net Income	Revenues	Net Income	Revenues	Net Income	Revenues	Net Income
2000	152,446	7,411	170,064	3,467	184,632	4,452	119,780	3,783	79,746	1,922
1999	151,035	5,785	160,658	7,237	176,558	6,002	100,990	3,747	75,525	2,534
1998	154,615	5,656	143,350	22,071	155,445	2,956	88,473	3,442	80,395	1,343
1997	61,147	2,805	153,627	6,920	178,174	6,698	99,730	3,143	63,664	765
1996	61,397	3,529	146,991	4,446	164,013	4,963	101,177	2,426	64,491	437
1995	53,195	2,025	137,137	4,139	160,254	6,881	89,715	1,458	61,168	233
1994	52,235	3,713	128,439	5,308	154,951	4,901	91,317	1,227	50,930	95
1993	43,596	-2,551	108,521	2,529	138,676	2,466	95,063	1,643	44,774	-1,134
1992	36,897	723	100,132	-7,385	132,429	-23,498	80,128	1,875	53,977	93
1991	29,370	-795	88,286	-2,258	123,056	-4,453	71,731	3,140	48,826	713
1990	30,620	68	97,650	860	124,705	-1,986	59,962	2,878	45,429	725
1989	35,186	359	96,146	3,835	126,932	4,224	61,440	2,652	37,606	597
1988	34,421	1,050	92,446	5,300	123,642	4,856	—	—	—	—
1987	28,353	1,290	79,893	4,625	114,870	3,551	—	—	—	—
1986	24,569	1,389	69,695	3,285	115,610	2,945	—	—	—	—
1985	22,738	1,610	57,616	2,515	106,656	3,999	—	—	—	—
1984	19,717	2,373	56,323	2,907	93,145	4,517	—	—	—	—
1983	13,240	701	44,500	1,867	74,582	3,730	—	—	—	—
1982	10,040	170	37,067	-658	60,026	963	—	—	—	—
1981	9,971	-476	38,247	-1,060	62,698	333	—	—	—	—
1980	9,225	-1,710	37,086	-1,543	57,729	-763	—	—	—	—
1978	13,618	-205	42,784	1,589	63,221	3,508	—	—	—	—
1976	15,537	423	28,840	983	47,181	2,903	—	—	—	—
1974	10,860	-52	23,621	361	31,550	950	—	—	—	—
1972	9,641	221	20,194	870	30,435	2,163	—	—	—	—
1970	7,000	-8	14,980	516	18,752	609	—	—	—	—
1968	7,445	291	14,100	627	22,755	1,732	—	—	—	—
1966	5,650	189	12,240	621	20,209	1,793	—	—	—	—
1964	4,287	214	9,670	506	16,997	1,735	—	—	—	—
1962	2,378	65	8,090	481	14,640	1,459	—	—	—	—
1960	3,007	32	5,238	428	12,736	959	—	—	—	—
1955	3,466	100	5,594	437	12,443	1,190	—	—	—	—

* Results for DaimlerChrysler beginning in 1998. SOURCE: Ward's Communications and company annual reports.

RESEARCH & DEVELOPMENT EXPENDITURES FOR SELECTED MANUFACTURERS, 1975-2000
(U.S. Dollars In Millions)

Year	Daimler-Chrysler*	Ford	General Motors	Toyota	Volkswagen	Year	Daimler-Chrysler*	Ford	General Motors	Toyota	Volkswagen
2000	5,347	6,800	6,600	4,196	3,855	1989	958	3,167	5,248	—	—
1999	7,628	6,000	6,800	4,771	3,806	1988	866	2,930	4,754	—	—
1998	7,853	5,300	7,900	3,367	3,343	1987	773	2,514	4,361	—	—
1997	1,714	6,327	8,200	3,723	2,555	1986	732	2,305	4,158	—	—
1996	1,602	6,821	8,900	—	—	1985	609	2,018	3,625	—	—
1995	1,420	6,624	8,200	—	—	1984	452	1,915	3,076	—	—
1994	1,303	5,811	6,900	—	—	1983	365	1,751	2,602	—	—
1993	1,230	5,618	6,030	—	—	1982	307	1,764	2,175	—	—
1992	1,053	4,332	5,917	—	—	1981	250	1,718	2,250	—	—
1991	955	3,728	5,887	—	—	1980	278	1,675	2,225	—	—
1990	908	3,558	5,342	—	—	1979	358	1,720	1,950	—	—
						1975	161	748	1,114	—	—

Data reflects DaimlerChrysler beginning in 1998.
SOURCE: Compiled by Ward's Communications from company annual reports.

Use of Tax Revenues by State

STATE MOTOR USE TAX REVENUES, 2000 (In Thousands)

State	Total State Tax Revenue	State Tax on Motor Vehicle Fuel	State License Tax on Motor Vehicles	State License Tax on Motor Vehicle Operators	Total Motor Vehicle Fuel and License Taxes	Percent Motor Vehicle of Total Taxes
Alabama	$6,191,736	$501,720	$187,282	$13,484	$702,486	11.3%
Alaska	1,334,159	45,839	42,570	0	88,409	6.6
Arizona	8,136,166	608,890	239,504	10,670	859,064	10.6
Arkansas	4,380,756	393,625	107,000	12,453	513,078	11.7
California	88,371,636	3,102,823	1,924,371	141,229	5,168,423	5.8
Colorado	7,303,187	503,318	167,968	16,069	687,355	9.4
Connecticut	9,594,096	511,811	163,704	28,744	704,259	7.3
Delaware	2,093,089	91,158	13,682	154	104,994	5.0
Florida	25,162,515	1,606,847	964,087	120,683	2,691,617	10.7
Georgia	13,951,602	660,486	239,986	38,100	938,572	6.7
Hawaii	3,429,989	76,470	81,539	547	158,556	4.6
Idaho	2,485,954	204,126	117,295	7,388	328,809	13.2
Illinois	20,637,169	1,327,825	771,281	57,985	2,157,091	10.5
Indiana	12,800,801	811,211	109,168	13,689	934,068	7.3
Iowa	5,151,629	328,204	339,497	12,870	680,571	13.2
Kansas	4,895,136	358,648	147,089	12,538	518,275	10.6
Kentucky	7,003,450	433,227	130,396	5,976	569,599	8.1
Louisiana	6,374,243	544,377	58,133	14,569	617,079	9.7
Maine	2,652,972	187,757	70,945	10,373	269,075	10.1
Maryland	10,617,844	726,450	188,179	17,359	931,988	8.8
Massachusetts	16,666,350	658,020	233,525	61,883	953,428	5.7
Michigan	23,282,602	972,723	754,557	11,568	1,738,848	7.5
Minnesota	13,975,779	605,616	577,582	30,771	1,213,969	8.7
Mississippi	4,174,798	406,239	136,900	10,123	553,262	13.3
Missouri	8,696,596	680,491	241,145	18,888	940,524	10.8
Montana	1,449,359	198,237	34,058	4,110	236,405	16.3
Nebraska	3,042,951	285,131	81,486	8,277	374,894	12.3
Nevada	3,680,457	237,860	130,379	14,437	382,676	10.4
New Hampshire	1,228,926	116,371	65,258	8,750	190,379	15.5
New Jersey	18,741,903	514,813	350,648	30,490	895,951	4.8
New Mexico	3,864,148	199,723	129,462	7,646	336,831	8.7
New York	43,906,384	518,985	532,900	78,700	1,130,585	2.6
North Carolina	15,448,402	1,121,995	397,121	63,361	1,582,477	10.2
North Dakota	1,096,480	73,054	41,725	3,557	118,336	10.8
Ohio	20,914,811	1,397,728	599,535	39,479	2,036,742	9.7
Oklahoma	5,997,220	402,017	630,186	0	1,032,203	17.2
Oregon	6,151,721	392,395	334,128	21,956	748,479	12.2
Pennsylvania	22,939,370	799,905	779,083	55,083	1,634,071	7.1
Rhode Island	2,077,228	130,929	49,904	2,032	182,865	8.8
South Carolina	6,507,717	336,872	98,998	16,043	451,913	6.9
South Dakota	811,781	117,543	75,791	1,855	195,189	24.0
Tennessee	7,871,031	786,484	226,306	37,637	1,050,427	13.3
Texas	30,266,799	2,951,451	1,006,944	131,941	4,090,336	13.5
Utah	4,062,830	332,501	83,316	7,206	423,023	10.4
Vermont	1,105,790	61,880	36,817	3,881	102,578	9.3
Virginia	13,087,800	811,149	303,231	30,084	1,144,464	8.7
Washington	12,470,570	680,252	385,579	34,755	1,100,586	8.8
West Virginia	3,274,005	244,502	88,803	4,438	337,743	10.3
Wisconsin	11,604,500	738,559	291,258	35,161	1,064,978	9.2
Wyoming	1,205,130	76,365	50,799	2,005	129,169	10.7
Total	**552,171,567**	**$29,874,602**	**$14,811,100**	**$1,310,997**	**45,996,699**	**8.3**

NOTE: 2000 is preliminary
SOURCE: U.S. Department of Commerce, Bureau of the Census.

New Car Corporate Average Fuel Economy

NEW CAR CORPORATE AVERAGE FUEL ECONOMY, 1974-2000 MODEL YEARS
(Sales Weighted Combined City/Highway Miles Per Gallon)

Manufacturer	Final Sales Basis									Preliminary Sales Basis	
	1974	1985	1987	1989	1991	1993	1995	1997	1998	1999	2000
DOMESTIC FLEETS											
Chrysler	13.9	27.8	27.5	28.0	27.5	27.8	28.4	27.6	28.8	27.2	27.5
Ford	14.2	26.6	26.9	26.6	27.6	28.8	27.7	27.2	27.8	27.6	28.1
General Motors	12.1	25.8	26.9	27.3	27.1	27.4	27.4	28.2	27.8	27.7	27.9
Honda	—	—	—	—	—	—	—	28.5	32.7	33.5	35.1
Mazda	—	—	—	—	—	29.7	30.3	27.2	27.8	27.2	28.0
Toyota	—	—	—	—	—	—	28.5	28.8	28.0	28.3	33.5
IMPORT FLEETS											
Alfa Romeo	—	27.7	25.5	26.9	25.2	—	—	—	—	—	—
AMC-Renault	—	28.6	33.0	—	—	—	—	—	—	—	—
BMW	19.5	26.4	24.9	22.2	23.2	25.2	25.3	25.7	25.4	25.4	24.9
Chrysler	—	36.2	33.4	30.3	28.7	31.0	28.6	25.7	25.4	26.5	25.3
Ford	—	25.2	24.2	31.7	33.2	26.7	34.0	31.3	28.9	30.1	27.5
Fuji(Subaru)	25.7	32.6	31.0	32.5	28.4	29.6	28.9	28.3	27.8	27.5	28.0
General Motors	—	47.9	39.0	40.4	32.4	30.5	36.7	32.1	29.4	25.5	25.0
Honda	31.1	34.5	33.2	31.6	30.7	32.5	32.7	32.4	28.1	29.4	29.0
Hyundai	—	—	34.8	33.4	32.9	31.3	31.2	31.4	30.9	30.8	30.7
Isuzu	—	34.2	38.8	35.8	34.9	34.8	—	—	—	—	—
Kia	—	—	—	—	—	—	—	31.0	30.9	30.9	29.8
Mazda	13.6	30.3	29.6	29.8	30.5	31.0	31.4	31.3	28.9	30.1	27.2
Mercedes-Benz	15.3	23.6	22.3	21.4	22.3	22.9	24.7	25.2	27.2	—	—
MG-TREaguar	21.3	19.3	19.3	20.8	—	—	—	—	—	—	—
Mitsubishi	—	31.9	31.7	31.4	30.3	29.4	29.9	30.0	31.5	29.6	29.4
Nissan	24.0	30.1	29.7	30.4	29.2	29.4	29.5	29.9	30.7	29.9	28.3
Peugeot	19.0	25.2	24.1	25.5	26.3	26.2	—	—	—	—	—
Saab	19.8	26.4	26.2	26.6	—	—	—	—	—	—	—
Suzuki	—	58.7	50.4	36.9	43.2	45.6	40.8	35.2	35.9	35.5	35.0
Toyota	22.5	33.5	33.4	32.1	30.9	29.1	30.4	30.1	30.7	29.9	29.0
Volvo	19.4	27.2	26.4	25.0	25.3	25.9	26.0	25.8	25.6	26.2	—
VW-Audi	25.9	30.5	30.1	30.4	29.9	27.2	29.0	29.0	29.0	28.2	28.5
Yugo	—	—	33.7	33.6	34.6	—	—	—	—	—	—

NOTE: After 1979, domestic fleet excludes captive imports.
SOURCE: U.S. Department of Transportation.

NEW CAR CORPORATE AVERAGE FUEL ECONOMY, 1974-2000 (Sales Weighted Combined City/Highway Miles Per Gallon)

Model Year	Federal Standard	Domestic Fleet	Import Fleet	Total Fleet
1974	None	13.2	22.2	14.2
1976	None	16.6	25.4	17.5
1978	18.0	18.7	27.3	19.9
1980	20.0	22.6	29.6	24.3
1982	24.0	25.0	31.1	26.6
1984	27.0	25.6	32.0	26.9
1985	27.5	26.3	31.5	27.6
1986	26.0	26.6	31.6	28.2
1987	26.0	27.0	31.2	28.5
1988	26.0	27.4	31.5	28.8
1989	26.5	27.2	30.8	28.4
1990	27.5	26.9	29.9	28.0
1991	27.5	27.3	30.1	28.4
1992	27.5	27.0	29.2	27.9
1993	27.5	27.8	29.6	28.4
1994	27.5	27.5	29.7	28.3
1995	27.5	27.7	30.3	28.6
1996	27.5	28.1	29.6	28.5
1997	27.5	27.8	30.1	28.7
1998	27.5	28.6	29.2	28.8
1999(prelim.)	27.5	28.0	28.9	28.3
2000(prelim.)	27.5	28.6	28.3	28.5

NOTE: After 1979, domestic fleet excludes captive imports.
SOURCE: U.S. Department of Transportation.

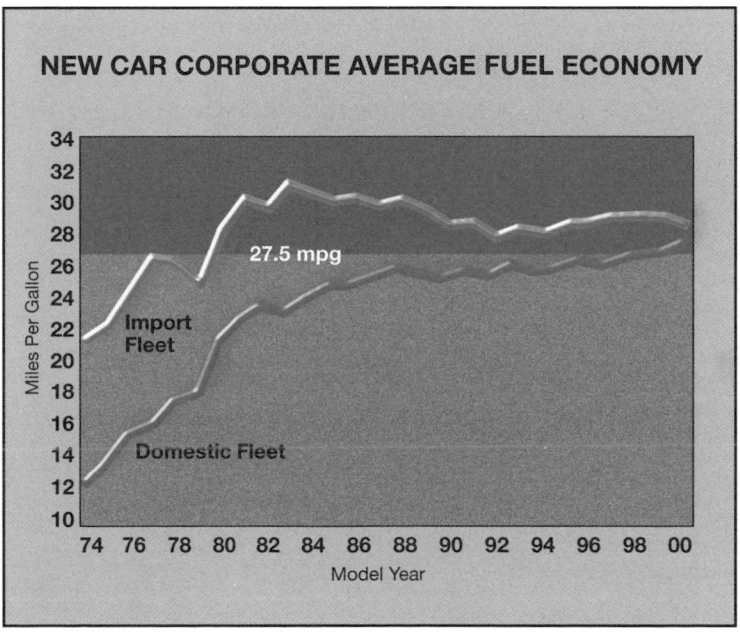

NEW CAR CORPORATE AVERAGE FUEL ECONOMY

New Light Truck Corporate Average Fuel Economy

NEW LIGHT TRUCK[1] FUEL ECONOMY PERFORMANCE, 1979-2000
(Sales Weighted Combined City/Highway Miles Per Gallon)

	2-Wheel Drive			4-Wheel Drive		
	Federal	Sales Weighted Average		Federal	Sales Weighted Average	
	Standard	Domestic*	Import	Standard	Domestic*	Import
1979	17.2	17.9	20.9	15.8	16.5	25.5
1981	16.7	18.6	28.3	15.0	17.1	24.3
1983**	19.5	19.6[2]	27.1[2]	17.5	19.6[2]	27.1[2]
1985**	19.7	19.9	27.4	18.9	19.6	24.7
1987**	21.0	20.4	27.5	19.5	19.4	25.3
1988**	21.0	20.6[2]	24.6[2]	19.5	20.6[2]	24.6[2]
1989**	21.5	20.4[2]	23.5[2]	19.0	20.4[2]	23.5[2]
1990**	20.5	20.3[2]	23.0[2]	19.0	20.3[2]	23.0[2]
1991**	20.7	20.9[2]	23.0[2]	19.1	20.9[2]	23.0[2]

	Federal Standard	Other(3)	Captive Import(4)	Total Fleet
1992	20.2	20.8	21.0	20.8
1993	20.4	21.0	24.3	21.0
1994	20.5	20.8	—	20.8
1995	20.6	20.5	—	20.5
1996	20.7	20.7	—	20.8
1997	20.7	20.4	—	20.6
1998	20.7	20.8	—	21.1
1999	20.7	—	—	20.8
2000	20.7	—	—	21.2

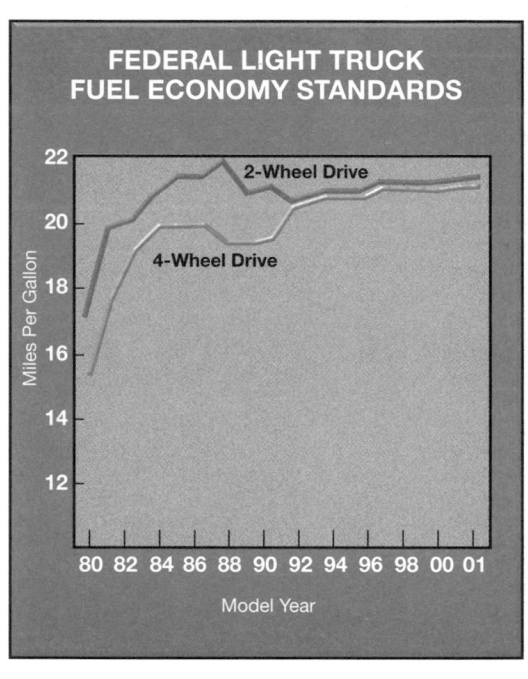

FEDERAL LIGHT TRUCK FUEL ECONOMY STANDARDS

* Captive imports are excluded.
** Manufacturers may elect to meet a single combined corporate fleet average of 19 mpg in 1983, 20 mpg in 1984, 19.5 mpg in 1985, 20 mpg in 1986, 20.5 mpg in 1987-89, 20 in 1990, and 20.2 in 1991.
(1) Light truck defined as 0-6,000 lbs. In 1979 and 0-8,500 lbs. in subsequent years.
(2) Combined 2-wheel and 4-wheel drive fleet average.
(3) Not a captive import light truck; 2 and 4 wheel drive combined.
(4) A light truck which is not domestically manufactured but imported by a manufacturer whose principal place of business is the United States; 2 and 4 wheel drive combined.
SOURCE: U.S. Department of Transportation.

NEW LIGHT TRUCK CORPORATE AVERAGE FUEL ECONOMY, 1993-2000[1] (Miles Per Gallon)

Manufacturer	1993 Model Year Combined	1995 Model Year Combined	1997 Model Year Combined	1998 Model Year Combined	1999 Model Year Combined	2000 Model Year Combined
Chrysler*	21.2	20.1	20.2	20.6	20.8	21.3
Ford*	20.9	20.8	20.0	20.4	20.4	20.9
General Motors*	20.2	20.1	20.5	21.2	20.3	20.9
Honda	—	—	26.9	26.9	26.1	25.3
Isuzu	21.8	20.3	19.6	21.4	21.5	20.9
Kia	—	24.4	23.7	24.4	24.4	23.5
Mazda	23.6	20.9	20.5	20.4	20.4	20.8
Mitsubishi	21.3	20.2	22.3	22.9	22.3	21.5
Nissan	23.7	22.4	22.3	22.3	21.2	21.1
Rover	15.5	16.3	17.2	17.2	17.0	17.0
Suzuki	28.9	28.1	27.4	27.4	23.8	22.9
Toyota	22.3	21.2	22.6	23.5	22.9	21.8
Volkswagen	21.0	19.6	18.5	—	19.1	19.2

* Captive imports are excluded.
(1) Trucks under 8,500 lbs. gross vehicle weight
SOURCE: U.S. Department of Transportation.

Gas Guzzler Tax Receipts, Automotive Fuel Prices and New Car Quality Improvements

NEW CAR GAS GUZZLER TAXES

Miles Per Gallon* At Least-Less Than	1980	1981	1982	1983	1984	1985	1986-90	1991 & Later
0-12.5	$550	$650	$1,200	$1,550	$2,150	$2,650	$3,850	7,700
12.5-13.0	550	650	950	1,550	1,750	2,650	3,200	6,400
13.0-13.5	300	550	950	1,250	1,750	2,200	3,200	6,400
13.5-14.0	300	550	750	1,250	1,450	2,200	2,700	5,400
14.0-14.5	200	450	750	1,000	1,450	1,800	2,700	5,400
14.5-15.0	200	450	600	1,000	1,150	1,800	2,250	4,500
15.0-15.5	0	350	600	800	1,150	1,500	2,250	4,500
15.5-16.0	0	350	450	800	950	1,500	1,850	3,700
16.0-16.5	0	200	450	650	950	1,200	1,850	3,700
16.5-17.0	0	200	350	650	750	1,200	1,500	3,000
17.0-17.5	0	0	350	500	750	1,000	1,500	3,000
17.5-18.0	0	0	200	500	600	1,000	1,300	2,600
18.0-18.5	0	0	0	350	600	800	1,300	2,600
18.5-19.0	0	0	0	350	450	800	1,050	2,100
19.0-19.5	0	0	0	0	450	600	1,050	2,100
19.5-20.0	0	0	0	0	0	600	850	1,700
20.0-20.5	0	0	0	0	0	500	850	1,700
20.5-21.0	0	0	0	0	0	500	650	1,300
21.0-21.5	0	0	0	0	0	0	650	1,300
21.5-22.0	0	0	0	0	0	0	500	1,000
22.0-22.5	0	0	0	0	0	0	500	1,000
22.5 & Over	0	0	0	0	0	0	0	0

NOTE: New car purchaser pays tax if car's combined city/highway fuel economy rating is lower than standard.
Combined city/highway rating.
SOURCE: Internal Revenue Service.

GAS GUZZLER TAX RECEIPTS

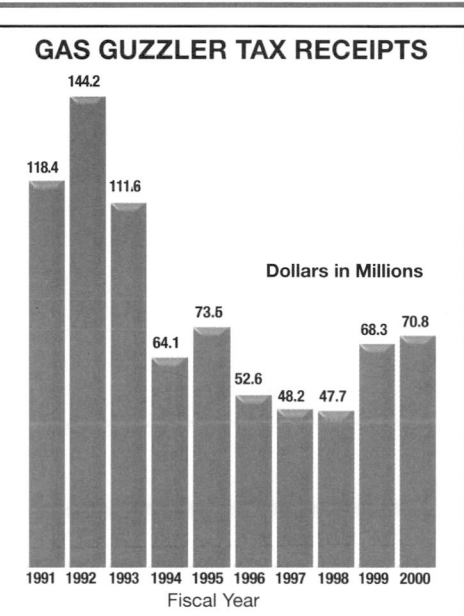

Dollars in Millions

1991: 118.4, 1992: 144.2, 1993: 111.6, 1994: 64.1, 1995: 73.5, 1996: 52.6, 1997: 48.2, 1998: 47.7, 1999: 68.3, 2000: 70.8

Fiscal Year

U.S. CITY AVERAGE RETAIL PRICES FOR AUTOMOTIVE FUEL, 1980-2000
(Cents Per Gallon, Including Taxes)

Year	Unleaded Regular	Unleaded Premium	All Types[1]	Diesel
2000	138.2	169.3	156.3	151.1
1999	116.5	135.7	122.1	112.0
1998	105.9	125.0	111.5	104.5
1997	120.0	138.1	124.5	120.0
1996	123.1	141.3	128.8	123.6
1995	114.7	133.6	120.5	110.9
1994	111.2	130.5	117.4	112.0
1993	110.8	130.2	117.3	114.8
1992	112.7	131.6	119.0	114.5
1991	114.0	132.1	119.6	124.3[2]
1990	116.4	134.9	121.7	134.3
1989	102.1	119.7	106.0	110.0
1988	94.6	110.7	96.3	104.6
1987	94.8	109.3	95.7	106.3
1986	92.7	108.5	93.1	99.9
1985	120.2	134.0	119.6	129.5
1980	124.5	N.A.	122.1	112.4

N.A. – Not available.
[1] Includes types of motor gasoline not shown separately.
[2] Price changed from "Full Service" to "Self Service."

AVERAGE RETAIL PRICE INCREASES FOR NEW CAR QUALITY IMPROVEMENTS, 1968-2001

Model Year	Requirements (Adjusted to 2000 Dollars)			
	Safety	Emissions*	Other**	Total
1968	$81.64	$44.06	-$1.93	$123.77
1969	37.95	0.00	-35.24	2.71
1970	19.75	14.49	86.92	121.16
1971	0.00	48.05	-63.22	-15.17
1972	5.10	15.31	30.63	51.04
1973	218.06	70.56	26.75	315.37
1974	259.43	3.38	21.46	284.26
1975	23.75	264.55	0.00	288.30
1976	27.96	15.86	-11.27	32.55
1977	13.78	28.36	75.15	117.29
1978	0.00	18.40	73.91	92.31
1979	9.81	20.65	48.64	79.10
1980	20.99	186.41	173.99	381.39
1981	6.39	695.24	89.26	790.89
1982	0.00	121.37	59.68	181.05
1983	0.00	90.34	88.58	178.92
1984	-16.42	79.97	85.93	149.49
1985	0.00	26.41	172.86	199.27
1986	34.61	0.00	200.79	235.40
1987	0.00	0.00	57.41	57.41
1988	78.12	0.00	215.12	293.24
1989	27.11	0.00	187.08	214.19
1990	205.26	0.00	44.41	249.66
1991	239.60	0.00	0.00	239.60
1992	37.68	0.00	244.77	282.45
1993	0.00	0.00	94.59	94.59
1994	188.94	40.50	143.81	373.26
1995	120.36	53.74	0.00	174.0:
1996	16.31	87.23	86.90	190.44
1997	8.97	20.45	153.35	182.78
1998	0.00	51.73	177.27	229.01
1999	0.00	76.61	408.25	484.86
2000	15.26	0.00	0.00	15.26
2001	25.16	67.65	0.00	92.81

*Includes changes to improve fuel economy and emissions control.
**Includes improved warranties, corrosion protection and changes in standard equipment.
SOURCE: U.S. Department of Labor, Bureau of Labor Statistics.

Federal Exhaust Emission Standards for Cars and Light Trucks

FEDERAL EXHAUST EMISSION STANDARDS FOR CONVENTIONALLY FUELED PASSENGER CARS AND LIGHT TRUCKS, 1991-2003 (Grams Per Mile)

Vehicle Type and Model Year	Useful Life	Percent of Fleet	NMHC	CO	CO Cold Start	NOx Gasoline	NOx Diesel	Particulates (PM-10)
LIGHT-DUTY VEHICLES(0-6,000 LBS. GROSS VEHICLE WEIGHT RATING)								
Passenger Cars								
1991-3	5/50	100	0.41[e]	3.4	—	1.0	1.0	0.20
1994	5/50	40	0.25[d]	3.4	10.0	0.4	1.0	0.08
1994	10/100	40	0.31	4.2	—	0.6	1.25	0.10
1995	5/50	80	0.25[d]	3.4	10.0	0.4	1.0	0.08
1995	10/100	80	0.31	4.2	—	0.6	1.25	0.10
1996-2000	5/50	100	0.25[d]	3.4	10.0[b]	0.4	1.0	0.08
1996-2000	10/100	100	0.31	4.2	—	0.6	1.25	0.10
1999-2003 "NLEV"	10/100	100	0.075	3.4	3.4[b]	0.2	—	0.08
Light-Duty Trucks(0-3,750 lbs. Loaded Vehicle Weight)								
1991-3	5/50	100	0.80[e]	10.0	—	1.2	1.2	0.20
1994	5/50	40	0.25[d]	3.4	10.0	0.4	1.0	0.08
1994	10/100	40	0.31	4.2	—	0.6	1.25	0.10
1995	5/50	80	0.25[d]	3.4	10.0	0.4	1.0	0.08 (40%)
1995	10/100	80	0.31	4.2	—	0.6	1.25	0.10 (40%)
1996-2000	5/50	100	0.25[d]	3.4	10.0[b]	0.4	1.0	0.08 (80%)[c]
1996-2000	10/100	100	0.31	4.2	—	0.6	1.25	0.10 (80%)[c]
1999-2003 "NLEV"	10/100	100	0.075	3.4	3.4[b]	0.2	—	0.08
Light-Duty Trucks(3,751 - 5,750 lbs. Loaded Vehicle Weight)								
1991-3	11/120	100	0.80[e]	10.0	—	1.7	1.7	0.13
1994	5/50	40	0.32[d]	4.4	12.5	0.7	1.7	—
1994	10/100	40	0.4	5.5	—	0.0	0.97	0.13
1995	5/50	80	0.32[d]	4.4	12.5	0.7	1.7	0.08 (40%)
1995	10/100	80	0.4	5.5	—	0.0	0.97	0.10 (40%)
1996-2000	5/50	100	0.32[d]	4.4	12.5	0.7	1.7	0.08 (80%)[c]
1996-2000	10/100	100	0.4	5.5	—	0.0	0.97	0.10 (80%)[c]
1999-2003 "NLEV"	11/120	100	0.1	4.4	—	0.4	—	0.10
LIGHT-DUTY TRUCKS (6,001-8,500 LBS. GROSS VEHICLE WEIGHT RATING)								
Light-Duty Trucks (3,751-5,750 lbs.Test Weight)								
1991-3	11/120	100	0.80[e]	10.0	—	1.7	1.7	0.13
1994	11/120	100	0.80[e]	10.0	12.5 (40%)	1.7	1.7	0.13
1995	11/120	100	0.80[e]	10.0	12.5 (80%)	1.7	1.7	0.13
1996	5/50	50	0.32[d]	4.4	12.5 (100%)	0.7	—	—
1996	11/120	50	0.46	6.4	—	0.0	0.98	0.10
1997-2003	5/50	100	0.32[d]	4.4	TBD	0.7	—	—
1997-2003	11/120	100	0.46	6.4	—	0.0	0.98	0.10
Light-Duty Trucks (Over 5,750 lbs. Test Weight)								
1991-3	11/120	100	0.80[e]	10.0	—	1.7	1.7	0.13
1994	11/120	100	0.80[e]	10.0	12.5 (40%)	1.7	1.7	0.13
1995	11/120	100	0.80[e]	10.0	12.5 (80%)	1.7	1.7	0.13
1996	5/50	50	0.39[d]	5.0	12.5 (100%)	1.1	—	—
1996	11/120	50	0.56	7.3	—	1.53	1.53	0.12
1997-2003	5/50	100	0.39[d]	5.0	TBD	1.1	—	—
1997-2003	11/120	100	0.56	7.3	—	1.53	1.53	0.12

NMHC-Nonmethane (reactive) hydrocarbons.
TBD-To be determined by EPA at level equivalent to car standard.

5/50   5 year/50,000 miles.
10/100   10 year/100,000 miles. In-use compliance is 7/75,000.
Test Weight = (GVWR + curb weight) / 2.
11/120   11 year/120,000 miles. In-use compliance is 7/90,000.

(a) The voluntary NLEV (National Low Emission Vehicle) program begins in nine of the thirteen states in the Northeast Trading Region (NTR) in the 1999 Model Year and begins in the rest of the country (37 states) in the 2001 Model Year.
(b) If by June 1997, six or more areas have a CO design value equal to or greater than 9.5ppm, then standards of 3.4 for cars, 4.4 for light trucks up to 6,000 lbs. GVWR, and a level of comparable stringency for LDTs equal to or greater than 6,000 lbs. GVWR, under cold start requirements shall apply beginning Model Year 2002.
(c) 100% in 1997 and thereafter.
(d) A set of intermediate in-use standards also applies during thephase-in period 1994-1997 for passenger cars and small light-duty trucks and 1996-1998 for larger light-duty trucks.
(e) Total hydrocarbons.
SOURCE: U.S. Environmental Protection Agency.

Federal Motor Vehicle Safety Standards

FEDERAL MOTOR VEHICLE SAFETY STANDARDS (FMVSS)

FMVSS NUMBER	Car	MPV	Truck	Bus	Equip.
100 SERIES Crash Avoidance					
101 Controls, Location & Identification	•	•	•	•	
102 Transmission Shift Lever Sequence	•	•	•	•	
103 Windshield Defrosting & Defogging	•	•	•	•	
104 Windshield Wiping & Washing System	•	•	•	•	
105 Hydraulic Brake System(1)	•	•*	•*	•*	
106 Brake Hoses	•	•	•	•	•
108 Lights & Reflectors	•	•	•	•	•
109 New Tires for Passenger Cars(2)	•				•
110 Tire Selection & Wheels for Passenger Cars	•				
111 Rearview Mirrors	•	•	•	•	
113 Hood Latch System	•	•	•	•	
114 Theft Protection	•	•	•		
115 Vehicle Identification Number (Location)	•	•	•	•	
116 Hydraulic Brake Fluids	•	•	•	•	•
117 Retreaded Tires					•
118 Power Operated Window Systems	•	•	•		
119 New Tires for Trucks, Buses, etc.					•
120 Tire Selection & Wheels for Trucks, Buses, etc.		•	•	•	
121 Air Brake Systems			•	•	
122 Motorcycle Brake System					
123 Motorcycle Controls, Displays					
124 Accelerator Control Systems	•	•	•	•	
125 Warning Devices					•
126 Truck-Camper Loading					•
129 Non-pneumatic Tires					•
131 School Bus Pedestrian Safety Devices				•	
135 Passenger Car Brake Systems(1)	•				
200 SERIES Occupant Protection					
201 Occupant Protection in Interior Impacts	•	•*	•*	•*	
202 Head Restraints	•	•*	•*	•*	
203 Steering Wheel Impact Protection	•	•*	•*	•*	
204 Steering System Rearward Movement	•	•*	•*	•*	
205 Glazing Materials	•	•	•	•	•
206 Door Locks & Hinges	•	•	•	•	
207 Anchorage of Seats	•	•	•	•	
208 Occupant Restraints	•	•	•	•	
209 Seat Belt Assemblies(2)					•
210 Seat Belt Anchorages	•	•	•	•	

FMVSS/CFR NUMBER	Car	MPV	Truck	Bus	Equip.
212 Windshield Mounting	•	•*	•*	•^A	
213 Child Restraint Systems					•
214 Side Door Strength	•	•	•		
216 Roof Crush Resistance	•*	•	•	•	
217 Bus Window Strength & Emergency Release				•	
218 Motorcycle Helmets					•
219 Windshield Zone Intrusion	•	•*	•*	•*	
220 School Bus Rollover Protection				•*	
221 School Bus Body Joint Strength				•*	
222 School Bus Seats				•*	
223 Rear Impact Guards					•
300 SERIES Post Crash Protection					
301 Fuel System Integrity	•	•*	•*	•*	
302 Flammability of Interior Materials	•	•	•	•	
303 Fuel System Integrity-CNG	•	•*	•*	•*	
304 CNG Fuel Container Integrity	•	•	•	•	•
49CFR PART NO. - Code of Federal Regulation (CFR) Parts					
– **Importation of Motor Vehicles & Equipment**	•	•	•	•	•
541 Theft Prevention	•*				•
565 Vehicle Identification Number (Content)	•	•	•	•	
566 Manufacturers Identification	•	•	•	•	•
567 Certification	•	•	•	•	
568 Vehicles Manufactured in 2 or More Stages	•	•	•	•	
569 Regrooved Tires					•
572 Anthropomorphic Dummy (Test Equipment)					•
573 Defect Reports	•	•	•	•	
574 Tire Identification & Record Keeping	•	•	•	•	
575 Consumer Information					
103 Truck Camper Loading			•		
104 Uniform Tire Quality Grading					•
105 Utility Vehicle		•			
577 Defect Notification	•	•	•	•	•
579 Defect & Non-Compliance Responsibility	•	•	•	•	•
580 Odometer Disclosure Requirements	•	•	•	•	
581 Bumper Damage Limits	•				
582 Insurance Cost Information	•				
583 Automobile Parts Content Labeling					•
595 Retrofit On-Off Switches for Air Bags					•

) Passenger cars may comply with either FMVSS or 135 until September 1, 2000 when FMVSS 135 becomes mandatory.
) Vehicle application is implied or is specified in other FMVSS.
Application or requirements vary for specific vehicle types or Gross Vehicle Weight Ratings (GVWR).
PASSENGER CAR: Motor vehicle with motive power, except a multipurpose passenger vehicle, motorcycle or trailer designed for carrying 10 persons or less.
MULTIPURPOSE PASSENGER VEHICLE: Motor vehicle with motive power, except a trailer, designed to carry 10 persons or less which is constructed either on truck chassis or with special features for occasional off-road operation.
TRUCK: Motor vehicle with motive power, except a trailer, designed primarily for the transportation of property or special purpose equipment.
BUS: Motor vehicle with motive power, except a trailer, designed for carrying more than 10 persons.
EQUIPMENT: Individual vehicle components or systems whether installed on a new vehicle or provided as a replacement.
SOURCE: Compiled by Ward's Communications.

Motor Vehicle Deaths by Type of Accident and Death Rates

MOTOR VEHICLE DEATHS BY TYPE OF ACCIDENT AND DEATH RATES, 1913-1999

Year	Total Motor Vehicle Deaths	Pedes-trians	Other Motor Vehicles	Rail-road Trains	Pedal cycles	Animal drawn Veh. or Animal	Fixed Objects	Deaths from Non-collision Accidents	Per 10,000 Motor Vehicles	Per 100,000,000 Vehicle Miles	Per 100,000 Popu-lation
1999*	41,300	5,800	18,800	300	900	100	11,100	4,300	1.89	1.54	15.1
1998	41,800	5,900	18,500	400	700	100	12,000	4,200	1.94	1.59	15.5
1997	43,458	5,900	19,900	371	800	100	12,000	4,400	2.05	1.70	16.2
1996	43,649	6,100	19,600	373	800	100	12,100	4,600	2.07	1.76	16.5
1995	43,363	6,400	19,000	514	800	100	12,100	4,400	2.11	1.79	16.5
1994	42,524	6,300	18,900	549	800	100	11,500	4,400	2.11	1.80	16.3
1993	41,893	6,400	18,300	553	800	100	11,500	4,200	2.12	1.82	16.3
1992	40,982	6,300	17,600	521	700	100	11,700	4,100	2.11	1.83	16.1
1991	43,536	6,600	18,200	541	800	100	12,600	4,700	2.26	2.00	17.3
1990	46,814	7,300	19,900	623	900	100	13,100	4,900	2.43	2.18	18.8
1989	47,575	7,800	20,300	720	900	100	12,900	4,900	2.48	2.26	19.3
1988	49,078	7,700	20,900	638	1,000	100	13,400	5,300	2.60	2.42	20.1
1987	48,290	7,500	20,700	554	1,000	100	13,200	5,200	2.63	2.51	19.9
1986	47,865	8,900	20,800	574	1,100	100	3,300	13,100	2.63	2.60	19.9
1985	45,901	8,500	19,900	538	1,100	100	3,200	12,600	2.59	2.59	19.2
1984	46,263	8,500	20,000	630	1,100	100	3,200	12,700	2.69	2.69	19.6
1983	44,452	8,200	19,200	520	1,100	100	3,100	12,200	2.62	2.68	19.0
1982	45,779	8,400	19,800	554	1,100	100	3,200	12,600	2.77	2.88	19.7
1981	51,385	9,400	22,200	668	1,200	100	3,600	14,200	3.13	3.30	22.4
1980	53,172	9,700	23,000	739	1,200	100	3,700	14,700	3.29	3.50	23.4
1979	53,524	9,800	23,100	826	1,200	100	3,700	14,800	3.35	3.50	23.8
1978	52,411	9,600	22,400	986	1,200	100	3,600	14,500	3.41	3.39	23.6
1977	49,510	9,100	21,200	902	1,100	100	3,400	13,700	3.33	3.35	22.5
1976	47,038	8,600	20,100	1,033	1,000	100	3,200	13,000	3.28	3.33	21.6
1975	45,853	8,400	19,550	979	1,000	100	3,130	12,700	3.33	3.45	21.3
1974	46,402	8,500	19,700	1,209	1,000	100	3,100	2,800	3.44	3.59	21.8
1973	55,511	10,200	23,600	1,194	1,000	100	3,800	15,600	4.28	4.24	26.3
1972	56,278	10,300	23,900	1,260	1,000	100	3,900	15,800	4.60	4.43	26.9
1971	54,381	9,900	23,100	1,378	800	100	3,800	15,300	4.68	4.57	26.3
1970	54,633	9,900	23,200	1,459	780	100	3,800	15,400	4.92	4.88	26.8
1969	55,791	10,100	23,700	1,495	800	100	3,900	15,700	5.19	5.21	27.7
1968	54,862	9,900	22,400	1,570	790	100	2,700	17,400	5.32	5.40	27.5
1967	52,924	9,400	22,000	1,620	750	100	2,350	16,700	5.35	5.50	26.8
1966	53,041	9,400	22,200	1,800	740	100	2,500	16,300	5.53	5.70	27.1
1965	49,163	8,900	20,800	1,556	680	120	2,200	14,900	5.36	5.54	25.4
1964	47,700	9,000	19,600	1,580	710	100	2,100	14,600	5.46	5.63	25.0
1960	38,137	7,850	14,800	1,368	460	80	1,700	11,900	5.12	5.31	21.2
1955	38,426	8,200	14,500	1,490	410	80	1,600	12,100	6.12	6.34	23.4
1950	34,763	9,000	11,650	1,541	440	90	1,300	10,600	7.07	7.59	23.0
1943-47 average	28,458	10,570	7,490	1,660	490	120	820	7,120	8.60	10.52	20.8
1938-42 average	33,549	12,430	9,500	1,624	748	140	1,048	7,848	10.41	11.49	25.4
1933-37 average	36,313	14,484	8,630	1,598	540	214	1,034	9,464	13.50	15.55	28.6
1928-32 average	31,050	12,300	5,700	1,850	—	274	700	9,100	12.10	15.60	25.3
1923-27 average	21,800	—	—	1,200	—	—	—	—	11.10	18.20	18.8
1918-22 average	12,700	—	—	—	—	—	—	—	13.90	11.9	
1913-17 average	6,800	—	—	—	—	—	—	—	23.80	6.8	

* Revised.
SOURCE: National Safety Council.

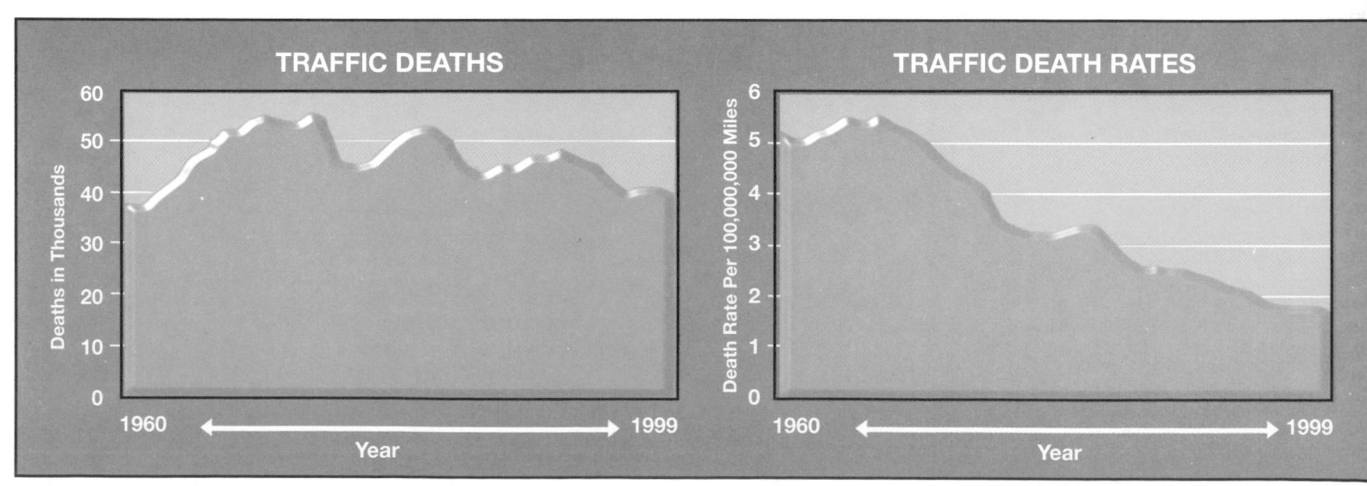

Motor Vehicle Traffic Deaths and Traffic Death Rates by State

MOTOR VEHICLE TRAFFIC DEATHS AND TRAFFIC DEATH RATES BY STATE, 1995-2000

State	Traffic Deaths						Traffic Deaths Per 100,000,000 Vehicle Miles	
	1995	1996	1997	1998	1999	2000	1999	2000
Alabama	1,111	1,142	1,181	1,069	1,083	950	2.0	1.7
Alaska	86	80	77	72	76	N.A.	1.7	N.A.
Arizona	1,040	903	961	980	920	931	2.2	2.0
Arkansas	631	615	660	625	602	652	2.1	2.3
California	4,165	3,972	3,377	3,161	1,755	1,959	1.1	1.1
Colorado	645	434	516	524	N.A.	646	N.A.	1.6
Connecticut	318	310	337	329	303	340	1.0	1.1
Delaware	123	120	147	115	103	128	1.2	1.5
District of Columbia ...	N.A.	N.A.	N.A.	58	46	N.A.	1.4	N.A.
Florida	2,812	2,813	2,847	2,804	2,867	2,934	2.1	2.1
Georgia	1,494	1,578	1,584	1,580	1,499	1,484	1.5	1.5
Hawaii	127	145	131	120	98	133	1.2	1.6
Idaho	263	258	259	265	278	272	2.0	2.0
Illinois	1,589	1,475	1,404	1,392	1,456	1,401	1.4	1.4
Indiana	960	981	N.A.	978	934	872	1.5	1.2
Iowa	527	465	468	444	486	433	1.7	1.5
Kansas	438	491	483	493	532	457	1.9	1.7
Kentucky	856	844	865	868	808	792	1.7	1.7
Louisiana	880	809	840	812	826	873	2.2	2.1
Maine	189	168	192	184	177	166	1.3	1.2
Maryland	682	614	609	606	587	609	1.2	1.2
Massachusetts	448	417	443	406	412	428	0.8	0.8
Michigan	1,537	1,505	1,446	1,367	1,329	1,340	1.4	1.4
Minnesota	597	576	598	650	616	619	1.2	1.2
Mississippi	868	811	861	948	926	N.A.	2.7	N.A.
Missouri	1,110	1,148	1,192	1,169	1,089	1,146	1.7	1.7
Montana	215	198	265	237	220	235	2.2	2.4
Nebraska	254	293	302	315	295	276	1.6	1.5
Nevada	312	348	347	360	349	318	2.0	1.8
New Hampshire	118	134	125	129	141	126	1.2	1.1
New Jersey	776	818	N.A.	755	727	734	1.0	1.1
New Mexico	485	481	484	424	461	436	2.0	1.9
New York	1,668	1,562	1,625	1,405	1,473	1,245	1.2	1.0
North Carolina	1,438	1,492	1,484	1,574	1,062	1,062	1.7	1.6
North Dakota	74	85	105	92	119	85	1.6	1.1
Ohio	1,357	1,393	1,439	1,421	1,337	1,248	1.3	1.2
Oklahoma	674	775	842	769	741	650	1.7	1.5
Oregon	572	524	521	538	414	449	1.2	1.3
Pennsylvania	1,480	1,470	1,562	1,485	1,549	1,196	1.5	1.2
Rhode Island	69	69	75	74	88	81	1.1	1.0
South Carolina	882	930	903	1,001	1,064	1,049	2.4	2.4
South Dakota	158	175	148	165	142	171	1.8	2.1
Tennessee	1,240	1,211	1,223	1,208	1,225	1,235	2.0	1.9
Texas	3,172	3,738	3,476	3,516	3,123	3,253	1.7	1.5
Utah	321	321	367	346	346	345	1.7	1.6
Vermont	106	88	96	104	92	N.A.	1.4	N.A.
Virginia	900	869	981	934	843	906	1.2	1.3
Washington	654	690	659	665	628	605	1.2	1.1
West Virginia	376	344	372	351	396	405	2.1	2.1
Wisconsin	739	759	721	709	745	805	1.3	1.4
Wyoming	170	143	137	154	189	152	2.3	1.9
Total*	43,363	43,649	42,400	41,800	41,300	41,300	1.5	1.5

2000 Data shows preliminary figures
N.A. - Not available.
*Total includes both traffic and nontraffic motor vehicle related deaths.
SOURCE: National Safety Council.

Traffic Accidents and Fatalities

MOTOR VEHICLE TRAFFIC DATA, 1988-1999

Year	Crashes	Injuries	Fatalities
1999 ...	6,279,000	3,236,000	41,611
1998 ...	6,498,000	3,251,000	41,501
1997 ...	6,764,000	3,399,000	42,013
1996 ...	6,842,000	3,511,000	42,065
1995 ...	6,699,000	3,465,000	41,817
1994 ...	6,496,000	3,266,000	40,716
1993 ...	6,106,000	3,149,000	40,150
1992 ...	6,000,000	3,070,000	39,250
1991 ...	6,117,000	3,097,000	41,508
1990 ...	6,471,000	3,231,000	44,599
1989 ...	6,653,000	3,284,000	45,582
1988 ...	6,887,000	3,416,000	47,087

TRAFFIC FATALITIES BY AGE AND SEX OF VICTIM, 1999

Age of Victim	Sex of Victim		Total
	Male	Female	
4 & under ...	405	328	733
5-9	461	334	795
10-15	833	570	1,403
16-20	3,981	1,936	5,917
21-24	2,934	950	3,884
25-34	5,006	1,815	6,821
35-44	4,716	2,002	6,719
45-54	3,415	1,491	4,908
55-64	2,076	1,156	3,235
65-74	1,804	1,258	3,063
75-98	2,263	1,762	4,025
Unknown ...	79	25	108
Total	27,973	13,627	41,611*

* Includes 11 fatalities of unknown sex

TRAFFIC FATALITIES BY AGE AND PERSON TYPE, 1999

Age of Victim	Person Type					Total
	Drivers	Passengers	Pedestrians	Pedalcyclists	Other	
4 & under	0	555	172	6	—	733
5-9	4	503	203	82	3	795
10-15	144	902	222	126	9	1,403
16-20	3,481	2,086	276	73	1	5,917
21-24	2,538	1,068	234	36	8	3,884
25-34	4,764	1,345	628	75	9	6,821
35-44	4,594	1,053	914	147	10	6,718
45-54	3,315	790	701	96	6	4,908
55-64	2,121	568	490	43	13	3,235
65-74	1,879	683	452	46	4	3,064
75-98	2,347	1,011	644	18	5	4,025
Unknown	22	32	51	3	—	108
Total	25,210	10,596*	4,987	750	68	41,611

* Includes 6 drivers and 4 passengers of unknown sex.

TRAFFIC FATALITIES BY HOUR OF DAY AND DAY OF WEEK, 1999

Hour of Day	Sun.	Mon.	Tues.	Wed.	Thurs.	Fri.	Sat.	Total
12 to 3 am	1,182	411	323	394	433	575	1,215	4,534
3 to 6 am	683	295	262	255	282	386	659	2,822
6 to 9 am	430	562	531	616	540	562	502	3,743
9 am to noon ..	461	551	521	493	525	578	585	3,715
noon to 3 pm ..	719	713	593	663	659	753	786	4,886
3 to 6 pm	842	840	845	851	864	1,042	948	6,232
6 to 9 pm	827	708	704	740	736	971	1,004	5,691
9 pm to 12 am .	628	562	580	574	689	991	1,079	5,103
Unknown	68	26	31	33	37	46	73	317
Total	5,840	4,668	4,390	4,319	4,765	5,904	6,851	37,043

* Including 6 fatal crashes that occurred on unknown days.

SOURCE: U.S. Department of Transportation, National Highway Traffic Safety Administration.

Traffic Deaths in Selected Countries and Countries with Safety Belt Use Laws

STATES WITH STANDARD/PRIMARY SEAT BELT ENFORCEMENT LAWS*

Alabama	Maryland
California	Michigan
Connecticut	New Jersey
District of Columbia	New Mexico
Georgia	New York
Hawaii	North Carolina
Indiana	Oklahoma
Iowa	Oregon
Louisiana	Texas

*The safety belt use law may be enforced independent of another violation.
SOURCE: National Highway Traffic Safety Administration.

TRAFFIC DEATHS IN SELECTED COUNTRIES, 1997-1999

				Traffic Fatalities	
				Per 100,000 Registered Motor	Per 100 Million Vehicle Miles
	1997	1998	1999	Vehicles	Traveled
Austria	1,105	963	1,079	24.8	N.A.
Belgium	1,364	1,500	N.A.	29.3	1.5
Canada	3,064	2,934	N.A.	16.0	N.A.
China	73,861	78,067	N.A.	609.9	N.A.
Denmark	589	499	500	22.4	1.8
Finland	438	400	427	17.9	1.5
France	8,444	8,918	8,487	25.6	2.8
Germany	8,549	7,792	7,772	16.0	2.2
Hungary	1,391	1,371	1,370	52.8	N.A.
Italy	6,724	6,326	N.A.	17.9	16.1
Japan	11,254	10,805	10,372	14.5	2.2
The Netherlands	1,163	1,066	1,090	15.8	1.6
Norway	303	352	304	14.2	1.9
Poland	7,310	7,080	6,730	74.0	7.1
Portugal	2,521	2,126	2,024	44.7	3.7
Spain	5,604	5,957	5,319	25.8	4.8
Sweden	541	531	570	13.4	1.4
Switzerland	587	597	583	15.4	1.9
Turkey	5,125	5,076	4,606	84.1	14.9
United Kingdom	3,743	3,581	N.A.	11.6	1.4
United States	41,967	41,471	41,345	19.4	1.5

N.A.-Not available.
Note: Data varies significantly between countries both definitionally and quantitatively.
SOURCE: Compiled by Ward's Communications from various sources.

COUNTRIES WITH SAFETY BELT USE LAWS

Country	Effective Date	Country	Effective Date
Australia	1/72	Colorado	7/1/87
Austria	7/76	Connecticut	1/1/86
Belgium	6/75	Delaware	5/22/91
Brazil	6/72	Dist. of Col.	12/12/85
Bulgaria	1976	Florida	7/1/86
Canadian Provinces		Georgia	9/1/88
Alberta	7/87	Hawaii	12/16/85
British Columbia	10/77	Idaho	7/1/86
Manitoba	4/84	Illinois	7/1/85
Newfoundland	7/82	Indiana	7/1/87
New Brunswick	11/83	Iowa	7/1/86
Nova Scotia	1/85	Kansas	7/1/86
Ontario	1/76	Kentucky	7/15/94
Prince Edward Island	1/88	Louisiana	7/1/86
Quebec	7/76	Maine	12/27/95
Saskatchewan	7/77	Maryland	7/1/86
Czechoslovakia	1/69	Massachusetts	2/1/94
Denmark	1/76	Michigan	7/1/85
Finland	7/75	Minnesota	8/1/86
France	10/79	Mississippi	3/20/90
Germany	1/76	Missouri	9/28/85
Greece	12/79	Montana	1/1/88
Hong Kong	10/83	Nebraska	1/1/93
Hungary	7/77	Nevada	7/1/87
Iceland	10/81	New Hampshire	
Ireland	2/79	New Jersey	3/1/85
Israel	7/75	New Mexico	1/1/86
Ivory Coast	1970	New York	12/1/84
Japan	12/71	North Carolina	10/1/85
Jordan	12/83	North Dakota	6/94
Luxembourg	6/75	Ohio	5/6/86
Malaysia	4/79	Oklahoma	2/1/87
Netherlands	6/75	Oregon	12/7/90
New Zealand	6/72	Pennsylvania	11/23/87
Norway	9/75	Puerto Rico	1/1/74
Poland	1/84	Rhode Island	6/18/91
Portugal	1/78	South Carolina	7/1/89
Singapore	7/81	South Dakota	1/1/95
South Africa	12/77	Tennessee	4/21/86
Spain	10/74	Texas	9/1/85
Sweden	1/75	Utah	4/28/86
Switzerland	1/76	Vermont	7/1/93
Turkey	10/84	Virginia	1/1/88
United States and Territories		Washington	6/11/86
Alabama	7/18/91	West Virginia	9/1/93
Alaska	9/90	Wisconsin	12/1/87
Arizona	12/31/90	Wyoming	6/8/89
Arkansas	7/15/91	United Kingdom	1/83
California	1/86	USSR	1/76
		Zimbabwe	7/80

SOURCE: University of Michigan Transportation Research Institute and the American Automobile Manufacturers Association.

INDEX

A

Accessories 10
Accidents, traffic 88-91
Age:
   Buyers, drivers 62,63,90
   Passenger cars in use 45
   Trucks in use 46
Air bags 10
Air conditioning 10
Air transportation 68
Anti-lock brakes 10
Assembly by city and state 8,9
Automotive businesses:
   Employees, payrolls 74-79
   Number and location 74-77
Automotive industry:
   Capacity utilization 80
   Consumption of materials 60,61
   Industrial production index . . . 80
   Profits 81
   Research and development costs 81
   Trade 54-59

B

Bodies, truck and trailer 11
Brakes, anti-lock 10
Buses:
   Employees 74
   Exports 54-57,59
   Factory sales 7,8
   Fuel consumption 70
   Imports 58,59
   Miles traveled 43,70
   Registrations 38,42-44
   School buses 42,43
   Travel by 43,68,70

C

Camper shipments 11
Canada:
   Exports and imports 7,59
   Factory sales 7
   Production 4,5,12
   Registrations 29
   Retail sales 29,30
Capacity utilization 80
Capital outlays for roads 73
Color popularity 28
Compensation, worldwide 79
Consumer credit 66
Consumer expenditures 67,68
Consumer price index 67
Corporate average fuel economy 82-84
Corporate profits 81

D

Dealers, retail automotive 77
Deaths, traffic:

United States 88-91
   Worldwide 91
Diesel fuel prices 85
Diesel truck sales 7
Drivers; licensed 63,72

E

Earnings 67,79
Emissions 86
Employment 74-79
Engines 10
Equipment 10
Expenditures:
   Average per new car 67
   Gasoline 68
   Operating costs, cars 65
   Passenger transportation 68
   Personal consumption 68
   Research and development . . 81
   Vehicle purchase 67,68
Exports:
   United States 7,54-57,59
   World 59

F

Facilities 74-77
Factory sales:
   Passenger cars 3,7,27
   Trucks and buses 3,6,7,27
Fatalities, traffic:
   United States 88-91
   Worldwide 91
Financing 64-66
Fleets 49
Fuel:
   Consumption 70
   Cost per mile 64
   Economy 83-85
   Expenditures 68
   Prices 83
   Taxes 82

G

Gas guzzler tax 85
Gasoline:
   Consumer price index 67
   Consumption 70
   Cost per mile 64
   Expenditures 68
   Retail prices 83
   Service stations 76
   Taxes 72,82
Government ownership 44

H

Highways:
   Capital outlays/maintenance . 73
   Rural and urban mileage 72
   Taxes, user 72,82

Vehicle miles traveled 70-72
Hourly compensation 79

I

Imports:
   Expenditures per new car 67
   Fuel economy 83,84
   Passenger cars 58,59
   Purchase characteristics 63
   Retail sales 15,18-26,28
   Trucks 58,59
Income:
   Hourly compensation 79
   Household 63
   Payrolls 76,77
   Personal 78
Industrial production index 80

L

License tax on vehicles 82
Licensed drivers 62,72

M

Maintenance of roads 73
Mass transit 68
Materials 61,62
Mexico:
   Production 14
   Sales 30
Milestones 27
Mode of transportation 68
Motor homes 11

N

New registrations 31-37

O

Operating costs, cars 64,65
Optional equipment 10
Overseas auto industry:
   Exports and imports 59
   Hourly compensation 79
   Production 12,13
   Registrations 50-53
Ownership of vehicles:
   Characteristics of buyers 63
   Government agencies 44

P

Paint, color popularity 28
Parts and accessories 10,76,77
Passenger cars:
   Assembly by city and state . . . 8
   Average expenditure 67
   Buyer characteristics 63
   By Age 45
   Consumer price index 67
   Exhaust emissions 86
   Exports 7,54-57,59

INDEX

Factory sales 3,7
Fleets 49
Fuel consumption 70
Fuel economy 83
Government ownership 45
Imports 58,59
In operation 45
Leasing 48
Materials per car 61
Operating costs 64
Optional equipment 10
Production 3-5,10,12-14,27
Registrations 38,42,43,47-53
Regulations 83-87
Retail sales 15-21,27-30
Scrappage 61
Top sellers 28
Payrolls 76,77
Personal consumptions expenditures . . 68
Personal income 78
Pickup truck sales 23,26,28
Plant locations 8,9,74,75
Price, average per new car 67
Production (see also Factory sales):
  By city and state 8,9
  Canada 4,5,12,13
  Facilities 74-76
  Mexico 14
  Milestones 27
  Passenger cars 3-5,12-14,27
  Trucks and buses 3,9,12-14,27
Profits 81
Public transportation 68

R

Records 27
Recreational vehicles 11
Recycling 61
Registrations:
  Buses:
    Government owned 42-44
    School 42,43
    Total 38,42-44
  Canada 29
  Passenger cars:
    By age 45
    By state 31-34,38,44
    Fleets 49
    New 31,34
    Total 38,44-47
    World 50-53
  Trailer 40
  Trucks:
    By age 46
    By state 35,36,38-41,44
    Combinations 40
    Government owned 44
    Light trucks 22,23,40,41
    New 31,35,36

Total 38-41,44,46,47
World 50-53
Regulations:
  Cost of 85
  Exhaust emissions 86
  Fuel economy 83-85
  Safety 87
Repair outlets 76,77
Research and development costs . . 81
Retail sales:
  Establishments 76,77
  Passenger cars 27-30
  Trucks 15,25-30
Retirement of vehicles 61
Roads (see Highways)

S

Safety belt use laws 91
Safety standards 87
Sales:
  Imports 15,18-27
  Passenger cars:
    By market class 21
    Factory sales 3,7
    Retail sales 15,21,27-30
    Top sellers 28
  Recreational vehicles 11
  Trucks:
    Body types 26
    By weight 7,8,25,26
    Diesel 7
    Factory sales 3,6,7
    Retail sales 15,22-30
  School buses 42,43
  Scrappage 61
  Service outlets 76,77
  Stolen vehicles 69

T

Taxes:
  Disbursements for highways . . 73
  State revenues 82
Taxis 68
Thefts 69
Tires 48,68,76
Tolls 68
Top sellers 28
Tractor trucks 40
Trade 54-59
Traffic fatalities 88-91
Trailers:
  Camping and travel 11
  Registrations 40
  Truck 11,40
Transit industry 68
Travel (see also Vehicle miles traveled):
  Auto/truck 70,71
  Bus 42,70,71
  By state 72

Rail 68
Rural and urban 71
Trucks:
  Assembly by city and state . . . 9
  Body types 26
  By age 45
  By weight 6,7,25,26
  Camper units 11
  Diesel 7
  Exhaust emissions 86
  Exports 7,54-57,59
  Factory sales 3,7,8
  Fuel consumption 70
  Fuel economy 84
  Government owned 44
  Imports 58,59
  In operation 46,47
  Leasing 48
  Optional equipment 10
  Production 3,9,12-14,27
  Registrations 44,46,47,49-53
  Regulations 84,87
  Retail sales 15,22-30
  Retirement of vehicles 61
  Scrappage 61
  Trailers 11,40
  Travel by 70,71
  Truck tractors 40
  Vehicle miles traveled 70,71

U

Used cars:
  Consumer price index 67
  Financing 66
  Purchases 68
  Sales 48
User taxes 82
Utility vehicles 22,26,41

V

Vans 26,41
Vehicle miles traveled:
  Average per vehicle 70,72
  Buses 43,71
  By state 71,72
  Passenger cars 70-72
  Trucks 70-72
  Urban and rural 71
Vehicles in use 45-47

W

Wages 79
Weights of trucks 6,7,25,26
Wholesale establishments 76
Wholesale shipments (see Factory sales)
Women buyers, drivers 62,63,90
World:
  Hourly compensation 79
  Production 12,13
  Registrations 50-53
  Trade in motor vehicles 59